THE LATIN-AMERICAN MIND

The
Latin-American
Mind

BY LEOPOLDO ZEA

*

*Translated from the Spanish by
James H. Abbott and Lowell Dunham*

NORMAN · UNIVERSITY OF OKLAHOMA PRESS

By Leopoldo Zea

El Positivismo en México (Mexico City, 1943)

Dos Etapas del Pensamiento en Hispanoamérica (Mexico City, 1949)

América en la Historia (Mexico City, 1957)

Latinoamérica y el Mundo (Caracas, 1960)

Democracias y Dictaduras en Latinoamérica (Mérida, 1960)

The Latin-American Mind (Tr. of *Dos Etapas del Pensamiento en Hispanoamérica* by James H. Abbott and Lowell Dunham, Norman, 1963)

Latin America and the World (Tr. by Frances K. Hendricks and Beatrice Berler, Norman, 1969)

Standard Book Number: 8061-0563-1

Library of Congress Catalog Card Number: 63-9955

Dedicated to Frances and Miss Gussie

—THE TRANSLATORS

Translators' Preface

THE WORKS OF LEOPOLDO ZEA belong to the same distinguished philosophical and intellectual tradition in Mexico as the works of such men as Benito Juárez, Ignacio Ramírez, Justo Sierra, José María Luis Mora, Gabino Barreda, Alfonso Reyes, Antonio Caso, and José Vasconcelos. Zea is linked to this tradition through his academic preparation, his professional activities, and his writings.

After completing his studies at the National Preparatory School and the National University of Mexico, where he specialized in philosophy, Zea began teaching philosophy in the National Preparatory School, El Colegio de México, and the Normal School for Women. In 1944, upon the recommendation of the great Mexican teacher and philosopher Antonio Caso, he joined the College of Philosophy and Letters of the National University as professor of history, and the philosophy of the history of America soon became his primary interest.

His concern with philosophical and historical currents led him to write *El Positivismo en México* (1943), which won him a place among the prominent scholars of Mexico, and he continued his study of positivism in *Apogeo y decadencia del positivismo en México* (1944). His interest in the philosophy of history also prompted him to write *Dos etapas del pensamiento en Hispanoamérica* (1949), of which the present volume is a translation.

For some time before the publication of this book, Zea had been occupied with an attempt to fix Mexican culture in its proper place in Latin America, and his studies of the culture of Mexico and other Latin-American countries had been directed toward this end. He

vii

was encouraged, and financial aid for completing the project was provided by a grant from the Rockefeller Foundation.

It happened that a number of Latin Americans had complained of inaccuracies and misinterpretations in a book on Latin-American thought published in the United States in the early 1940's. Among those who objected to portions of this book was the well-known Mexican writer Alfonso Reyes, who mentioned the subject to an official of the Rockefeller Foundation. It was then suggested to Sr. Reyes that if Latin Americans were dissatisfied with the book, they should write a better one themselves. The subsequent search for an author led rather logically to Leopoldo Zea because of his wide background in the culture of Mexico and other Latin-American countries.

The book which resulted from Zea's studies is brought to the English-speaking world in this translation because we, the translators, believe that it offers the best picture yet to appear of the difficulties that Hispanic Americans have faced since their independence, and we believe also that it presents succinctly the main currents of thought proposed by various Spanish American philosophers as a solution to their problems. Unfortunately, many English-speaking Americans, along with the majority of Western Europeans, are not well informed on cultural and philosophical movements in Latin America. How many, even among university graduates, are aware that there have been as avid followers of Hegel, Kant, Comte, and Spencer in Latin America as in North America, or that positivism was a vital philosophical movement in Latin America? A well-known European writer, when told of Zea's book on a recent visit to the University of Oklahoma, exclaimed, "Positivism in South America? Why, I had to come to Oklahoma to learn that!" A young doctoral candidate in a great American university upon being informed of the translation, asked, "How does it happen that we never hear of those Latin-American thinkers and philosophers in our classrooms?" The reactions of the writer and the doctoral candidate both point up the need for a book like Zea's for English-speaking people who do not read Spanish. The translation will also allow the English-speaking world to see Latin Americans seriously facing their overwhelming problems, analyzing them, and suggesting significant solutions of their own making.

Translators' Preface

This translation has been undertaken because of a kind of missionary zeal or enthusiasm which often compels translators to carry the message of an author to a wider reading public. Zea's *Dos etapas del pensamiento en Hispanoaméricana,* to which we have given the more inclusive title *The Latin-American Mind,* is a vital book for twentieth-century Americans. We trust that it will provide a better understanding of Latin America and her problems and that it will be useful to diplomats, politicians, businessmen, social and political scientists, and others who wish to understand the Latin-American nations. We trust, also, that the translation has not done too much violence to the original and that it will add something to the already commanding stature of one of Spanish America's most competent and serious thinkers, who hopes that *"mi libro ayude a establecer comprensión entre norteamericanos y latinamericanos."*[1] His efforts, like those of many of the men he discusses in his book, are directed toward understanding and helping "our America."

James H. Abbott
Lowell Dunham

NORMAN, OKLAHOMA

[1] Personal letter from Leopoldo Zea, July 17, 1962.

Acknowledgment

THE TRANSLATORS are especially indebted to the author for personal interviews granted and for extensive correspondence in which he was kind enough to help clarify passages presenting some difficulty. We are also indebted to our colleagues at the University of Oklahoma, the late Olive V. Hawes and Professors Ruben Landa and Antonio de la Torre, and to Professor Abelardo Villegas M., of Mexico City, for assistance in the translation of other troublesome passages; to Frances Ranson Dunham for her help in improving the English version, and to Frances Murtha for her contribution.

James H. Abbott
Lowell Dunham

Author's Preface

IN RECENT YEARS there has been a notable and apparently ever increasing interest in the study of the history, culture, and thought of Ibero-America. As a result of this interest, many books have already been published or are in preparation. Some of them present an over-all picture of the history of Latin-American ideas, while others deal with only a segment of this thought. Among these works the most notable analyses are those of Pedro Henríquez Ureña, Ramón Insúa Rodríguez, William Rex Crawford, Ezequiel Martínez Estrada, and Aníbal Sánchez Reulet.

The present book seeks to present a comprehensive picture of one on the most important stages in Hispanic-American thought, a stage during which there were ardent discussions of the problems presented by the incorporation of Hispanic America into the new social, political, and educational currents, once political independence had been won from Spain. This period was regarded as the incorporation of Hispanic America into civilization. There followed a discussion of the problems arising from the formation of a new order that was to be a worthy substitute for the repudiated colonial order.

Perhaps no other period in our history expresses a mode of being proper to the Hispanic-American man better than the one already mentioned. During this time the problem arose of the man who finds himself with a being or mode of being already made for him which he does not consider his own, which he regards as something given to him, or, worse, as something which has been imposed upon him. It is a period during which the disarticulation of the Hispanic-American man becomes evident: he is in conflict with himself without any possibility of resolving this conflict, considering the enormous contradictions which appear to exist. It is a time of transition in which we still seem to find ourselves, in spite of all the efforts made to emerge from this period. Many of the problems posed during this epoch continue to reappear in our own time, without any solution having been found to date. It is necessarily a critical period for Hispanic-American man, passing as he was from one mode of being imposed by three centuries of colonial rule, struggling to reach by more violent means another mode of being. It is a stage in which one finds the roots of many of our good qualities and of many of our defects.

The present book, it goes without saying, does not pretend to be exhaustive. On the contrary, the lacunae that can be found in it are numerous, perhaps too numerous. Indeed, the research for a book of this type cannot be propertly completed until the history of the thought, the culture, and the philosophy of each one of our countries has been recorded and the qualities deduced which characterize these countries as members of the community called Hispanic America, Ibero-America, or America. The work that has been done and is being done in this field by diligent researchers such as Roberto Agramonte and Medardo Vitier of Cuba, Arturo Ardao of Uruguay, Guillermo Francovich of Bolivia, Jorge Muñoz Rayo of Chile, and others in various countries will provide additional and perhaps greater enlightenment. A thorough investigation must be the responsibility of many scholars in the different countries of our America. I hope that my work may help to stimulate them in completing this task.

This book was conceived as a continuation of research I did some time ago on positivism in Mexico. After seeing how Mexicans reacted to and assimilated positivism, I found it interesting to compare their reception of it with that of other countries of Ibero-America in which it had also been influential. The first comparisons, as might be expected, revealed the difference that exists between Brazil and the Hispanic-American countries; the latter, in spite of their division into various nations, have much in common. There is among them a unity which does not exist in the case of Brazil. The historical circumstances and situations which gave rise to Brazil were different from those which created Hispanic America. For the present, therefore, it seemed urgent to discover what gave that unity to the Hispanic-American countries in order to search later for any unity that might exist between them and Brazil. I devoted myself to the first task. As for Brazil, there are several projects that have been completed or are in progress concerning its history, culture, and thought, outstanding among them the work of Professor Cruz Costa of the University of São Paulo.

Once my investigation of positivism in Hispanic America was begun, it became evident that the movement could not be explained or even given meaning without analyzing the period that preceded it. To this period is applied the general term "romanticism," even though it is not very precise. But while it may not be exact from the point of view of philosophical influences, I have accepted it because it is exact from the point of view of the attitude taken by the different members of the generation of Hispanic-American scholars who from 1840 to 1860 gave it a spiritual significance and unity. The bases for explaining the acceptance and adoption of positivism in all the Hispanic-American countries are found in the thought of this generation. A knowledge of their ideas and the problems posed is necessary to explain the rapid spread of the influence of positivism in Hispanic America.

For that reason this work has been divided into two parts: one devoted to the so-called romanticism in Hispanic America and the other to positivism. In both I have attempted to avoid treating the subject by nations. To be sure, lack of sufficient information would have made it impossible for me to do so; however, it seemed more important to stress a series of ideas in which there was evident a unity of spirit expressed in a unity of problems and the attempts to solve them. I have tried to make the analyses given here valid not for a specific country in our America, but for all Hispanic America. This was not difficult in the case of romanticism, for the similarity of the problems and the solutions proposed was obvious. Hispanic America had just shaken off the political yoke of Spain and was trying to destroy habits and customs imposed by the mother country during the long colonial period. From the romantic thought in Hispanic America I have chosen the most representative ideas, for it is in this period that the ideas which prepared the way for the adoption of positivism in different American countries become most obvious.

For the period during which positivism was adopted, this unity continues to be evident, but now with national differences. The problems and the solutions are similar, but the solutions must be adapted to specific circumstances. Diversity of historical circumstances will stimulate a series of no less diverse situations of social and political reality. Within its unity Hispanic America will begin to produce a variety of situations that take on national characteristics. Positivism, regarded as a philosophy for the establishment of a new order in Hispanic America, will continue to adapt itself to different specific circumstances that demand it. The interpretations and adaptations of positivism will be in accord with these situations and circumstances. Hence in dealing with positivism a national sequence has been followed, in contrast to the method employed in discussing romanticism, but emphasis is placed on a series of general traits that the reader will easily comprehend. The analysis of positivism given here is limited to those countries in which there appear both general characteristics and special characteristics which give a certain originality and diversity to its interpretation.

In the course of this work I have relied primarily on the financial assistance of El Colegio de México and the Rockefeller Foundation. During my travels in North and South America I received valuable suggestions as well as encouragement from many individuals and cultural institutions. I shall not list their names in order to avoid any lamentable omission, but to them I dedicate this book.

Unfortunately, it has not been possible to make the bibliography as exhaustive as I would have preferred. In the libraries visited, I attempted, within the limited time at my disposal, to take notes from sources that were impossible or difficult to consult in more accessible places. At the same time I tried to obtain the greatest possible number of books related to my research, sending them to Mexico to study on my return. Most of them were delivered, but some were not, probably because of the confusion existing in transportation facilities shortly after the end of World War II. I am not attempting thereby to justify the lacunae that may be found here. I am simply setting forth the reason which in part prevented me from reducing these gaps.

Leopoldo Zea

Contents

Contents

THE LATIN-AMERICAN MIND

Introduction

The Feeling of Dependence

HEGEL, in his *Lectures on the Philosophy of History*, referring to the American continent, said: "America is the land of the future. In the coming years its historical importance will appear perhaps in the struggle between North and South America. It is a land longed for by those who are weary of the historical museum of old Europe." But, he added, "America must sever its ties with the land where, up to the present time, universal history has developed. What has happened there heretofore is only the echo of the Old World and the reflection of an alien way of life." But this is something which belongs to the realm of the future, and "as a land of the future, America does not interest us since the philosopher does not make prophecies." In this way the German philosopher dismissed our continent, assigning it to historical oblivion.

For Hegel, who conceives of the history of ideas as a dialectical movement in which every accomplishment is at the same time a negation and a conservation, America has no history and, because it has no history, no reality. What we call history on this continent is only the echo or reflection of the history of the Old World, its appendage. According to Hegel, America will acquire history, it will exist, when it is capable of entering into that dialectical movement through which the spirit develops; that is, when it is capable of denying a past which is no longer its own, but through a dialectical negation, by way of an act of assimilation. Within the realm of dialectical logic, negation

3

does not mean to eliminate but to assimilate—to preserve. According to this logic, what one is, one is fully, so that there is no necessity for *becoming* again. When something is assimilated completely, it is not felt as something belonging to another, a hindrance, an obstacle, but something which is one's very own, natural. That which has been assimilated forms a part of one's own being, in such a way that it does not hinder the continuity of existence. That which has been, the past, becomes a part of experience which makes it possible to continue being. When something has been assimilated, there is no need at all to repeat the experiences of the past. Historical consciousness offers this experience, making its repetition useless. History is the objective expression of this assimilation, the most obvious expression of the dialectical negation. Such is the history of Europe, the history of the European man. Hegel has sought the meaning of this history by showing in his philosophy what has been and what is. The history of the Old World is the history which, some day, according to Hegel, America will have to deny if it wants to begin its own history. As long as such negation or such assimilation is not carried out, America will continue being a continent without history, a dependency of European history.

The Spanish philosopher José Ortega y Gasset was referring to the Hegelian interpretation when he said: "European man has been democratic, liberal, absolutist, feudal, but he is no longer any of these things. Does this mean, strictly speaking, that he in no way continues to be so? Certainly not. European man continues to be all of these things, but only because he has been all of them. If he had not had these experiences, if he did not have them behind him and did not continue being them in that particular way of having been them, it is possible that, faced with the difficulties of present political life, he would resolve to try hopefully one of these attitudes. But having been something is the force which most automatically prevents being it."[1] We may now ask for our own satisfaction: Is this valid for America? Or, more concretely: Can we Hispanic Americans speak in this way?

We Hispanic Americans have been, during our past, conquerors and conquered, colonials, enlightened, liberals, conservatives, and

[1] Ortega y Gasset, *Historia como sistema*, *Obras Completas*, VI (Madrid, 1947).

revolutionaries. But have we really been all of these in the sense that, because of having been them, we have no need of being them again? Or, in other words, are the problems which the Conquest, the Colony, the Independence created and those which have continued to be created in Hispanic America—are they problems which have already been solved in such a way that there is no necessity of formulating them again? Are they already past in the fullest sense of the word? The Conquest, Colonization, Independence, and all of our struggles for freedom—are these for us already a mere historical experience? The answer to these questions has to be no. If it were not, if in truth all of that past were an authentic past, it would mean that we had begun to realize our history in the dialectical sense which Hegel pointed out.

No, this history is not yet a history of denials. We have not yet assimilated it. We Hispanic Americans still have, on the surface, the conqueror and the conquered, the colonist, the romantic liberal, and all of the things which were our past. What is more, in spite of the fact that we claim to have been all of them, we are still not fully any of them. We have taken these attitudes only as a matter of form. Actually such attitudes have served only to mask, to conceal, a reality not yet assimilated, the colonial reality being the first of which the Hispanic American was aware—that is, his reality as a dependency, his knowledge of being an entity dependent upon a reality which he does not yet consider his own, his dependency upon something which he considered foreign to him.

The Hispanic American of the twentieth century continues discussing passionately, affirming or denying, this reality. The Conquest and colonization remain alive in his mind, and about them revolve, after all is said and done, all of his discussions. Sometimes we see him defending the rights of the conquered, at other times defending the conquerors; at times justifying the colonies, at other times justifying independence. He always takes the same point of view, in spite of disguising it with different ideological labels or different terminology. The problem of the dependence and the independence of the Hispanic American is always evident. The enlightened, the liberals, the conservatives, the positivists, and the revolutionaries have done nothing but express in different periods and with different language

5

the same and ever latent problem. Our past always amounts to that. This past is Spain, and with Spain, Europe. We have not yet been able to assimilate this past because we still feel it as something foreign to ourselves; we do not feel it in our veins, in our blood, we do not feel it as our own. Or, in other words, our past still has not become a real past; it is still a present which does not choose to become history.

Instead of trying to solve our problems by the dialectical method, we Hispanic Americans have only accumulated them. The contradiction between conqueror and the conquered was still not resolved when we decided to become republicans, liberals, and democrats according to the model which great modern countries, especially Anglo-Saxon ones, gave us. Following that, and without resolving the new contradictions which faced us, we aspired to establish a *bourgeoisie* similar to the great European *bourgeoisie* without succeeding in being anything but insignificant servants of the latter. While in our time we have not yet attained the economic power which makes possible the disintegration of that *bourgeoisie sui generis*, we are faced with the problems of a class struggle. Of course, one cannot deny that this struggle between the oppressed and the oppressor exists, but it does not exist in the terms in which the Conquest formulated it: the struggle of the conquered against the conqueror, the struggle of the colony against the mother country. Formerly it was a struggle against Spain; now it is a struggle against our new mother country, the United States, for we are still a colony. It is always the same, a struggle for our independence. At one time it was a political struggle against Spain; then it was a spiritual struggle against Spain's habits and customs, and later an economic struggle against the *bourgeoisies* of which we are only the tools. It was also a struggle against our cultural dependence, for we are faced with a past which we have not come to regard as ours through a dialectical assimilation.

Antonio Caso said of the history of Mexico: "Our national problems have never been solved as they arose. . . . Mexico, instead of following a uniform and graduated dialectical process, has proceeded accumulatively. . . . Deeply rooted causes, which had developed before the Conquest, as well as others arising later, and all of them working together, have created the formidable national problem, so abstruse and difficult, so dramatic and hopeless. . . . We still have not solved the problem which Spain bequeathed us with the Conquest; neither have we yet solved the problem of democracy, and now we have on the agenda of historical discussion socialism in its most acute and urgent form."[2]

This matter of being blind to our problems, seeing them only in the light of European solutions, led Hegel to state that we were living as an echo and reflection of the Old World, as its shadow and not as a reality. Echoes and reflections of another way of life. Nevertheless, reality is always more powerful than man's imagination. In this case Hispanic-American reality, as we may call it, is more powerful than the desire of the Hispanic American to escape it. In spite of all the subterfuges used to elude it, it is always evident. Apparently the Hispanic American formulates the same problems and looks for the same solutions which he has learned from European culture; but obviously he does not formulate the same problems nor does he give the same solutions, in spite of the fact that he imagines he does. Reality is always more powerful, and it forces him to formulate problems which are his own and to look for his own solutions. He does all of this without being aware of it, doing one thing while he believes that he is doing another. It is in our time that he begins to realize this fact. The day that he becomes fully aware of the situation he will decide to resolve the problems in a direct way, hoping that the solutions will be conclusive, as has happened in all true philosophy.

Negative Renunciation of the Hispanic-American Past

HISPANIC-AMERICAN man, as he became more and more aware of his dependent relationship with a world which he did not consider his own and with a past which he considered foreign, tried to break once and for all with that world and that past. But instead of denying them in accordance with a dialectical logic, he did it with a formal logic; that is, according to a logic which does not admit contradiction, a logic in which there is no room for history. With this logic as a point of departure, the Hispanic American had no choice but to deny

[2] Antonio Caso, *México, apuntamientos de cultura patria* (México, 1943).

his history, to renounce it, considering it as alien to him. His history, his past, was considered as something which did not belong to him because it had not been his work. The past appeared to him as completely negative, as that which the Hispanic American ought not to be, not even in the sense of having been it at one time.

The Hispanic American, upon analyzing himself, found that he was a man of many contradictions, and because he felt incompetent and incapable of effecting a synthesis of these contradictions, he chose the easiest way out, amputation. He chose one form of his being and attempted to sever it from the other, once and for all. But the contradiction was still there without even an apparent solution. He regarded the past as the root of all his misfortunes, the source of all of his troubles. This past was and still is the colony. He looked upon the history of the Colonial period as something totally alien to him. Spain had created this past and Spain alone could answer for it. Of his ancestral defects only this one should be called to account; the Spanish American could not make up his mind to break with the past. Accepting this past as something of his own meant for him only the acceptance of his dependence. Since his past had been made by Spain, it was impossible for him to have any other attitude than rejection or submission. Not for a moment did the way of denial by assimilation occur to him.

In this way the Hispanic American compromised himself in a difficult, almost impossible, task: that of tearing himself away from a very important part of his being, his past. He surrendered to the difficult task of no longer being that which he was, in order to become, as if he had never existed, something entirely different. The leaders of the intellectual independence of Hispanic America sought a complete reformation of the Spanish and the colonial heritage. Our heritage, they added, is the complete opposite of what we want to be and what we should be. We carry our defects in our blood; let us rid ourselves of this blood if necessary. The social emancipation of Hispanic America, they said vehemently, will not succeed if we do not completely repudiate our Spanish heritage, our past.

Spain, the past, was in the mind, in the habits and customs of Hispanic-American man. It was so deeply rooted in him that he felt he was unable to develop as other peoples were doing. He felt that all his efforts to transform his past had failed. He could do nothing to change it. He felt that everything attempted toward this end was futile. The Hispanic American had struggled to attain his political emancipation, but this, too, was futile because it lacked prior intellectual emancipation. The past, Spain, was always present in the flesh and blood of the liberators themselves. They, who had aspired to give to Hispanic America a form of life that was alien to Spain, had failed because in their own blood they carried the very roots of this failure. It was all to no avail; the colonial past imposed by Spain always appeared. The Hispanic American continued as if no change had taken place. And in truth none had. Nothing real or conclusive seemed to have been gained. The political freedom which had been attained was only a formality. The new forms only covered up past and permanent defects. Hispanic America had gained its independence from the Spanish crown, but never from Spain. Spain continued alive, influencing every action of the Hispanic American, who continued living as if nothing had changed. Every Hispanic American sought only to take the place left by the conquistador. From the dominated man which he was, he aspired to be the dominator of the weakest.

The leaders of the new Hispanic-American emancipation were fully aware of this situation and hoped to end it. The revolution of independence, they said, had been animated more by the Hispanic imperial spirit than by the spirit of liberty. It had been a political revolution, argued the leadership, and not a social revolution. They had only sought to replace one master by another. The scepter had been wrested from Spain, but they kept its spirit. The legislative bodies of the period of liberation, the liberators, and the soldiers of the political emancipation of Hispanic America had acted only in accordance with the spirit which Spain had imposed upon them. The struggle had not been between America and Spain, but between Spain and Spain. A younger Spain, but Spain, after all, had conquered the old Spain. Nothing had changed, the same old privileges continued to exist, the liberators themselves had seen to it that it would be so. Hispanic America continued to be a colony.

Thus the new emancipators of Hispanic America were aware of the harsh reality and determined to eliminate it once and for all.

9

In their efforts to destroy it, they were caught up in that rare spectacle of men intent upon eradicating a part of their very being, their history. And they devoted themselves to this difficult task with the same rage, courage, and tenacity that they had inherited from Spain. In their violence to root out the past they acted like worthy sons of that Spain they were seeking to deny. The native Spanish steadfastness, as Andrés Bello would say, was evident in the very zeal of the Hispanic American to cease being a Spaniard. The same push and valor that the Spaniard had exerted to dominate these lands and to impose on them his habits and customs, the Hispanic Americans had used to liberate them and to eradicate such habits and customs. They answered one violence with another and one imposition with another.

Nevertheless, the past is not something which can be eliminated in that way, without further ado. The past, if it is not completely assimilated, always makes itself felt as present. In each gesture, in every act carried out by the Hispanic-American man, the past becomes evident. The political parties took on various names, new ideas were discussed, new philosophies seemed to guide them; but in the background the past remained alive, latent, ready to put in an appearance at the first opportune moment. They were but new names with which they disguised old problems. Meanwhile the rest of the world marched forward, progressed, and made history. Hispanic America continued to be a continent without history, without a past, because the past was always present. And if it had a history, it was not a conscious history. Hispanic America continued to refuse to consider as part of its history a past which it had not made. The colony was not its history, but neither did it accept as such the series of struggles to free itself from this history. This was pure anarchy of which it was ashamed. It wanted nothing to do with that series of struggles, upheavals, violence, and intermittent dictatorship and anarchy. In past history it found nothing constructive, nothing of what it aspired to be. Nevertheless, and in spite of all this, the Hispanic American kept making history, not the history that he would have liked to make, but his history—a very special history without dialectical negations or assimilations, a history full of contradictions which never became synthesized, but a history after all. It now falls to the lot of the Hispanic American at mid-twentieth century to deny dialectically this history; that is, to assimilate it.

Hispanic America and Its Zeal to Make a New History

THE DESIRE to begin as if nothing had been done, to make history from its very beginnings, is among "attitudes that have appeared" in the history of culture and also in the particular histories of individuals, such as biographies. That desire to begin anew normally appears in times of crises or great disillusionment. Man, in certain periods of his life, is wont to feel this desire; it is one of the most effective means of escaping his circumstances, his reality. In this way he thinks that he can elude the compromises that his situation in the world has imposed upon him. On these occasions, during which the upheavals of history seem to become "involved" and complicated, man feels impelled to escape from the entanglement. Instead of devoting himself to the difficult but not impossible task of untangling his situation, he prefers to escape and to take no cognizance of the complex conditions. He then begins to imagine worlds without complications, worlds without previous history, worlds in which each individual can begin to realize his history as he would have it. In these worlds liberty appears in its maximum expression. It is a question of worlds in which the individual has no compromises; in them everything is done to perfection. In these imaginary worlds man has no other obligation but to live freely, without limitations. Or these worlds appear as virgin worlds in which everything is still to be done and thus full of possibilities. In short, they seem to be utopias, which are ideal states, or utopias in which everything is yet to be created. In both, man can escape his past, his compromises, his obligation to answer for the compromises of a past which he did not make. In one utopia everything is already completed; in another everything is yet to be done; but neither represents a compromise. And since there are no compromises, there are no problems.

Hence we see that during the great crises of humanity man is wont to assume one or both of these two attitudes. Sometimes he decides upon the ideal of a world in which everything is resolved. In accordance with such an ideal, man finds no compromises. Liberty in this world is at a maximum, since everything which represents a compromise that restricts liberty has been abandoned to a providence which foresees everything and resolves everything. Such is the attitude assumed by man in the world in which so-called pagan culture reached a crisis. At other times man desires an entirely new world in which everything has to be done. In this instance there is no rejection of action. Action exists—indeed, there is complete freedom of action— and since it is completely free, it is also irresponsible. There is nothing to hinder this action since nothing is done. That is what so-called modern man attempted when Christian culture reached a crisis. Man, disgusted with the historical museum of old Europe, aspired to create an entirely new world. His utopia was no longer placed in transcendent worlds in which everything is foreseen, but on the earth itself. But this was a virgin land, a new country, where man who inhabited it lived in a complete state of nature, that is, without history; it was a new land in which the action of the individual was still not compromised by the action of others. The virgin land and the noble savage represented the ideals of modern man who was already tired of having to answer for the actions of his predecessors. This was the man who with the greatest of effort tried to realize a history in which he was the principal protagonist as well as initiator. History, the past, seemed to disappear in an apparent obscurity.

Something similar happened in Hispanic America, the land which the Europeans have looked upon as the realization of their utopia. At a certain historical juncture the Hispanic American rebelled against his past, and hence against the responsibilities that it implied. He attempted to make an immediate break with that past. He denied it, by attempting to begin a new history, as if nothing had been accomplished previously. He also created his utopia. He found the ideal to which he aspired in the great Anglo-Saxon countries, England and the United States, or in France, in what it contributed to the advancement of civilization. Their political constitutions, philosophy, literature, and culture in general were models by which the Hispanic Americans sought to mold a new history.

The past or the future was the dilemma which faced them. In order to attain an ideal future, it was necessary to renounce the past irrevocably. The Hispanic-American past was but the absolute negation of its own ideals. The new ideals were an absolute contradiction of the inheritance of the past. The new civilization was an absolute denial of colonial Spain. It was necessary to choose one or the other; it was necessary to renounce the future or the past. Republicanism or Catholicism, shouted the Chilean Francisco Bilbao. Democracy or Absolutism, civilization or barbarism, were the choices given by Domingo Sarmiento. Liberalism or tyranny, there was no other choice; it was one or the other. This terrible dualism, these men said, will lead us to death if we are unable to choose one of the two. It was necessary to choose between the absolute dominance of the colony or the absolute dominance of the new ideals of liberty. No reconciliation was possible; to conceive of one would be the greatest of errors. They held that one of these extremes would necessarily predominate at the expense of completely eliminating its opposite. And while the Latin Americans were engaged in this reasoning, they were in the process of exterminating one another. One half stood in the way of the other. In this manner the history of the nineteenth century evolved, a history in which a minority filled with faith in the future chose to reject all of its past.

Nevertheless, the past was always with the Hispanic American; it was a part of his being. The future never became present; the past never became the past. Utopia, instead of becoming an actuality, receded farther and farther every day. In spite of all the efforts which the Hispanic Americans made, they continued being Hispanic Americans, products of that circumstance and reality called Hispanic America. The past continued to be present in the diverse forms of life of those men who struggled in vain to extirpate it. With a present and a past which had never become an actuality, history, our history, did not exist. Hispanic America, through its own history, became a people without a history. The most it could expect to become, as Hegel held, was a country of the future. Hispanic America, in the realm of reality, resigned itself to being an echo and a reflection of something which it wanted to be, but which in fact it was not. It became an alien project, a utopia of a Europe also exhausted by its history, a utopia of people disgusted with the old European museum. In this way, in keeping with a plan which was not his own, once more the Hispanic American continued being a colonial; he renounced his true history and with it his reality.

But reality is always more powerful, and, in spite of everything, the renunciation was futile. In spite of all the efforts made, the Hispanic American retained his reality (a dangerous reality) because it was based on a past which he had not been able to assimilate. The longer he postponed assimilation, the more dangerous it became. The old forces from which he thought he had liberated himself continued so boldly latent that they did not even conceal their intention to dominate openly his reality. The fact that he had not been able to assimilate this past at the proper time gave it its strength.

And so we see that, while Europe was discussing its future, we in Hispanic America were still constrained to continue discussing our past. While Europe was struggling to realize a history which would represent one stage in the progress of its dialectical movement, Hispanic America still had to look to the past to defend liberties which appeared to be already won. A hundred years later, Hispanic America still had to defend the work of a Juárez or of a Sarmiento against the ever present and latent forces that make possible the defenders of past privileges or of the new Rosas. While Europe devoted itself to searching for a type of community which it must adopt in the future, Hispanic America was still discussing the Conquest, independence, and liberalism. Only among peoples like the Hispanic American, where the past is still present, can political forms, like the colonial ones, which appear to be already abandoned, remain controversial issues. Only peoples who have not assimilated their history can continue to feel threatened by their past. Hence the urgent necessity of effecting this assimilation. Of necessity we Hispanic Americans must make of the past something which no longer has any need to exist simply because it has existed. Of necessity we must make our history—that is, we must be conscious of it—a history which will indicate to us the paths that our past has taken, so that we will not feel the necessity of following them again because we know them through experience. Of necessity we must be able to look at the past as something that was and not as something that no longer exists. Of necessity we must live the past in retrospect, as a past experience, as something, in short, which we *are* for having lived and not as something which we will be by continuing to live.

This is, in part, what will justify the history which will develop later. If, in truth, we do not want to repeat the experiences of our past by living them as something present, we shall have to experience them as history, as a past that is. And the best way to do so is by assimilation; we must assimilate our past; we must become conscious of it. Europe has always done so; that has always been the task of its historians and philosophers. They are the creators of its so-called universal history. History is not made of facts alone, but rather of the awareness which one has of facts. It is this that we still have not attained; it is this for which Hegel reproaches us. But now it seems that we are at least aware of its necessity. Such an awareness explains the ever increasing interest in the history of our ideas. We have now only to do our part, however small it may be.

II. ROMANTICISM IN HISPANIC AMERICA

Intellectual Autonomy

THE PREOCCUPATION of the Hispanic Americans with their reality had been developing in a series of stages whose origins go back as far as the conquistadors themselves. In the middle of the eighteenth century, however, because of a series of historical and cultural circumstances, this preoccupation became more evident. The philosophical ideas then in vogue lent theoretical support to this realization, ideas which were grouped under the generic name of the Enlightenment. The new philosophy began by destroying the principle of authority upon which scholasticism, the official philosophical doctrine, rested. The Hispanic-American men of the Enlightenment tried immediately to separate religion from philosophy. In the field of religion the principle of authority was valid because it was based upon faith; but this was not so in the field of philosophy. Here the only method for attaining knowledge was through experience. Religion belonged to the divine world, philosophy to the human. The two were not to be confused.

The Hispanic American, without neglecting the salvation of his soul, set out immediately to know the world in which it had fallen his lot to live. Armed with the new scientific experimental method, he began this difficult task. The American flora, fauna, earth, and sky became the object of his knowledge. He would lose little time in realizing what this reality he experienced meant. America had its personality; it possessed a rich individuality in all fields. The Hispanic-American men of science were the first to teach us to know and love this reality. Their direct contact with this reality, which they looked upon fondly, led them to become deeply attached to it. That world which they were observing and discovering so carefully was their world. Facing them was a reality, physical at first, moral and social later, which was not necessarily inferior to that of other peoples. They very soon passed from the problems of a naturalist to problems of a political nature. America was not inferior to Europe simply because it was different. Each of the various regions of the Spanish colony had its own personality, from which there arose problems that only the natives could understand. They soon began to talk openly, if not of independence, at least of autonomy. And in the face of Spain's incomprehension the idea of political independence soon became a program. In Mexico, in New Granada, in Peru, Chile, and the Plate region, those who only yesterday were men of science now became conspirators and soldiers; telescopes, microscopes, and other scientific instruments were exchanged for rifles and cannons, and scientific treatises became proclamations of liberty. In Santa Fé de Bogotá and other Hispanic-American cities, many men of science who only a short time before had been favored by the viceroys were sacrificed.

The political independence of Hispanic America was the positive result of this reaction. Nevertheless, the liberators, carried away by a mirage, were unable to see clearly the reality that they were to face and to liberate. Like good men of the Enlightenment, they executed plans by which they intended to remake and orient the liberated peoples. They looked upon the latter as clay easy to mold. The Hispanic-American people understood that they were still not prepared to enjoy the fruits of their liberty, but that their liberators, now turned governors, would assume the responsibility of preparing them. Enlightened despotism was the redeeming formula. The American peoples were to be taught by force to be free. In the name of liberty

Bolívar imposed his power upon the peoples whom he had liberated. O'Higgins did the same in Chile, Iturbide in Mexico, Rivadavia in Argentina, and Dr. Francia in Paraguay. Henceforth, any dictatorship would be justified for the liberty and well-being of the people. But in the shadow of the dictatorships there were always the old colonial interests unwilling to yield. To escape continual anarchy, the people were forced to choose between liberal dictatorship and conservative dictatorship. Liberty, bandied about in the proclamations of the revolutionaries, became more and more restricted. It was liberty only when compared to rule by the mother country, liberty that did not imply in any form whatsoever a change in the social structure of the Hispanic-American peoples. There had been only one change: a national dictator took the place of the Spanish. That was the only thing that independence offered.

The optimism preceding the independence movement became a deep pessimism. Everything was the same except politically. New privileges were only added to the old ones. Hispanic-American reality displayed other aspects to which American men of science at the end of the eighteenth century had been blind. There was something in that reality which made it impossible for the countries to follow the path of the great European nations and the United States. There was something innate in the Hispanic American that made it impossible for him to be really free. It was necessary to recognize this something, since only by recognizing it could it be extirpated. The generation following the one which carried out political independence would devote itself to this task. It began to probe its soul with almost sadistic passion, and so initiated a new experience in Hispanic-American reality. The spectacle which the new generation offered was something really grievous and discouraging: countries decimated by long and endless revolutions, anarchy and despotism experienced alternately in a vicious circle. The revolutions were the result of the tyrannies and the tyrannies the result of the revolutions. One violence was pitted against another. Order was necessary, not so much for governing as for survival. Violence was the method by which one ruler in Hispanic America followed another. The only interest of these rulers was to maintain themselves in power for the sake of power. The future of Hispanic-American society no longer seemed important to anybody; the only thing that mattered was how to seize the command abandoned by the former representative of the Spanish government.

Where did the root of this evil lie? How could an end be put to it? These were the problems which the new generation was to face. They would find the cause of them in the colony, for it existed in the very soul of the Hispanic American. The colony had formed the mentality that now stultified progress. There lay all the difficulty. To eradicate it, it would be necessary to remold that mentality from its very beginnings. There was an urgent new task: the mental emancipation of Hispanic America. The new generation would devote itself to this task. Intellectual autonomy was its new standard.

Romanticism and the Sense of Originality

BOTH French and German romanticism inspired in the Hispanic Americans a preoccupation with the reality which appears in history and culture. The concern for national values became a concern for values appropriate to America. They realized that it was necessary to remake this reality that had fallen to their lot, but they also realized that they could remold it only if they departed from what it really was. They objected to the idealism characteristic of the rationalism of the Enlightenment. This rationalism failed in Spanish America because it had failed to see the reality that was evident there. Romanticism inspired also a concern for national *destiny*—in this case, the American destiny. But while the Europeans found in their own national histories the justification for such a destiny, the Hispanic Americans found in European history the negative elements of this destiny. All of these forces were in the past, in the colony whose continued existence now hindered the progress of the Hispanic-American people. Therein lay what was stagnant in the present America's own destiny.

Just as the European had turned to history to find the source of his future destiny, so the Hispanic American had turned to history to discover what prevented the realization of his own destiny. There began to appear in the different countries of this America a series of historical works that revealed the negative reality of Hispanic America. Penetrating historical and sociological analyses of this reality were written. Prominent among them was Sarmiento's *Facundo*. The first edition, published in 1845, bore the significant title *Civilization and Barbarism, the Life of Juan Quiroga: The Physical Aspect, Customs, and Habits of the Argentine Republic*. Moved by the same absorbing interest, José Victorino Lastarria delivered a lecture in 1844 at the University of Chile; entitled *Investigations of the Social Influence of the Conquest and the Colonial System of the Spanish in Chile*, this lecture provoked great discussion. It brought a quick reply from Andrés Bello, who took it upon himself to point out the positive elements of the colony, absolving it of all the errors it had committed and the defects which they implied.

In Mexico, in 1837, José María Luis Mora wrote his *Political Review of the Various Administrations Which the Mexican Republic Has Had up to 1837*. He clearly demonstrated that the majority of the errors committed by these administrations had originated in the colony. In Cuba, José Antonio Saco, in *The History of Slavery* and in works such as his treatises on *Indolence in the Island of Cuba*, goes to the heart of the evils which the island suffered. In these and many other works appearing throughout the nineteenth century the Hispanic Americans kept pointing out that the past should be denied, while the Europeans, in contrast, were pointing out in similar works of history and sociology that the past should be affirmed.

But, concurrently with this concern for the negative, there arose also a concern for the positive, for that something proper to Hispanic America that ought to be effected. Hispanic Americans must realize that they had a destiny. They began to talk of nationality, but this, they knew, could not be based on their own history as it was among the European nations. The desire for a common goal, not land and history, makes a nation. This must be emphasized: What is the common undertaking essential to the Hispanic-American peoples? Unity must be found in a future yet to be realized, not in what has been realized, for that is negative. The national destiny was a thing of the future without any negative ties to the past. It was something which they wanted to be in order to cease being what they had been. To realize this objective was the task proper to the peoples of Hispanic America. They soon began to talk about the necessity of developing an American culture, a literature, a grammar, and a philosophy. All this was something to be realized, not something which had already been done; but it was there, nevertheless, waiting to be aroused.

Political independence from Spain was not enough; it was necessary to take a new and decisive step: a step toward cultural independence from Europe. Hispanic Americans said that there was no longer much to be learned from Europe. Europe still kept the feudal spirit alive, the same spirit from which Hispanic America sought to free itself. Europe at first meant Spain in the mind of the Hispanic Americans; later it meant a France and an England with colonial ambitions. That same Europe had bombarded the coasts of Chile and Peru and had invaded Mexico in the name of civilization. America had nothing to learn from that Europe. America would have to turn its attention to itself. Within this negative world that Hispanic America seemed to be, something positive would have to be found upon which a new culture could be built in the future.

The members of this new generation of Hispanic Americans began to talk in this manner and to discuss the urgent necessity of realizing this culture. The Spanish American countries, they said, should have their own literature and their own grammar. The reality experienced by the writers—that is, the reality of the peoples of which they were a part—should furnish the themes for this literature. As for the grammar, the people, ever wise, had left their traces on the Spanish language by introducing new forms of expression. As for history, why continue to speak of a history that was alien to our peoples? Weren't our Hispanic-American historians capable of speaking with more authority about the facts of which they were so much a part? In the field of the sciences there were many completely original experiences which could be contributed by our scientists. In the realm of philosophy, while accepting its universality from a formal point of view, they considered their reality, of which it must be an expression, to be original and unique. Each people should have a philosophy that would conform best to its own reality.

Philosophical Influences

MANY varied philosophical movements were to exert an influence on this period in which the future of our American peoples was under discussion. A multitude of philosophical currents, contradictory in many aspects, replaced the philosophy of the Encyclopedists. The reality of the Hispanic-American problems under discussion drew these currents together. Ideology, French traditionalism, eclecticism, utilitarianism, the Scottish school, and the romantic socialism of Saint-Simon furnished the ideological arms of the generation which sought to effect the new Hispanic-American emancipation. Many of the men of this generation had firsthand knowledge of these philosophies. Bello, during his diplomatic residence in London, knew Bentham and James Mill, and the philosophy of these two men left a deep impression on the Venezuelan educator. This same thought had a powerful influence upon the Mexican José María Luis Mora. The Argentine, Esteban Echeverría, in Paris from 1825 to 1830 also came under the influence of the various romantic currents then in vogue. The social romanticism of Saint-Simon, through his student Pierre Leroux, can be seen in Echeverría's *Dogma Socialista*. Echeverría's influence soon became evident among several members of his generation. Juan Bautista Alberdi assimilated these influences and those of utilitarianism, idealism, and eclecticism. Sarmiento also assimilated all of these influences and defended them in frequent debates in the neighboring republic of Chile. The ideas of Echeverría, Alberdi, and Sarmiento spread into Uruguay. The *Révue Encyclopédique* and *Le Globe,* in which the socialist ideas of Saint-Simon and his followers were published, were read and quoted in Argentina, Chile, and Uruguay. The Chilean Francisco Bilbao studied in Europe under Lamennais, Quinet, and Michelet. José de la Luz y Caballero, the Cuban teacher, while in Europe studied German idealism and its French expression, Victor Cousin's eclecticism, in Europe. This knowledge led him to oppose these doctrines as prejudicial to the desire for independence on the island of Cuba. The literary aspect of romanticism also offered a series of ideas to justify the desires of the new Hispanic-American generation. Victor Hugo's and Lamartine's lyricism expressed these men's desire for liberty. In Chile, Lamartine's *Los Girondinos* organized the generation which was to fight for the ideas of liberalism in their country. Lastarria was known as Brissol; Francisco Bilbao, Verigaud; Pedro Ugarte, Dantón; Manuel Bilbao, Saint-Just; and Santiago Argos, Marat.[3]

Alberdi is an example of the diversity and the vagueness of the influences under which these men came. "From Echeverría, who had been educated in France," Alberdi says, "I first learned of Lerminier, Villemain, Victor Hugo, Alexander Dumas, Lamartine, Byron, and of everything that was then known as romanticism as opposed to the old classical school. I had studied philosophy in the university as a result of reading Condillac and Locke. For years I had been engrossed in reading at random Helvecio, Cabanis, Holbach, Bentham, Rousseau. To Echeverría I owed the change which took place in my mind with the reading of Victor Cousin, Villemain, Chateaubriand, Jouffroy, and all the eclectics from Germany in favor of what was called spiritualism." With regard to other influences, which Alberdi and his generation owed to Echeverría, he said: "In Buenos Aires he introduced the *Revista Enciclopédica* published by Carnot and Leroux, and with it the social spirit of the revolution of July. Through him we first became acquainted with the books and liberal ideals of Lerminier . . . and the doctrinarian philosophies and publicists of the Restoration."[4]

Each of these diverse philosophical doctrines was to furnish the necessary and adequate means for the solution of the no less diverse problems which were confronting the Hispanic Americans in their desire to reconstruct their reality. In the French traditionalists, Maistre, Chateaubriand, Benjamin Constant, and De Bonald, they would find the arms to combat the naïve utopianism into which the men of the Enlightenment had fallen. In them they studied the theses of the inability of people to govern themselves. The will of the people, they said, has nothing to do with the existence of government. It exists because it is necessary. There is no social contract; society did not arise as the result of a decision of a group of individual wills. On the contrary, the individual was a part of society even against

[3] Benjamín Vicuña Mackenna, *Los girondinos chilenos* (Santiago de Chile, 1902).

[4] Juan Bautista Alberdi, *"Autobiograía," Escritos póstumos.*

his will, for he must assume responsibility for things which he had not done. This was the situation in which the Hispanic American found himself; he was part of a society which he had not made, a society which he would have to change if he wanted it to be his own. Traditionalism offered a critical means to combat false ideas such as those which made of the people a mere legal entity or a means to combat constitutions which attempted to transform by decree a reality rooted in several centuries of colonial domination.

Social romanticism, on the other hand, provided the positive instruments for the same reaction: the people did not exist as an ideal individual, but they did exist as a difficult and complex reality. Social romanticism aroused in the Hispanic Americans a desire to make a positive science of social studies. From it they likewise derived their interest in finding a way to liberate the people from misery, in this case interest in making the Hispanic-American people capable of attaining the same social well-being and the same economic means that made the Anglo-Saxon people the leaders of civilization. They also spoke of socialism, such as Echeverría had in his *Dogma,* but this had nothing to do with the socialism which was spreading throughout Europe. The socialism of the Hispanic Americans was a romantic and individualistic socialism, a bourgeois socialism. Alberdi points out the difference between the socialism which he calls American and the socialism which was beginning to grow in Europe. "There is an abyss of difference between the two," he said; "they have nothing in common but the name," a name that the French socialists or demagogues did not invent, since society and socialism, as they have existed throughout time, express inevitable facts universally recognized and sanctioned as good. All good men have been and are socialists, as Echeverría and the youth of his time were. His system was not a system of exaggeration; he never sought to change existing society from its foundation up. His society is the same that we know today, devoid of abuses and defects that no honest man would authorize.[5] Socialism was, therefore, for the Hispanic Americans the expression of a desire more moralistic than social. From

[5] Alberdi, in "Prólogo" to *Los ideales de Mayo y la tiranía,* by Esteban Echeverría.

the school of Saint-Simon they derived their interest in economic and industrial liberalism as means for eliminating poverty among these peoples.

The historical school and French eclectic spiritualism contributed their propensity for emphasizing the originality, the individuality, and the irreducibility of the spirit within the historical and geographical circumstances that are proper to it. Herder and Hegel, through their French interpreters such as Cousin and Leroux, made the Hispanic Americans aware of the importance that history has in the make-up of the spirit. Lerminier, a follower of Savigny, helped them in their reaction against universalist and formalist illuminism. These contributions led them to take more stock in their own social and historical reality; this they thought was negative, but they knew that they could only count on it as a reality, to be remade. Within this same reality they were to search for positive elements with which it was to be reformed. Our reformers had before them the great models by which they were trying to remake their America; but they were fully aware that such a thing would be achieved only so far as the circumstances of that reality would permit. They no longer dreamed as their predecessors had; reality had made them more cautious as they learned to deal with it.

The liberalism found by the Hispanic Americans in the Enlightenment remained in the ideology which would continue to influence them. But the other currents mentioned and their own experience made them turn towards a less formal liberalism, to a liberalism more adapted to the circumstances of Hispanic America. The ideologist's analysis made by reason was compensated for by the romantic's intuitive analysis. To individualism, devoid of history, was joined romantic socialism, which knows that man, as an individual, is not enough. The Scottish school gave still more balance to the romantic enthusiasm which had taken hold of this generation. Common sense made them more cautious in their enthusiasm. They dreamed, but at the same time they considered carefully the domain where such dreams were to be fulfilled. They were not disposed to suffer any more disillusion. William Hamilton, Thomas Brown, Dugald Steward, and Thomas Reid were continually quoted, sometimes directly and at other times through the French eclectics whom they had influenced, such as Roger-Collard, Jouffroy, and Laromiguière. As for these influences and their indirect form of assimilation, Alberdi had said, "The most important consequences of Scottish and German philosophy have been fused fortunately in present-day French philosophy; and since we have been oriented in that philosophy, we can be sure that we are not far from Scottish and German ideas."[6] The utilitarianism of Jeremiah Bentham and James Mill completes the practical vision of the Hispanic Americans. Their concern with attaining "the greatest happiness for the greatest number" led them to analyze the motives for the actions of the individuals of this America, thus emphasizing their innate defects. Once these motives were recognized, the subsequent problem was their correction by means of an adequate education. Hispanic Americans, they thought, would be happy when they knew how to co-ordinate their actions with those of others. Each individual must work out his own happiness, for by doing so he also contributes to society's happiness. The Hispanic American should be concerned with directing his efforts towards industrialization and the wealth that arises from personal work, abandoning politics and its by-products, such as the mania for holding public office.

All these diverse currents: French traditionalism with its conservative spirit, eclecticism with its historic sense, Saint-Simonianism and its preoccupation with society, ideology, the Scottish school, and utilitarianism and its preoccupation with the experimental and positive would prepare the way for the adoption of positivism. Many of the members of this generation, which we can call pre-positivist, would be greatly surprised to find that their ideas coincided almost exactly with those of positivist philosophy, in spite of their having no previous knowledge of it. In fact, Auguste Comte had summarized in his philosophy the entire body of philosophical currents with which he had come in contact. There was nothing surprising about the rapidity with which its influence was felt in Hispanic America. By working with the same European philosophical currents, the precursors of our intellectual emancipation struggled to attain in Hispanic America the same synthesis which positivist philosophy had

---

[6] Juan Bautista Alberdi, *Ideas para presidir a la confección del curso de filosofía contemporánea en el Colegio de Humanidades* (Montevideo, 1840).

attained in Europe. It was not surprising that the Americans agreed with the Europeans or that the former should see in positivism the philosophy that they had struggled to attain through their own means.

III. POSITIVISM IN HISPANIC AMERICA

Positivism as a Philosophy for a New Order

AFTER scholasticism no other philosophical movement has gained the importance that positivism has had in Hispanic America. Scholasticism's entrenchment and vigor were due to the concept of life and the world held by the people who conquered and colonized this part of America. The Iberian Peninsula, Spain and Portugal, had become, at the time of the discovery and colonization of America, one of the last strongholds of that concept of the world which was already in retreat before what was known as modernism; England was the very embodiment of this concept. Spain and Portugal brought the Roman Catholic religion to the New World and with it the philosophy that justified it rationally. Scholasticism, as a philosophy which gave organization to the mind, completed the work which Catholicism was carrying out from the religious point of view and which Spain and Portugal established as a political power: the colonization of Ibero-America. Other philosophical currents also reached this part of America, the same ones that in Europe had been undermining, when they were not destroying, the authority of Catholic philosophy. Cartesianism, sensualism, the Enlightenment, eclecticism, ideology, and utilitarianism were such currents. Under the influence of these philosophical movements imposed upon them by the colony, the Ibero-Americans began a countermovement against the philosophy which they regarded as colonial. But none of these philosophies gained the importance of positivism. While the philosophical doctrines already mentioned were only destructive instruments, with no purpose other than that of freeing the Ibero-Americans from the body of ideas which had been imposed upon them, thus breaking the intellectual restrictions which colonialism had attempted to force upon them, positivism claimed to be something else, a philosophical doctrine which would replace scholasticism. While the other doctrines were regarded as destructive or instruments of combat, positivism was regarded as constructive, as an instrument of order. Positivistic philosophy tried to be in our independent America what scholasticism had been in the colony—an instrument of intellectual order. Those who advocated it attempted to carry out something which had not been possible up to that time in spite of political emancipation: intellectual emancipation. The problem of this emancipation was posed more dramatically in Hispanic America than in Portuguese America.

Different historical circumstances led the Hispanic American countries along a very different path from that followed by Brazil in its social and political evolution. Hispanic America tried to break violently with its colonial past; Brazil evolved in almost a natural way through various stages leading to independence. The political emancipation of Hispanic America was followed by violent internal wars, while in Brazil political emancipation, as well as other political changes, was achieved in a completely orderly manner: one fine day the nation that had gone to bed as a colony awakened as an independent empire, only to awake the following day as a republic.

The Hispanic Americans regarded positivism as a redeeming philosophical doctrine. They looked upon it as the instrument most suitable for attaining their full intellectual freedom and with it a new order which was to have repercussions in political and social fields. They regarded positivism as the philosophy suitable for imposing a new intellectual order which would replace the one destroyed, thus ending a long era of violence and political and social anarchy. The Brazilians, on the other hand, looked upon positivism as the doctrine most suitable for bringing into focus the new realities which arose in their natural social evolution. The Hispanic Americans regarded positivism as an instrument for changing an established reality; for the Brazilians it was only an instrument at the service of the reality which faced them. The Hispanic Americans tried to guide their reality; the Brazilians tried to adapt themselves to theirs.

The men of Hispanic America, even when they attempted to reestablish order, always acted as revolutionaries, for they struggled to change the mentality, habits, and customs inherited from the colony. The Brazilians, like men of order, sought only to raise their country to the level of the new circumstances.[7] Thus positivism in Spanish America was to be only, after all was said and done, an instrument for creating a great new utopia, while in Brazil it was the proper instrument for a specific reality. By following the path of evolution and not revolution, the Brazilians were true positivists. They did not experience the violent outbreaks in their evolution which took place in our countries. The Roman Catholic philosopher Jackson de Figueiredo said of positivism in his country, "If instead of positivism some other philosophical spirit had inspired the founders of the republic, where would demagogic enthusiasm have carried us? As a Brazilian, I, unlike many people, look favorably upon the more or less effective influence of positivism on our twenty-six years of republican life. Positivism knows what it wants in the midst of the confusion of ideas and egotistical feelings."[8]

In their struggle for freedom the Hispanic Americans always reacted violently; they always tried to eradicate once and for all any influence which they considered foreign. They attempted to destroy all traces of their so-called colonial heritage, as if such a thing were at all possible. They thought that they could put an end to all the evils that afflicted them by extirpating that heritage, implanting in its place new forms of understanding and facing life. By following positivism, the Mexicans thought that they could put an end to the almost perpetual anarchy which kept them in turmoil. In Argentina, positivism was considered a good instrument for eliminating the absolutist and tyrannical mentalities which had scourged them. The Chileans considered positivism an effective means of converting the ideals of liberalism into reality. In Uruguay, positivism was regarded as a moral doctrine that could put an end to a long era of military uprisings and corruption. Peru and Bolivia found in positivism a doctrine which would strengthen them after the great national catastrophe which they had suffered in their war against Chile. The Cubans looked upon it as a doctrine that would justify their desire

[7] For positivism in Brazil, see João Camilo de Oliveira Torres, *O positivismo no Brasil?* (Rio de Janeiro, 1943); Cruz Costa, *A filosofia no Brasil* (Porto Alegre, 1945); Antonio Gómez Robledo, *La Filosofía en el Brasil* (México, 1946); Guillermo Francovich, *Filósofos Brasileños* (Buenos Aires, 1943).

[8] See Francovich, *Filósofos Brasileños*.

for independence from Spain. Positivism was in every case a radical remedy which Hispanic America attempted to use to break away from a past that was overwhelming it. The Brazilians, in contrast, adopted only those aspects of positivism which their reality required. It was reality itself which demanded this doctrine, and not the doctrine which sought to impose itself upon reality.

Positivism and Its Varied Interpretations in Hispanic America

HISPANIC-AMERICAN countries interpreted positivism in various ways, always in keeping with the most urgent problems which they were attempting to solve. The interpretations were in direct relation to these urgencies and always depended upon the series of historical circumstances surrounding the problems they were trying to solve. Hence, although certain similarities can be found among the different interpretations, their most prominent common characteristic is their great diversity. One can say that there is a Hispanic-American positivism, but it is just as accurate to say that there is also a Mexican, Argentine, Uruguayan, Chilean, Peruvian, Bolivian, or Cuban positivism. In each interpretation there was always the core of problems peculiar to those who made the interpretations.

All of these interpretations rejected the Comtian religion of humanity. In this sense Hispanic Americans differed from the Brazilians, whose adaptation did accept it.[9] We find, to be sure, isolated figures, like Agustín Aragón, Horacio Barreda, and José Torres in Mexico, who followed French positivism in its entirety, although such devotion never attained major importance.[10] In Chile the brothers Juan Enrique, Jorge, and Luis Lagarrigue strove unsuccessfully for the acceptance of Comtian sociocracy. In the rest of the Hispanic American countries the humanitarian religion was definitely rejected; and in Cuba, Comtism was completely rejected because of the negative implications which the humanitarian religion might have for the revolution of independence.

The adaptation which was made of positivism as an educational doctrine was also uniform. In some countries positivism was considered the best means of forming the new type of Hispanic Amer-

[9] See bibliography cited in note 7 above.
[10] See my work *El positivismo en México* (México, 1943).

ican who would not be much different from his Anglo-Saxon model. In other countries it was looked upon as a good instrument to rid students of the so-called body of superstitions which they had inherited from the colony. It was thought that by means of a positivistic education a new type of man could eventually be created, free from all the defects he had inherited from the colony, a man with a great practical mind such as had made the United States and England the great leaders of modern civilization.

On the political level the differences would depend upon the given situation which the theoricians of Hispanic-American positivism would encounter. For example, the rejection of Comtism in Cuba and the adoption of English positivism has a direct relation to the political interest pursued by the promoters of political emancipation on the island. In Mexico, Comtism was accepted in the field of education, as it was embodied in the reforms carried out by Gabino Barreda; in the political field, on the other hand, the Mexicans followed English positivism, principally that of Spencer, thus providing the policies of the Porfirio Díaz regime with certain theoretical elements.[11] In Argentina, Comtism influenced education, while English positivism was influential in administration and politics. In Uruguay, Anglo-Saxon positivism was emphasized as a means of implementing morality in the republic. In Chile both Comtism and English positivism were interpreted from a liberal point of view. Bolivia, Peru, Paraguay, Colombia, Venezuela, and Ecuador also considered positivism a liberal doctrine.

The influence of positivism, of course, was not felt with the same vigor in all the Hispanic-American countries, although its influence was evident in all these countries. Its influence in Mexico was powerful; it impregnated an entire cultural and political era known as *porfirismo*. In this country its outstanding proponent was Gabino Barreda, who introduced positivism into Mexico and reformed the Mexican system of education; in the political field and in the field of education, Justo Sierra is eminent. Sierra, along with a group of new politicians schooled in positivism, came close to being the educational and political theorist of the era of Don Porfirio. In Argentina positivism was likewise a powerful influence. There were three outstand-

[11] See my work *Apogeo y decadencia del positivismo en México* (México, 1944).

ing groups. One comprised the so-called positivists *sui generis,* or pre-positivists, the most prominent of whom were Sarmiento, Alberdi, and Echeverría. The second was the Comtian Paraná school, whose principal influence was in the field of education through the normal schools; prominent in this group were Pedro Scalabrini, Alfredo J. Ferreira, Angel C. Bassi, Maximio Victoria, Leopoldo Herrera, and Manuel Bermúdez. Another powerful group was formed at the University of Buenos Aires, which combined Comtian positivism with English positivism, especially that of Spencer. This group was distinguished by the application which it made of scientific criterion and of the principles of evolution to various political, administrative, and educational problems. Positivism also took on in Argentina the character of an advanced and socializing liberalism. Such was the positivism of José Ingenieros and of Juan B. Justo, who were members of the Argentine Socialist party. The latter combined the evolutionism of Spencer with Marxism, thereby establishing the theoretical bases of this Socialist party, of which he was also the founder. Other Comtian positivists were to turn to the principles of this same party, among them Américo Ghioldi. In Chile, José Victorino Lastarria, one of the first positivists, was drawn to Comte by what he considered an affinity of ideas. Positivism for Lastarria was a liberal ideology, and he made it an instrument for the defense of the political liberties of his people. Another Chilean, Valentin Letelier, continued this interpretation of positivism. Opposing these positivists, who could be considered heterodox, there arose another group, the orthodox, who followed Comtian philosophy in its entirety, including its religious aspect; the Lagarrigue brothers were in this group. As will be seen later, Chilean history would offer both camps the opportunity of displaying their respective attitudes when faced by the same fact, the *coup d'état* of President Balmaceda.

In Uruguay positivism arose in opposition to the so-called spiritualist movement. The dispute revolved around the capability of both doctrines to raise the moral level of the country, torn by many military uprisings and corruption of all kinds. In Peru positivistic philosophy also had a strong influence in fomenting administrative and educational reforms. Among the outstanding men there were the sociologist and parliamentarian Mariano Cornejo, Javier Prado, and the educator Manuel Vicente Villarán. Positivism also had great influence in Cuba, where its chief exponent was Enrique José Varona. Spencer, not Comte, was the positivistic philosopher whom they followed. Comte had only one Cuban follower, Andrés Poey, who lived in France and wrote in French. For political reasons peculiar to the island, Varona and his followers had rejected Comtism. As is well known, Cuba was the last Hispanic-American country to gain its independence from Spain; hence all of its scholars, throughout almost all of the nineteenth century, were possessed by a single aim, the emancipation of the island. There existed a clear and definite line of thought among all these scholars and educators, a line that stems from Agustín Caballero, is continued in Félix Varela, culminated in José de la Luz y Caballero, and fulfilled in Varona. All of these men were prompted by the same motive: to educate and give Cubans a set of ideas which would prepare them for independence at the first opportunity that arose. Therefore, they were concerned with the choice of philosophies which they taught. Not all doctrines were suitable to awaken in their students a sense of independence and a desire to atain it. Indeed, certain philosophical doctrines could have exactly the opposite effect by influencing students to conform to the given reality. This was the case with the positivism of Auguste Comte. His idea of a semi-theological order could justify the order imposed by Spain. Spencer, on the other hand, with his doctrine of an evolution that culminates in the complete freedom of the individual and his scientific analysis of social reality justified the desire of the Cubans for freedom and led them to recognize the evils produced by the colony.

Positivism's influence began to be felt in Bolivia, as in Peru, after the Bolivian defeat in the war with Chile in 1880. This war cost Bolivia its only outlet to the sea. The Bolivians placed the blame for their defeat on their own education and intellectual training, which they considered idealistic. In opposition to this past, which was unable to measure the real forces of Bolivia, there arose a realistic and positivistic doctrine. Agustín Azpiazu was the principal figure of the positivistic movement in the republic of Bolivia. In the remainder of the Hispanic-American countries, positivism, although a powerful influence, never attained the importance that it did in the countries discussed above. In general it was regarded as an instrument of liberal ideology and of the anticlerical movement. Its principal exponent in Paraguay was Cecilio Báez; in Venezuela, Gil Fortoul; in Colombia, Nicolás Pinzón and Herrera Olarte; in Puerto Rico, the venerable educator Eugenio María de Hostos. In all of these countries French positivism was combined with English positivism, with the latter, especially Spencer's, predominating.

The Hopes and Failure of Positivism

IN EACH and every one of the instances cited, the Hispanic-American reformers regarded positivism as the best instrument by means of which they could attain their greatest goal: the intellectual emancipation of Hispanic America; that is, a complete change in the mind and character of Hispanic Americans. They thought that it was possible, through adequate education, to destroy the spirit which Spain had imposed upon its colonies. Once this spirit had been eliminated, they thought, Hispanic America could rise to the level of the great civilized nations. To the north they saw the ever more powerful model of what the nations of America should become. They attempted to destroy the spirit that made anarchy and despotism possible. They tried to put an end once and for all to a history of which all Hispanic Americans were ashamed.

As a result, between 1880 and 1900 a new Hispanic America seemed to arise. It was a Hispanic America that apparently no longer resembled in any way the Hispanic America of the first fifty years following its political independence. A new order arose in each country, but it was no longer the theological and colonial order which they had repudiated. It was now an order based upon science, an order concerned with the education of its citizens and the attainment for them of the greatest material comfort. Railroads began to be built and industry grew. An era of progress and, with it, an era of great optimism followed. In politics "liberty," "progress," and "democracy" based on science and positivism became the new watchwords. Great waves of immigration into various Hispanic-American countries made these nations realize what such an influx had meant in the United States of North America. Wealth, derived from industry, seemed to be the best stimulant for the growth of the new

America. The ideal of the liberators of Hispanic America seemed to be fulfilled.

Soon, however, a mute discontent was felt in many social spheres, and there was talk of the materialism of the age, of egotism as its personification. Education was not reaching all the social classes. Comfort was not enjoyed by all members of society. Soon great social differences would appear. Oligarchies arose that monopolized public affairs for the benefit of individual economic interests. There were also new forms of tyranny, such as that of Porfirio Díaz in Mexico. Railroads and industries grew, but they were in hands other than Hispanic American. The *bourgeoisie* in Hispanic America was but a tool in the service of the great Europeon and North American *bourgeoisie* which had been its model. The colonial spirit reappeared and with it all of its repudiated defects. Liberalism and democracy were still far from their models; they were but names which continued to disguise old forms of government. The same colonial forces continued to dominate, although they had changed their language and appearance.

These forces again raised their heads, this time in the service of new imperialisms. *Coups d'état*, revolutions, and military uprisings continued to dominate our America. Militarism and clericalism continued as negative forces, now allied with the interests of the different Hispanic American pseudo-*bourgeoisie*. All of the evils which they had attempted to eliminate by means of a positivistic education arose again, encouraged and increased in many aspects by the interests of the new empires, of which Hispanic America came to be a colony. The problem seemed insoluble: Hispanic America again appeared, as in the past, divided into two great parts, one still facing a colonial past, the other looking toward a future without a reality. They still could not bridge the gap between these two points of view. This link was the only thing that could make them fully aware of their past while still looking forward to the realization of their coveted future.

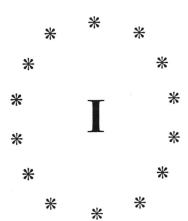

Mental Emancipation

The Revolution of Independence and the Colonial Reaction

As SOON AS political independence had been won, Hispanic Americans realized that this kind of freedom was not enough. The Venezuelan teacher and thinker Andrés Bello (1781–1865) remarked: "We snatched the scepter from the monarch, but we did not rid ourselves of the Spanish spirit: our congresses obeyed, without knowing it, Gothic inspirations. . . . even our soldiers, adhering to a special code, which was in opposition to the principle of equality before the law, revealed the predominance of the ideas of the same Spain whose banner they had trampled."[1] Hispanic America had won her political independence, but Spanish habits and customs remained firmly rooted in the mind of the Hispanic Americans.

The revolution of independence had only brought about a change of power. The revolutionists had not sought the welfare of the community, but simply power for the sake of power. The Creole had demanded from the Spaniard his right to govern because he was a native of these lands. The American revolution, said the Argentine Domingo Faustino Sarmiento, was motivated only by "a passing desire to take advantage of an opportune time to substitute local administration for a peninsular one."[2] The colonial spirit which still re-

---

[1] *Investigación sobre la inflencia de la conquista y del sistema colonial de los españoles en Chile* (Santiago de Chile, 1842); collected in *Antología del pensamiento de lengua española en la edad contemporánea*, by José Gaos (México, 1945).

[2] *Conflicto y armonía de las razas en América.*

37

mained in the mind of the Hispanic American was not long in becoming evident at the first opportunity. "Scarcely had the revolution of independence ended," said the Chilean Victorino Lastarria, "when, as a natural result of the laws of society, the reaction of the colonial spirit and of the interests which that revolution had defeated began to appear. The leaders who had served that revolution carried that spirit in their training and in their hearts."[3]

This reaction immediately sought allies in all possible areas. There began to appear the ecclesiastical-military reaction, an exponent of the conservative forces in Mexico, the provincial *caudillos* with their followers in Argentina, and the *pelucones* or conservatives in Chile. The church and army together soon took it upon themselves to establish the only order advantageous to their interests. This order was none other than the Spanish, but without Spain.

In the name of the people, and for their welfare, Doctor José Gaspar Rodríguez Francia imposed upon Paraguay one of the cruelest dictatorships the world has ever known. In Argentina, Juan Manuel de Rosas, a rancher and military man, waving the banner of liberty and provincial rights, established another historic dictatorship. In Mexico, General Antonio López de Santa Anna, sometimes under one banner, sometimes under an opposite one, established an equally nefarious dictatorship. In Ecuador, Gabriel García Moreno set up a kind of theocracy, and in Chile, Diego Portales succeeded in establishing a governmental mechanism, which imposed an impersonal but none the less effective order similar to Spanish order, and so, in other countries, the men of colonial mentality continued to establish the order that took the place of the Spanish.

Repudiation of the Colonial Heritage

IN OPPOSITION to this order, there arose a group of Hispanic-American reformers. Their ideal was to transform this mentality and destroy its habits and customs for the purpose of attaining an authentic independence, which they would call intellectual emancipation. "Society," Lastarria held, "had the duty of correcting the experience of its ancestors in order to assure its future." Hence, he asked, "Is it not necessary then to correct the civilization that Spain has given

[3] José Victorino Lastarria, *Recuerdos literarios* (Santiago de Chile, 1885).

us? . . . It," he continued, "must be completely reformed because it is the complete opposite of the democracy which we have established."[4] And in Argentina, the exiled Esteban Echeverría affirmed: "American social emancipation can only be attained by repudiating the heritage which Spain has left us."

In Mexico, José Luis Mora (1794–1850) had said that the habits of the Mexicans must be changed if the reforms were to be permanent. It is necessary that every revolution, if it is to be effective, be accompanied or prepared for by an intellectual revolution. "It is necessary," he said, "for the stability of a reform that it be gradual and that it be characterized by intellectual revolutions, which extend to society and which modify not only the opinions of certain people but also those of all the masses."[5]

Francisco Bilbao (1823–65), a romantic Chilean rebel who opposed the colonial institutions which continued after independence, said that if the governments had understood that the development of equality was a sacred legacy of revolution, they would not have succumbed, the people would have followed and supported them. "And then, with legitimate authority they would have been able to lay the foundation, by means of a general education, for a complete renovation of the people, who had kept their old beliefs."[6] It was then necessary to change the mentality of the Hispano-American people, remodel them completely, revolutionize their minds. All traces of the Spanish heritage must be extirpated. In the Spanish heritage lay all the evils. The Argentine Sarmiento (1811–88) exclaimed with his customary violence: "Do not laugh, oh, people of Hispanic America, at seeing so much degradation! Remember that you are Spanish, and the Inquisition educated Spain in that manner! We carry this disease in our blood!"[7] Perhaps none of those reformers tried as hard as Sarmiento to destroy what they considered a disease.

And so the new struggle which began with this generation was an educational and spiritual struggle which often had to resort to arms. There was, however, no longer any concern with power for the sake

[4] *Ibid.*

[5] *Obras sueltas* (Paris, 1837).

[6] *Sociabilidad chilena* (Santiago de Chile, 1844).

[7] *Facundo.*

39

of power, but only with the power to change the people of Spanish America. The idea of intellectual emancipation encouraged these men. They discussed it in their university classrooms, in their newspaper articles, in their manifestos, and in their speeches. A generation, romantic in ideals, began this struggle for the new emancipation. Belonging to this generation are the Argentines Esteban Echeverría, Domingo Faustino Sarmiento and Juan Bautista Alberdi; the Venezuelan Andrés Bello, the Ecuadorian Juan Montalvo (1833–89), the Peruvian, Manuel González Prada, the Chileans Francisco Bilbao and José Victorino Lastarria; the Cuban José de la Luz Caballero, and the Mexican José María Luis Mora, plus the champions of reform and still others in various Hispanic-American countries.

These men opposed the despotism of the past as their parents and grandparents had opposed the despotism of the Spanish government. Lastarria (1817–88) had said: "The despotism of the kings had fallen, and the despotism of the past remained alive with all its vigor. The revolution of independence was over and the war against the powerful spirit which the colonial system had inspired in our society was just beginning."[8] Andrés Bello, with characteristic balance, understood that although the movement for political independence had been precipitated, it was nevertheless necessary. The second phase of political independence, that of intellectual emancipation, would have to be the work of the American people. "We have the alternative of taking advantage of the first opportunity or of prolonging our servitude for centuries." We could no longer expect from Spain "the education that prepares one to enjoy liberty. . . . we should educate ourselves, no matter how costly the effort."[9]

Esteban Echeverría (1805–51), in speaking of the same thing, said: "The American generation is infested with the habits and tendencies of another generation. On their faces they show the recent scars of their past enslavement, if not the dejection of the slave." It was against this slavery that they must fight. It was necessary to root it out of the mind of Hispanic Americans; otherwise, the political emancipation of the Hispanic American would have been futile. In

---

[8] *Investigaciones sobre la influencia social de la conquista y del sistema colonial de los españoles en Chile* (Santiago de Chile, 1844).

[9] Bello, *Investigación . . . de la conquista.*

this generation, said Echeverría, "the body has been emancipated, but not its mind." Independent America still wears, "as a sign of vassalage, traces of the imperial trappings of what once belonged to its mistress, and adorns itself with its moth-eaten livery. . . . The arms of Spain no longer oppress us, but its traditions still weigh us down." It was necessary to oppose this spirit and it was necessary to be freed from it. "The revolution marches on," he said, "but with shackles." "A political emancipation" and "a social emancipation" must take place in every authentic revolution. Echeverría considered social emancipation as the revolution which was to change the entire social and mental status imposed by Spain; this was precisely the revolution that was lacking.

How was it to be affected? Echeverría answered, "The American social emancipation can only be attained by repudiating the heritage that Spain left us."[10] The May revolution, that is, the revolution for Argentine independence, he said, had as its purpose "political emancipation from Spanish domination," a triumph that was completely successful when Spain was defeated. But it also had a further intent: "The founding of an emancipated society on a principle different from colonial rule."[11] This had not been attained. This, then, was the task which was imposed upon the new generation; it was the same task which other groups in other countries attempted to carry out. The new generation tried to complete the work done by the liberators, with the realization that it had been incomplete and insufficient.

The Colony in Hispanic-American Mentality

SPAIN was a part of the mind and the habits of Hispanic Americans. She was the cause of all the troubles they had suffered. Mental vassalage continued, and the vassals acted only in accordance with the limitations that the mother country had imposed upon them throughout long centuries of mental, political, and social domination. It was this same intellectual domination that produced the useless slaughter in which the Hispanic Americans had engaged after they had cut their political ties with Spain. They had tried futilely to establish in

[10] *Dogma socialista de la Asociación de Mayo* (Buenos Aires, 1838).
[11] *Mayo y la enseñanza popular en el Plata* (Montevideo, 1844).

their countries forms of government in which liberty and democracy would thrive. The Hispanic Americans were not ready for either. The ideals of liberty and democracy on their lips were but words, simple pretexts, by which they sought their right to govern; that is, to impose their wills upon the wills of others. Each Hispanic-American *caudillo,* without regard for his mottoes or his banners, only aspired to occupy the place abandoned by the conquistador.

The revolution of independence, Bello remarked, had been animated by the imperial Hispanic spirit. It had been a political revolution, not a liberal revolution. The spirit of the liberators was only an ally, not the ultimate end which they sought. "In our revolution liberty was a foreign ally which fought under the standard of independence and which, even after victory, has had to do a great deal to consolidate and entrench itself."[12] The idea of a liberal revolution was completely alien to Hispanic-American mentality, and in order to achieve it, it was necessary for the legislators to take into account, above all, the reality within which it was to develop. It was a reality that was opposed, or at least alien, to such an idea. And it could only be a success, said Bello, when it was adapted to the harsh Iberian reality. "The work of the soldiers is over; that of the legislators will not be ended until this idea imported from abroad penetrates more deeply into the hard and tenacious Iberian temperament."

Bello continued, "The Americans are better prepared for political emancipation than for freedom of the domestic hearth." In the revolution of independence two ideas animated each of the movements: "one spontaneous," the political; "the other imitative and foreign," the liberal—"one often standing in the way of the other, rather than helping it." While "the foreign principle produced progress," the native "produced dictatorships." One principle created the desire to raise Hispanic America to the level of the times; the other caused the liberators and *caudillos* of the struggles for independence to believe that Hispanic America was still far from that ideal, and that it should therefore continue to be subjected to forms of government that made such progress impossible.

All Hispanic America was divided into two great camps: those

12 Bello, *Investigación . . . de la conquista.*

who sought to make it a modern land and those who believed that the time for this had not yet come and that only a government similar to the Spanish government could save it. Unitarians against Federalists in Argentina, *pelucones* against *pipiolos* in Chile, Federals and Centralists in Mexico, Colombia, Venezuela, and other countries. Nevertheless, no matter who won, the spirit inherited from Spain soon reappeared. Some wanted only to re-establish Spanish order, but without Spain, while others, now in power, considered that it was first necessary to prepare the Hispanic Americans for liberty and that dictatorships were a necessary preparation. In 1810, said Echeverría, the people became sovereign without limitations, but this was but a standard to attract them. It was soon discovered that they were unfit for this liberty. They had no civic or cultural talents. The "enlightened" emancipators found no solution other than tyranny.

Spanish tyranny or enlightened tyranny, but always tyranny. Rosas, Portales, and García Moreno; Francia and Rivadavia; or Santa Anna. "The Unitarian party," said Echeverría, "had no local rules of social criterion; they looked for it in the cities, but it was in the country. They were unable to organize it, and they, therefore, were unable to control it. [The party] had no faith in the people." On the other hand, among the extreme opposition, "Rosas was shrewder; he seized the democratic element, exploited it skillfully, and relied on its power to establish tyranny. The Unitarians were able to do the same thing to establish the rule of law."[13] Nevertheless, in spite of their enlightened ideals, the Unitarians only alienated themselves from the people, forcing Rosas, who was waving the banner of federalism—that is, the autonomy of the provinces—to impose one of the most historic dictatorships in Hispanic America. "For Dorrego the North American constitution was a beautiful ideal of federal organization," Echeverría said, "and Moreno, the most doctrinaire of the opposition in the congress, never stopped invoking it; but for both of them the North American federation was an arm of reaction and combat, rather than a norm for organization."[14]

Sarmiento was aware also of the futility of the hypothetical ideals held by the parties. Actually their sole aspiration was power for the

[13] Echeverría, *Dogma socialista*, 1846.
[14] Echeverría, *Mayo y la enseñanza*, in *Obras Completas*.

sake of power. It was useless to speak to the Argentines of unitarianism or federalism; the terms never had the same meaning for them as they did for Europeans. Hidden behind these parties were the abiding interests which had always animated the men of the colony. Behind them were hidden the desire for personal rule, the rule of the *caudillo,* the exploitation of the weak, absolutisms and fanaticisms. Every Hispanic American, whatever banner he followed, aspired only to political control, to the elimination of those who did not think as he did. "We have spent twenty years trying to find out if we are to be Federalists or Unitarians," said Sarmiento, "but what kind of organization can you possibly give to an unpopulated country, to one million men scattered over a limitless extension of land?" And, "so in order to be Unitarians or Federalists, it was necessary for some to eliminate others; it was necessary for some to kill others or persecute them or exile them. Instead of increasing the population of the country, they have diminished it; instead of advancing knowledge, they were intent upon persecuting the most educated."[15] The Hispanic Americans continued to be just as the Spaniards had made them; the defects of the latter continued to be their defects. While the North American revolution, added Sarmiento, was waged in defense of constitutional rights, the South American revolution was motivated by the obvious desire to take advantage of the propitious opportunity to substitute a local administration for the peninsular.

II. THE MIDDLE AGES AND MODERNITY IN AMERICAN CULTURE

Hispanic America, Bulwark of the Middle Ages

THE GENERATION concerned with the intellectual emancipation of Hispanic America considered this struggle as a continuation of the one that took place in Europe between the forces of the Middle Ages and the forces of modernity; it was a struggle between theocratic absolutism and liberal democracy, between the forces of retrogression and those of progress. It was Spain's lot to represent the forces of the Middle Ages. Hispanic America had thus become, through the work and influence of its conquerors, one of the last bulwarks of theocratic and feudal imperialism.

[15] D. F. Sarmiento, *Argirópolis.*

Esteban Echeverría had shown that the political independence of Argentina had been but one of the first steps taken in America to continue the struggle which in Europe had ended with the triumph of the forces of modernity. Spain had resisted the Reformation and the Renaissance, the sixteenth-century philosophical manifestation of the struggle, with the spirit of absolutism and with the Inquisition. This spirit had left its imprint in Hispanic America, closing it off from all possible contact with the modern world which in Europe was winning ground on all sides. Spain, "ruling and conquering by arms, but without a comprehensive intelligence, had been unable to establish anything either beautiful or robust, nothing for herself, and nothing for the other peoples, since the force that destroys does not create anything." Spain, preoccupied now with her own defense, with the defense of the concept of the world and of life of which she was the heir, was no longer concerned with creating but only with preserving what had already been done. A Spain ossified and hardened by resistance was America's heritage from her conqueror.

This America, declared Echeverría, "was infinitely more backward than Spain," for she had taken great care that no influences should enter which might destroy her empire. Because Hispanic America was hedged in and isolated, the difficulties in the way of its intellectual regeneration would be many. "Separated from Europe by an ocean and walled in by a prohibitive system, with the Inquisition in its midst," said Echeverría, "Hispanic America vegetated in darkness."[16] The Hispanic Americans themselves, using their own resources and committing many errors in the process, were forced to bring about their political as well as their intellectual emancipation. The new generation sought only to complete and put in order the work already done by the liberators. Echeverría and the men of his generation likewise looked upon themselves as continuers of the work carried out by the political emancipators of Argentina, and in their honor they called their group the *Asociación de Mayo*.

Modernity in Hispanic-American Mentality

Juan Bautista Alberdi (1810–84), discussing the influence of Europe in America, felt that the latter was entering a second stage

---

[16] E. Echeverría, *Antecedentes y primeros pasos de la revolución de Mayo*.

of its cultural life, a stage that Europe had transcended with the so-called modern epoch. In Europe two forces had struggled against each other: Gothic and Modern. "Who then was the winner in this struggle?" he asked. It was the Europe of France and England which represented the civilization of the last centuries. "This civilization," he added, "after triumphing on the other continent, passed to this one, where today it is struggling for new victories, but of another kind and by other means."

In order to defend itself and the civilization which it represented, Spain had taught the Hispanic Americans to hate Europe. But when speaking of Europe, Spain was referring to the part which she did not represent. "The kings of Europe," said Alberdi, "taught us to hate as foreign anything that was not Spanish." The first Hispanic-American liberators inherited this hatred, for they considered Spain an expression of European culture. "The liberators of 1810, regarding Spain as a part of Europe, taught us to hate, as an enemy of America, everything that was European. The question of war was formulated in these terms: Europe and America. Spain called this first hatred 'loyalty,' the liberators called the second one 'patriotism.'"

America against Europe was the argument bandied about in the struggle unleashed between Rosas' and Alberdi's generations. Rosas came forward as the champion of Argentine nationalism rooted in the American soil, as the defender of an order suitable for America—that is, the feudal order that Spain had maintained for centuries. Alberdi's generation would not accept this order; they wanted for America, in general, and for Argentina, in particular, the civilization and the order which Europe had attained after conquering the medieval forces.

Patriotism does not figure in this struggle at all. "The fatherland," said Alberdi, "is not the land. We have had the land for three centuries, but we have only had a fatherland since 1810." There was no fatherland in the colony. The fatherland was born with independence. Hence, the fatherland is a special idea. "The fatherland is liberty, order, wealth, civilization on the native soil, organized under the very essence and in the name of the soil itself." These ideas, he added, this way of regarding the fatherland, "was brought to us from Europe." The indigenous had no knowledge of these things. This was but the transfer of an idea which had triumphed previously on the old continent. The Americans, as long as they aspired to realize such an idea, continued to be Europeans. For Alberdi, Americans were only Europeans transplanted to America. Hence the same struggle which had taken place in Europe took place in their minds. "Everything in the civilization of our land is European," said Alberdi. "We could define civilized America by saying that it is Europe established in America. . . . We who call ourselves Americans are but Europeans born in America."

The revolution had not done anything and would not do anything but emancipate the Americans from the same forces from which the Europeans had already been emancipated. "The Spanish Europe which bequeathed us a nascent civilization from another continent came to an end in America with the revolution. . . . We Americans today are but Europeans who have changed mentors: English and French initiative has succeeded the Spanish." Modern forces have supplanted Gothic forces, and democracy has followed theocracy. The new forces came only to complete the civilizing work of Europe in America which was initiated by Spain. A new Europe, an evolutionized Europe had taken the place of the one that discovered, conquered, and educated America, thus completing the civilizing work. "Contemporary Europe comes today to complete in America the work of medieval Europe." Such an act was necessary "because the work of our civilization is incomplete; it is just now at the halfway mark: Europe, the author of the first half, must also be the author of the second."[17] A new age was beginning in America. The period of warlike conquests and arms had ended. America could no longer be conquered by arms, but by ideas, which were influential in the second American emancipation.

Civilization against Barbarism

"IN THE ARGENTINE REPUBLIC," said Sarmiento, "there are two different civilizations on the same soil: one, a nascent civilization, is correcting the ingenious and popular efforts of the Middle Ages; another is attempting to put into effect the latest achievements of European civilization. The nineteenth and the twelfth century live

[17] J. B. Alberdi, *Acción de la Europa en América.*

together: one in the cities, the other in the country." These two forces are engaged in a tragic struggle for American soil, just as they struggled for European soil. Sarmiento called one "civilization," the other "barbarism."

"There were," he said, "before 1810 in the Argentine Republic two different, rival, and incompatible societies, two different civilizations—one Spanish, European, and civilized; the other barbarous, American, and almost indigenous. The revolution of the cities would only serve as a cause, a motive, for these two ways of life of a people to oppose each other, to attack each other, and, after many years of struggle, for one to absorb the other." Spain was thus, according to Sarmiento, the first civilizing agent in America. In contrast to autochthonous and barbarous America, Spain represented European civilization. The first step toward civilization was taken when theocratic and medieval Spain absorbed barbarous America. But this first step was not enough. European civilization had made new advances, in the light of which Spain was already a backward and outmoded nation. As for Spanish America, absorbed by medieval Spanish civilization, it was not only outmoded, but it was the expression of a new barbarism. Hence it was necessary for America to take a new step toward civilization, a step that would mean a new liberating and civilizing epoch.

In America it was the cities that felt most urgently the need for this new civilizing task; not so the rural areas, which remained Spanish and faithful to the Spanish spirit. Hence "the revolution," said Sarmiento, "except in its exterior symbol, independence from the king, was interesting and understandable only in the cities of Argentina; it was strange and without any prestige in the rural areas." The rural areas accepted political independence, but they were not ready to accept a change in their way of thinking.

The Argentina war of independence had a double character: On one hand, there was the European aspect, a "war of the cities, initiated by European culture against the Spaniards, for the purpose of extending this culture." This was the war of the modern spirit against the old spirit represented by Spain. On the other hand, there was the American aspect, a "war of the *caudillos* against the cities, for the purpose of freeing themselves from all civil restraint, for developing their character and unleashing their hatred against civilization. This was the war of the Spanish spirit, which remained in the rural areas, against modern civilization, centered in the cities. In the first war the spirit of modernity triumphed, and, as Sarmiento said, "The cities triumphed over the Spaniards." In the second war the colonial spirit triumphed, the heritage of imperial Spain won. "The rural areas defeated the cities." Buenos Aires had conquered Spain, but Rosas, the *caudillo* of rural feudalism, conquered Buenos Aires. The modern spirit, conqueror of the medieval European spirit, was conquered by American medievalism.

The struggle continued in this manner. Civilized Americans had now to complete the work effected by the modern spirit in Europe and the task begun by the American liberators of 1810. Sarmiento's generation looked upon itself as the heir to this new task. It had to complete the work that the *caudillos* of May could not finish; it had to take the revolution of the cities to the country in order to destroy the pernicious influence of colonial medievalism. "Why do we fight?" Sarmiento asked. "We are fighting to return to the cities their own way of life." His generation attempted to restore the spirit of modernity to the cities by defeating the medieval spirit.

Buenos Aires was the representative of the modern spirit. Its struggle was the struggle of this spirit. Its mission was to conquer in America the medieval world in the same way that it had been conquered in Europe. The struggle that was carried on in America was but a continuation of the struggle that had taken place in Europe. "Buenos Aires," said Sarmiento, "looks upon itself as a continuation of Europe, and if it does not confess frankly that it is French and North American in spirit and tendency, it denies its Spanish origin."[18]

Catholicism or Republicanism

FRANCISCO BILBAO regarded the vital forms of the Middle Ages and modern times as two forces which were struggling against each other and tearing the soul of Hispanic America apart. It was a struggle between two contradictory ways of life, expressed in the two formulas "Catholicism" and "republicanism." Instead of supporting each other, they contradicted each other. "Religion," said Bilbao,

[18] *Facundo.*

"should support politics, and politics religion. This is the basis of lasting peace and of strength." But when they do not, "when religion denies politics and politics religion, the poles of the moral universe are inverted." This was the cause of anarchy and of weakness. What was the happening in Hispanic America? "Catholicism is the religion of South America. The republican form of government was the political policy of South America." Catholicism denied the fundamental principles of a republic, the sovereignty of the people and the sovereignty of reason in all men. For its part, "republicanism denies the dogma which imposes blind obedience upon it," and likewise it does not recognize any authority which forces it to give such obedience.

"This is," said Bilbao, "the dualism of South America, a dualism that will destroy us if we do not make one of the two propositions prevail." Agreement was practically impossible; the Hispanic American must choose. "Either Catholicism triumphs, and monarchy and theocracy rule America, or republicanism triumphs, with free reason and the religion of law dominating the conscience of every man." A feudal monarchy or a liberal republic! The medieval forces and the modern forces each seek their own political forms. "Either Catholic dogma builds its political world, a monarchy, or the republican principle rises and affirms its dogma, rationalism." Both Catholicism and republicanism search for their complement within their own sense of life. "The Catholic religion searches for its form of government. The republican form of government searches for its religion." The policy of the first is monarchy; the religion of the second is rationalism.

The struggle between these two forces became more and more open. Bilbao warned America of the danger that was awaiting it. The church was no longer content with spiritual power; it sought and struggled openly to attain material power. "The Catholic religion," he said, "tired of spiritual supremacy, wants and aspires to temporal supremacy." Mexico was in that situation, where the church, supported by a revived French theocracy incarnate in Napoleon III, had set up a monarchy. "The time has come," he added, "for America to think of its destiny. Its destiny is to maintain the balance of justice against despotism and demagogy, against socialist utopias, and against dying religions. . . . Its destiny is to provide bread and justice for the hungry multitudes of Europe." But, he added, all this would be lost if we did not make the Mexican cause the American cause.

In this struggle "the republican form of government aspires and seeks to found its principles on the eternal axiom of liberty." It finds its perfection in liberty. Nevertheless, the struggle is difficult in Hispanic America for the republican forces, because their followers still do not have a sense of freedom. "I know very well," continued Bilbao, "how much the American mind resists the stimulation of free thought. The Americans still do not consider themselves free, and like nocturnal birds, they search for darkness to carry on their activities." But it was no time to hesitate, the Hispanic Americans would necessarily have to choose between one form or another: to accept domination or freedom. And it would be necessary to choose if they sought a strong America. "In order to strengthen America, either the absolute predominance of Catholicism with all its consequences, as in Rome, or the predominance of liberty, as in the United States, would be necessary."[19] Rome and the United States were for Bilbao the two citadels of the forces in conflict.

Progress against Retrogression

The Mexican José María Luis Mora noted also that two forces were in conflict, representing two antagonistic ways of life: the colonial and the modern. The war between the forces of progress and those of retrogression followed the war of political independence. "The revolution of independence," said Mora, "was a universal and effective disintegrating force that put an end not only to caste distinctions but also to old family ties, privileges of nobility, and opprobrious "distinctions." But that was not enough, because the independence proclaimed by the pretentious priesthood increased the power of the clergy; and independence, whose most visible manifestations were fought for and won by material force, created a predominance of the military and the habit of considering brute force and priestly aspirations as the only powers."

The forces of progress were identified with liberal ideals, while the forces of retrogression were but the continuation or remnants of

---

[19] *La América en peligro.*

habits imposed by the forces represented by Spain. The clergy and the military, heirs of these forces, tried to maintain inherited privileges in Hispanic America, while the forces of progress tended to carry out "more or less rapidly" the seizure of the property of the clergy, the abolition of the privileges of both the clergy and the military, the extension of public education among the people absolutely independent of the clergy, the suppression of monastic orders, the absolute freedom of opinion, the equality of foreigners with natives in civil law, and the establishment of a jury in criminal cases. The struggle was therefore between one force which upheld the interests of a group and another which sought the protection of public interest. Mora was not opposed to the clergy and the military, but he was opposed to the spirit which they attempted to maintain. "No cultured or religious nation," he said, "can exist without a clergy or an army." But both must be in the public service, at the service of the people, and not the contrary. "Every Mexican should ask himself daily if the people exist for the clergy or if the clergy was created to satisfy the needs of the people."[20]

III. THE SPANISH HERITAGE IN HISPANIC AMERICA

The Esprit de Corps against National Interest

THE PRINCIPAL CAUSE, it has been said, the reason which has prevented the Hispanic American from becoming a completely modern man is to be found in his Spanish heritage, from which he had not yet been able to free himself fully. José María Luis Mora, in speaking of the constitution of Mexico, blamed the habits inherited from Spain for the inability of the Mexican to understand the modern meaning of nationalism. Among these habits, he said, there figured and still figures as one of the principal ones "the *esprit de corps* permeating all classes of society." It is this *esprit de corps* which has a "noticeable debilitating effect or which destroys the national spirit."

Either because of a premeditated plan or as an unforeseen result of unknown causes brought into play, the fact is that "in the civil realm of old Spain there was a marked tendency to create corporations and to accumulate about them privileges and exemptions from

[20] *Obras sueltas* and *Ensayos, ideas y retratos*, selected by Arturo Arnáiz y Freg (México, 1941).

the common law." Only within the framework of these privileges did the Spaniards and Mexicans act. The feeling of nationalism did not exist; there was only the feeling of the group with all the privileges which it signified. "If independence," Mora added, "had been achieved forty years ago, a man born or living in the territory would have had no respect whatsoever for the word 'Mexican,' and he would have considered himself alone and isolated in the world, if he counted only upon this designation." For this man the title of *oidor* or any other "would have been more highly regarded, and one must agree that he would have been right, since it stood for something more positive."

To have discussed "the national interests" with this type of man "would have been like speaking to him in Hebrew. He did not recognize, nor could he recognize, any interests other than those of the special group or groups to which he belonged, and he would have sacrificed, in order to uphold them, those of the rest of society. . . . If then a congress had convened, who doubts that its members would have been elected by the special groups and not by the electorate, who doubts that each one of them would have considered himself a representative of these groups and not of the nation, and that there would have been a hundred thousand arguments over the rights, privileges, etc. . . . and that nobody would have bothered about what might interest the masses?"

This heritage, this *esprit de corps*, made it impossible for Mexicans to place national interests above their private interests. "Thus we see," said Mora, "the class interests destroying public interests." This spirit impedes the march of progress, which has as its goal the common good of all society. "An *esprit de corps* produces and supports an inversion of social principles." Nothing exists beyond its own interests. "The class," declared Mora, "is offended and dishonored when one of its members appears delinquent; hence the zeal to hide the crime or save the culprit, to remove him from the hands of authority or to prevent his punishment." But it must not be otherwise, for no member should "fail to meet the obligations peculiar to his class," because then, "even though they are of little or no interest to society, a dispute arises that public authority quite often cannot settle."

This attitude has done nothing except completely pervert all the principles of public morality when it created obligations that should not exist and that are alien to this morality, "disregarding in many cases, much too frequently, all human society. . . . Here again the *esprit de corps* weakens public morality and loses sight of the ideas which should be held concerning public morality."[21] It is against this spirit, against this heritage, that the generation following political emancipation would struggle.

"Even though the basis of Mexican character is entirely Spanish," said Mora, "since it could not be anything else, the mutual motives of anger which for twenty years have been fomented between both peoples by barbarism and prolongation of the struggle for independence have caused the Mexicans to show the greatest zeal in renouncing everything that is Spanish. For they do not consider themselves completely independent if, after having shaken off the political yoke, they find themselves subject to habits and customs of the former mother country."[22] A struggle for intellectual independence and freedom from old habits and customs was to follow political independence.

Atrophy of the Faculty of Thinking

THE ARGENTINES, seeking the cause of all the evils from which Spanish America was suffering, likewise gave the same answer: Spain. "The evil," shouted Sarmiento, "is within us!" We Hispanic Americans are but the heirs of all the defects of the Spanish race. In addition to these defects, we must add those of the races with whom we have mixed in America, the indigenous and the Negro. Sarmiento said: In America, "we shall see what a mixture of pure Spanish, European elements, with a good portion of the Negro race, all diluted into an enormous mass of indigenous, primitive men with little intelligence, will produce." And these three racial elements had scarcely "any practice in the political liberties which constitute a modern government."

As for the intelligence of the Spanish people, Sarmiento added, it "became atrophied by a kind of mutilation cauterized with fire."

[21] Mora, *Revista política de las diversas administraciones que la República ha tenido hasta 1837.*

[22] In *Ensayos, ideas y retratos.*

54

For it has already been established through the study of comparative anatomy that "a muscle not used for centuries . . . becomes atrophied through lack of use." If we are to accept the fact, continued Sarmiento, that the exercise of intelligence enlarges the brain, "one can well believe that the Spaniard's has not increased any since the fourteenth century, before the Inquisition began to function." As for the Hispanic Americans, it is to be feared that "in general their brain is smaller than the peninsular Spaniard's because of the mixture with races that are known to have smaller brains than the European races." On the one hand, added the Argentine scholar, there are the Indians, who "do not think because they are not prepared for it"; and on the other hand, there are the white Spaniards, who have "lost the habit of exercising the brain as an organ. . . . The Spaniards, and more so the South Americans, are born enervated by this atrophy of governmental faculties already acquired by the human race." It was this heritage that made it impossible for the Hispanic American to attain the wealth that civilization had already given to other races.

Democracy, and with it the liberty which it presupposed, were as a result impossible among people inheriting a mentality diminished by despotic forces. "A Spaniard or an American of the sixteenth century," said Sarmiento, "should have said, 'I exist, therefore I do not think.' " For he would not have lived if he had had the misfortune to think for himself. "The barbarians triumphed with the kings of Castile and Aragon, for compared with the kings of Granada and Córdoba, the kings of the interior of Spain were barbarians." Only barbarous people could conceive of imposing beliefs by means of fire and torture. "Phillip II was the embodiment of the Mohammedan-Spanish principle of the unity of beliefs. He, and not the Pope, established the Inquisition." This institution was nothing but Mohammedan heritage. "Without Mohammed there is no Inquisition in Spain. . . . The Pope kept the Inquisition alive without fire. But only in Spain and with former Mohammedans could they build altars to cannibalism and to the aversion to witchcraft which savages have kept."[23] Such is the mentality inherited by Hispanic America; such is the disease that we have in our blood. "Terror is within us."

[23] *Conflicto y armonía de las razas en América.*

Esteban Echeverría, on the other hand, said: "Two fatal legacies from Spain were the principal forces in checking the progressive movement of the American revolution: its customs and its legislation." Its habits and its forms of government—these inherited customs and legislation arrested the advance of the revolution. "The great thought of the revolution has not been realized. We are independent, but not free." From inherited habits and laws anarchy has risen and, with it, the counterrevolution. The Hispanic American, trained to obey, did not know what to do with liberty when he got his independence, and he surrendered to chaos. Those who held to the old idea of order were to take advantage of this chaos in an attempt to re-establish that order. "The static idea," said Echeverría, "the Spanish idea, coming out of the dark lair, raises again triumphantly its stupid head and hurls anathemas against the reforming and progressive spirit." But, he concluded, filled with faith in progress, "its triumph will be ephemeral. . . . it is God's will that today not resemble tomorrow and that the present century not be a monotonous repetition of the previous one . . . and that in the moral world as in the physical, in the life of man, as in the life of peoples, all will march forward and progress."[24] This progress will come about, as far as Hispanic America is concerned, through its repudiation of the Spanish heritage.

Juan Bautista Alberdi, considering this nefarious heritage, prophesied: "Many states of America will have their Rosases. I say their Rosases, because they will have them; not in vain was Rosas called 'man of America.' He is, in truth, the man of America, because he is a political type that will be seen throughout America as a logical product of what produced him in Buenos Aires and of what exists in other Spanish American countries. Rosas is a product of the American soil, a product of what it has become as a result of the work of Spanish colonization. . . . Everywhere when an orange tree reaches a certain age, it produces oranges," continued Alberdi. "Wherever there are Spanish republics formed out of former colonies, there will be dictators when the development of affairs reaches a certain point."[25]

[24] *Dogma socialista de la Asociación de Mayo.*
[25] *La República Argentina 37 años después de su revolución de Mayo.*

Vices Inherited from the Colony

THE FEUDAL SPIRIT and Catholicism which opposed the modern spirit of liberal democracy we have inherited from Spain, declared Bilbao. "Our past is the Spain of the Middle Ages." The body and soul of the Middle Ages was "Catholicism and feudalism." This is what the Hispanic Americans have inherited, a Catholicism that glorifies slavery. "A mountain of snow upon the fire of individual dignity. This is the glorification of slavery." We, the Hispanic Americans, have "emerged from the Middle Ages of Spain." The Middle Ages were fulfilled in Spain; there they reached their maximum development. America became Spain when it received her stamp. "Slavery, degradation . . . . This is the past!"

In contrast to this heritage is "our revolution or past with a future"; it emerged as the "New Age," from Europe. "The New Age," said Bilbao, "first appeared in France"; therefore it was necessary for us to link our thought to French revolutionary thought if we wanted to free ourselves from the Middle Ages. Intellectual freedom is natural to all men; it is not in itself a contradiction of the work of God. "Does God, who has given us a head where such great potentialities exist, then authorize the possessors of his law to make it so small that it will hold only what they wish?"[26] No, he answered. The limitation of the mind is something alien to nature and creation. It is the work of a given way of thinking, the way that Spain developed to its maximum.

In his book *Influencia social de la conquista,* Victorino Lastarria said: "The Spaniards conquered America, soaking its soil in blood, not to colonize it, but rather to take possession of the precious metals that it produced so abundantly." America was just a booty of war. But when Spain attempted to colonize it, she transplanted into Hispanic America "all the vices of her absurd system of government, vices that multiplied infinitely as a result of causes that had their origin in the system itself."

To these vices was added the scorn that the peninsular felt for the new owner of the American soil, the *mestizo.* The *mestizo* became

[26] Bilbao, *Sociabilidad chilena.*

the bastard of America. "What greater insult could taint the man of the times," said Lastarria, "what crime could dishonor him more atrociously than the mixture of blood!" The *mestizo* carried on his brow the mark of degradation and infamy; his birth condemned him to the misfortune of being the pariah of society. His social position was a thousand times worse than that of the Indian. He was the one who, with the Indian, had to endure the harshest and most degrading tasks. While the Spaniards and the Creoles shunned all types of work and grew wealthy, the Indians and the *mestizos* were employed exclusively as workmen "because they were condemned to hard work as a result of their degradation." Work became therefore punishment, something degrading. This, said Lastarria, is "the reason that the immoral and pernicious custom of scorning all those who devote their labors to industry has been perpetuated to our day."

This attitude has made it impossible for the Hispanic American to join the march of progress, since progress has as its basis personal work. Such is the fatal consequence of this habit left by Spain. Lastarria's generation struggled against it, and many other habits. By focusing its attention on the reality inherited from Spain, the new generation realized the difficulties that the Hispanic American would have to overcome to gain his true independence. Was or was not our society prepared to enter a new kind of life? Lastarria asked. Could it subject itself to a system diametrically opposed to the one that had guided it for three centuries and under which its very being had taken shape? "Certainly not," he answered, "the colonists had been educated precisely to live in servitude and not to desire or even know a condition better than that to which they had been subjected. Both laws and customs conspired to conceal from them their importance and to destroy their individuality; the colonists, in short, had no consciousness of themselves, and they were entirely, their lives and their interests, absorbed by the royal and theocratic power upon which they completely depended."

In order to attain political independence, Lastarria said, the Hispanic-American revolutionaries had to disguise their aspirations by saying that they were serving their king held prisoner by the French. "The revolutionaries disguise and continue their activities, but the idea of the sovereign disappears slowly, losing prestige on account of events until it is replaced by the idea of national independence, when the conflagration becomes general and the majority of the nation takes part in the movement." The reason for this attitude of the revolutionaries may be explained by something which had no relation whatsoever to liberal democracy, which later became their banner. "It is still a problem for me," said Lastarria, "whether, in this manner of proceeding, the wisdom of the promoters of the revolution had any influence or not, or whether it was the fear of meeting abruptly difficulties which they had no means of overcoming, or whether, instead, it was the limitation of their aspirations, reduced, perhaps solely, to the advantage of not being governed by a foreign power not invested with the majesty of kings."[27] Hispanic-American mentality conditioned to obey the theocratic power of the kings of Spain was unable to recognize any authority that was not invested with such trappings.

Favorable Aspects of the Spanish Heritage

ANDRÉS BELLO objected to the above theses, especially to Lastarria's interpretation of the influence of the Conquest in America. It must not be forgotten that the Hispanic Americans are sons of Spain and America. This is a reality which one must always keep in mind. Everything was not necessarily negative in this reality; there also existed some positive elements which ought to be utilized. For Bello the ills of Hispanic America did not necessarily proceed from race, nor were they ills that could be attributed to the Spanish influence in the colony. These evils are common to all of humanity; they were the weaknesses of humanity.

"Injustice, atrocity, perfidy in war," he said, "were not common to the Spaniards alone, but to all races in every country." Spanish barbarism is the same barbarism that all people in similar circumstances have employed or could have employed. Barbarism is still practiced, he said, even though other means to perpetrate it have been used. "The horrors of war have been partially mitigated, not because humanity is more respected, but because material interests are better calculated." That is why "it would be madness to enslave the vanquished, if more can be gained by making them tributaries and forced

[27] *Influencia social de la conquista.*

59

providers of the conqueror's industry." We must not accuse any nation of these evils, but instead "of human nature."

Spain's contribution to the colony was not entirely negative. "America still owes everything that there is of grandeur and splendor in its public buildings to the Spanish government." And we must confess with shame that we have been able to keep little of this. As for the war of independence, the Hispanic American owes much to the spirit he inherited from Spain. To be sure, said Bello, accepting the thesis of Sarmiento, Lastarria, and other thinkers, our revolution was animated by the Spanish spirit: it was a political and not a liberal revolution. Liberalism was only an ally of the first objective. But, sparking the revolution, there was something more, of a positive character, something that was also inherited from Spain. "A people thoroughly vilified, completely crushed, devoid of all virtuous sentiment has never been able to execute the great deeds that glorified the campaigns of the patriots, the heroic acts of abnegation, the sacrifices of all kinds with which Chile and other American sectors won their political emancipation." The spirit that animated this abnegation and sacrifice was inherited from Spain; it was this spirit that defeated Spain herself.

"Whoever observes philosophically the history of our struggle with the mother country," added Bello, "will quickly recognize that it was precisely the Iberian element that made it possible for us to defeat her. . . . Native Spanish persistence clashed with the inborn stubbornness of the sons of Spain. The patriotic instinct in the hearts of Americans led them to deeds similar to those of the Spaniards at Numancia and Zaragossa. . . . The captains and the veteran legions of European Iberia were defeated and humiliated by the *caudillos* and improvised armies of another young Iberia which, rejecting its name, maintained the indomitable spirit of the ancient defense of its homes."

What was alien to this spirit was the modern meaning of what has been called "the republican spirit." "Republican elements did not exist," said Bello; "Spain had not been able to create them; its laws produced, doubtlessly, an entirely different orientation. But deep down in their hearts there were seeds of magnanimity, of heroism, of proud and generous independence; and if the customs were simple and modest . . . , there was something more in those characteristics than the stupidity of slavery." Bello recognized that evils did exist, that the Hispanic American was still not prepared to enjoy fully the liberal spirit; but these shortcomings did not invalidate in any way the positive qualities which might have been inherited from Spain. The first and most urgent act was political independence; the second and truly decisive act would have to be intellectual independence. The latter would have to be the work of educators once the conflict was over. "No one," he said, "loved liberty more sincerely than General Bolívar, but he, like everybody else, was caught up in the nature of things. Independence was necessary for liberty, and the champion of independence was and had to be a dictator. Hence the apparent and necessary contradictions that characterized his acts. Bolívar triumphed; the dictatorships triumphed over Spain; the governments and the congresses still waged war against the customs of the sons of Spain, against the habits formed under the influence of the laws of Spain. It was a war of vicissitudes in which ground was won and lost, an insensible war in which the enemy had many powerful allies among us."[28] This is the second step toward emancipation.

IV. THE URGENCY OF POLITICAL EMANCIPATION

From Limited Sovereignty to Despotism

POLITICAL emancipation, even without intellectual preparation, was a necessary and urgent first step. Intellectual emancipation was necessarily the work of the Hispanic Americans themselves. They could expect nothing from Spain. What Spain had not done during centuries of colonial rule, said Bello, was not going to be done afterwards. History had afforded the Hispanic Americans an opportunity for political independence; if they had not taken advantage of the opportunity, it would have been impossible to achieve it later. The Hispanic Americans only took advantage of the opportunity. Later they would have the task of emancipating their minds, and this was to be the work of the new generation. The sole purpose of the political liberators had been the destruction of a political order which was the first obstacle to the intellectual independence of Americans.

---

[28] Bello, *Investigación . . . de la conquista.*

"The American revolution," pointed out Esteban Echeverría, "like all the great revolutions of the world, was solely concerned with tearing down the Gothic structure erected by tyranny and force during centuries of ignorance, and it had neither time nor a period of peace sufficient for rebuilding a new structure." The urgency of the era kept Hispanic Americans from building at the same time they were destroying. That this was so did not mean that the leaders of American independence did not aspire to another type of order; this was not their principle objective, even though they had not had time to realize it. The revolution "proclaimed truths" which were to serve "as a basis for the reorganization of modern societies." But they put first things first, political independence from Spain. "In order to establish liberty, it was necessary to emancipate the fatherland first."

This first emancipation was, of course, difficult and dangerous. The people, although desiring liberty, did not know what liberty was or what to do with it. The enjoyment of liberty required a special education, but they did not have time for it. The leaders of the independence, continued Echeverría, "knew, doubtless, that the mind of the people was not prepared to evaluate its importance; they recognized that there were in their sentiments, in their customs, in their way of thinking, certain reactionary instincts against everything which was new and which they did not understand." They knew that reactionary forces would take advantage of these instincts and these habits, but it made no difference; the essential thing was to begin. "It was necessary to set to work, and they did."

To attract the people, they offered them an unlimited liberty, a liberty that was only possible through education; but there was no time to argue if the opportune moment had arrived. The important thing was to act. "They needed the people . . . and they gave them unlimited sovereignty." This was nothing but a "necessity of the times." "It was necessary to attract the votes and the strength of the multitudes to the new cause by offering them the bait of omnipotent sovereignty." But this right, given to a people not educated to enjoy it, would soon cause disasters which would allow the negative forces to regain power and implant tyrannies. Liberty without education could only bring anarchy.

"But once the people began to exercise their sovereignty, after having destroyed the tyrants," continued the Argentine scholar, "it was difficult to curb them. Sovereignty was a privilege acquired at the cost of blood and heroism." Only anarchy, carried to the extreme of disaster, would cause them to lose their sovereignty. Colonial despotism, latent in the minds of various Hispanic Americans, would again seize power. "The principle of the power of the masses would produce all the disasters that it has produced, and would end in the sanction and establishment of despotism."

But this evil would finally become a blessing. The new despotism would teach them, with an unforgettable lesson, that liberty is a blessing that one must know how to enjoy. The new despotism would teach them to love the liberty that they had tasted and not to risk turning it into libertinism. "These people, dazzled until now by the majesty of their omnipotence, will recognize, once they have come to, that it was not given to them by God except to practice it within the limits of the law as an instrument of good." This lesson, though harsh, would begin the period of definitive liberation, the period of the intellectual enlightenment of the people: "The people will be enlightened: the principles of the revolution . . . will finally penetrate their minds and will become the norm of their actions."[29] The habits and tendencies inherited from other generations would begin to disappear.

Civil War, anarchy, was but the result of the struggle which had begun among the Hispanic-American people: the colonial spirit against the modern spirit. The people, inspired by a new idea, had thrown themselves into the struggle to achieve liberty and sovereignty; but within themselves there existed contradictory elements which would lead them to anarchy and then to despotism. "Civil war," said Echeverría, "was the monstrous fruit of the clash between the principle of May and the colonial spirit, which was defeated but not annihilated." In the absence of any preparation or education, the Hispanic-American revolution took a different path from the great North American revolution. "Our revolution, because of the inevitable linking of events of the period, began where it should have ended, and has gone in a direction opposite to that of the revolutions of other countries. Consider, on the other hand, the United States,"

[29] Echeverría, *Dogma socialista de la Asociación de Mayo.*

he continued. "At the fall of colonial power, democracy appears organized and beautiful, radiant with intelligence and youth, springing from the head of the people as Minerva from the head of Jupiter."[30] In Hispanic America, where there was no such organization, it was necessary to educate the people for it. The Hispanic Americans, once they had achieved political freedom, would need the intellectual emancipation which accompanied political freedom in the United States.

Evolution and Revolution

COULD the Hispanic Americans aspire to anything other than their political emancipation? "Since society was not prepared to receive the generating impulse," said Lastarria, "it was inevitable that it should limit itself solely to fighting for its political liberty, because if it had come forward to break abruptly with the past, to proclaim its complete regeneration . . . it would have clashed with a thousand powerful resistances and would not have attained its triumph except by complete extermination." The urgency of the moment would permit nothing else. The work of complete emancipation from the past and regeneration had to take place later, and for that task very different weapons were necessary. It was no longer a war against physical despotism, but against the despotism that remained in the hearts and souls of the Hispanic Americans. Once the visible power was destroyed, it was necessary to destroy the invisible power which had its roots in the Hispanic Americans. The men who attained political emancipation could not do all this; the time which they had at their disposal was scarcely enough for the first task. But, once the political war was ended, it was necessary to start the new war: "The war against the powerful spirit which the colonial system inspired in our society was beginning." Once political emancipation had been achieved, such a war became more urgent and necessary. The colonial spirit attempted to gain control of the nation by availing itself of the power that it had in the Hispanic-American mind. "The influence of the Spanish system," said Lastarria, "taking advantage of the calm, appears at times in a violent clash with regeneration and raises against it all the petty passions, fanaticism, and errors of the masses."

[30] *Mayo y la enseñanza.*

That is when "the hatreds of the revolution are regenerated, lines are drawn, and political parties are even formed, and a true crisis is in the making."[31]

This second stage in the revolution was a disadvantage for Hispanic America, since it obliged Hispanic America to make certain efforts which North America did not have to make to attain full independence. The North Americans, in contrast to the Hispanic Americans, did not have to free themselves from habits and customs inherited during the colonial period. They did not have to stop being English. The habits and customs they had inherited from the English, instead of being an obstacle to the attainment of their liberties, were the best stimulant and the principal reason for their success.

Lastarria, referring to the necessity of the Hispanic Americans to free themselves even from Spanish literature, pointed out that such a step was not necessary for the North Americans. He said: "When the United States won its political freedom, the people did not free themselves from the influence of English literature; they could use it and, in effect, did, for their new situation, because their sentiments and their ideas, their interests and their social necessities continued to be British, with the sole difference that their social organization would be better served by a republican organization; and it could be so because it was not a violent innovation, but progress, a natural development." The North American revolutionaries only took advantage of the natural evolution of the British heritage in American lands. Hispanic-American revolutionaries had to take advantage of the first opportunity which they found, regardless of whether the people were prepared or not for their political freedom.

The continuation of the despotic order, even without Spain, was natural in Hispanic America. "The entire interest of the political organization, for example," said Lastarria, "was summarized in the magical word 'order,' which for public opinion represented the tranquility that facilitates the course of affairs, in addition to the peace which prevents unexpected attacks, by reconciling the peace of the home with that of the streets. For the statesmen and petty politicians it signified the domination of an arbitrary and despotic power, that is, the political possession of an absolute power which in the peaceful

[31] *Influencia social de la conquista.*

times of the colony enriched the representatives of the Spanish king."

And so, while the habits and customs which the North Americans inherited from England led them through a natural evolution to political independence, the habits and customs which the Hispanic Americans inherited from Spain led them into a new colonialism. This "situation," said Lastarria, "openly ran counter to the objectives of the American revolution, and instead of aiding us to correct our past and to prepare our regeneration, it tied us to the point of departure, thus rehabilitating the colonial system."[32] Hispanic-American independence, if it was to be a success, had to be complete; it was necessary to shake off all the past, without exception. If the Hispanic Americans wished to be completely free, they must renounce everything that was Spanish. In contrast, the North Americans found in their English heritage the source of all their possibilities and the roots of their future power.

The Inability of the Liberators to Establish a New Order

"OUR REVOLUTIONARIES," said Bilbao, "equipped only with a critical philosophy, were faced with a responsibility they could not discharge. Since this philosophy was formulated to destroy and to attack, they were unable to establish the bases for a new order. Once the colonial order had been destroyed, they failed to set the foundation for a modern, liberal order. Complete disorder followed the revolution of independence, and with that disorder the urgency for any kind of order arose in the minds of the Hispanic Americans, including the liberators, who were forced to establish dictatorships when they had promised complete liberty." O'Higgins, the liberator of Chile, said Bilbao, "attempted to organize the social elements, that is to say, the Chilean traditions, on the basis of the new ideas and the power which would put them into effect. But in this effort he met opposition, and when he only attempted to organize power, he became a despot."

When the urgent task of winning political independence for Hispanic America had been completed, the shadow of despotism appeared again, this time in the person of the liberators themselves. The very nature of things led them to create, or to claim, a power as

[32] *Estudios literarios.*

all inclusive as the one they had defeated on the battlefields. "Human weakness in such cases," said Bilbao, "turns to the past and establishes itself firmly on the remnants of the very structure which it had torn down." The very urgency made it impossible for them to find a new order, and so they paradoxically re-established the past in order to save liberty.

The people saw only the immediate result of the revolution of independence, political emancipation as opposed to Spanish power. They did not see the ultimate objectives of this revolution: As far as their sentiments were concerned, the people belonged to the past; they kept their old beliefs. Not for one moment did they ever think of questioning them. But the problem of true liberty lay in these beliefs, for it was something more than political liberty. Their freedom depended upon the rejection of these beliefs. "The men who promoted our revolution," continued Bilbao, "were men of rejection, while the people were spontaneous." But "the people, who had felt only political exaltation in the conquest of civic rights, saw in political liberty only a solitary fact separated from the other questions that reflection had destroyed; the people remained in the past."

The men who carried out the revolution were unable to endow the people with new beliefs which corresponded to the liberties they had won. The contradiction became immediately evident: liberty in a liberal sense did not correspond to what was understood as liberty in Catholicism. The people could not be both liberal and Catholic at the same time. It was a matter of two contradictory conceptions of the world. The liberators, who had not yielded to Spanish political power, yielded to its spirit, to its idea of order. "The men who led the philosophical revolution," said Bilbao, "finding it impossible to organize beliefs logically related to political liberty, became reactionaries in matters of religion and politics concerning the people." There arose what was called constitutional despotism, a new name for an old form of political organization.

These men, according to Bilbao, had neither faith in the people nor faith in the ideas for which they had fought. Lacking faith, they did not bother to preserve the liberties they had already won or to achieve those promised; they were only concerned with keeping the power they had seized. "If the governments had understood that the development of equality was a sacred testament of the revolution," said the Chilean thinker, "that equality is a historical necessity in the development of the revolution, they would not have succumbed." The people would have followed them and supported them, since in that way they would have gained support for themselves. Backed by the people and therefore counting upon a legitimate authority, "they would have been able, by means of general education, to lay the foundation for a complete regeneration of the people."[33] Education carried out with the support of the people would have brought about, in a short time, the second stage of emancipation which was vitally necessary for the Hispanic Americans. But the lack of faith led them again into despotism and, with despotism, to blocking the path that would lead them to the liberty that had been promised them.

V. THE NEW GENERATION AND ITS PROGRAM

The Third Party

THE GENERATION of the political liberators was followed by a new generation which, as has already been seen, attempted to do in education what the liberators had done in politics. This new generation had nothing in common with the political parties then in conflict. These parties struggled only for the sake of political interests. The new generation, on the contrary, considered politics as only an instrument to be used for more lofty aims, educational ones. This generation tried to complete the work that the liberators had left unfinished because of the urgency of circumstances. It was neither federalist nor centralist, neither unitarian nor federal, neither liberal nor conservative.

The men of this generation began by forming the basis of a third party which would break away from the narrow interests of the parties in conflict up to that time. Their standard was *liberalism*. It was not the form of government that was important to them, but rather the content. They attempted to transform man himself. Liberalism was not just a political banner, but a program to educate the Hispanic American, to make of him a man different from the one the colony had produced.

[33] *Sociabilidad chilena.*

In 1837, said Esteban Echeverría, Argentine society was divided
into two great groups, the Federals, victors at that time, and the
Unitarians, the defeated minority. The former were supported by
the semibarbarous instincts of the masses; the latter were defeated,
in spite of their good intentions, as a result of their "haughty impulses toward exclusivism and supremacy." But, in the meantime,
a new generation had grown up without becoming involved in the
struggles that the older groups carried on among themselves. This
new generation did not share their hatreds, nor did it take part in
their fratricidal war. "The Federalists looked upon this new generation with distrust and ill-will, because they found it unwilling
to accept its trappings and its domination; they saw it thumbing
through books and wearing frock coats." On the other hand, "the
leaders of the Unitarian party, isolated in Montevideo," looked upon
"this new generation with pity and scorn, because they thought it
had become federalized and busied itself only with frivolities."

The new group in Argentina, Echeverría tells us, had a program
of "beliefs similar to that of young Italy." This program decreed
that "progress is the law of development and the necessary end of all
free society. . . . But every people, every society, has its laws or conditions peculiar to its existence, which arise from their customs, their
history, their social state, their physical, intellectual, and moral necessities, from the very nature of the soil which providence willed
that they should inhabit and live on perpetually. . . . Normal, true
progress means that a people moves toward the development and
exercise of its activity in accordance with those conditions peculiar
to its existence."

In this way the new generation goes to the heart of the question—
its reality. It is a partisan of liberalism, but a liberalism which con-
forms to Hispanic-American reality. In this way these men sought
to overcome, to avoid, the obstacles which had lain in the way of the
liberators. The latter failed because they were too utopian, because
they could not grasp reality. They felt stronger than this reality,
and they tried to mold the people according to their ideas; and when
they failed, they abandoned the people to their destiny. The Hispanic Americans would be capable of practicing liberalism if, above
everything else, they were cognizant of the reality in which they

lived. A few years later several members of this new American generation discovered and identified themselves with a philosophy that attempted above all to take cognizance of reality. This philosophical doctrine was positivism.

The Hispanic-American people had their first opportunity on the day they declared their political independence. "In May," said Echeverría, "the Argentine people began to exist as a people . . . as a slave people, they were outside of the law of progress, as a free people, rehabilitated, they came within the province of this law." But their politicians, the leaders of the parties who fought over the right to lead them were blind to reality. Unitarians and Federals failed to recognize conditions basic to all authentic progress. Instead of stimulating it, they kept destroying it, going as far as the "annihilation of national activity: the Unitarians perverted it and wasted their energy in a vacuum; the Federals suffocated it under the weight of a brutal despotism; both of them resorted to war."[34] Instead of stimulating the liberalism of the people, they set in motion the traditional forces which had permitted despotism in the past. The mania for governing on the one hand and, on the other, the real or imagined apathy of the people for maintaining their political rights and the imagined incapacity of the people led the parties to the gradual establishment of a new despotism, of a monstrous centralization. In the face of disorder, in the face of the anarchy which followed political independence, a new but despotic unity was established.

We also, said Echeverría, are moving toward *unity*, but down a different road from that followed by the Federals and Unitarians. We aspire neither to the unity of form of unitarianism nor to the despotic unity of federalism, but to the unity that comes from the concentration and action of the physical and moral capabilities of all the members of a political association. That is, to a responsible unity, arising from the people themselves, from their own circumstances, from their own reality. Such was the program of the third party.

The Progressive Party

IN CHILE the generation of José Victorino Lastarria aspired also to form a party that would go beyond the limited interests of the

[34] *Dogma socialista.*

conservatives and the liberals. Lastarria himself hoped to form what he considered a "progressive party" by opposing especially the causes of the old hatreds and resentments. This new party was to be formed by the new generation which was being educated in democratic ideas. It was necessary, he said, that it be led so that it would not be contaminated by the old rancors or by the interests and hatreds of the moment or by the backward doctrines now popular. The action of this party must take place within the law. There was to be no violence whatsoever; violence only engenders violence. The fact that the classical party had not acted in this way had led to violence. Lastarria wanted to reform the society of his day, but peacefully. He himself had already set an example when he opposed in the parliament the abuse of authoritarian power in the Chilean constitution of 1833, established by Diego Portales. This constitution had placed in the hands of the president a power similar to that which the Spanish kings had held in the colony.

Lastarria, in a confidential letter,[35] speaking of the *pipiolos,* the most progressive party of its time, which had been defeated by the *pelucones,* or conservatives, said: "I looked at the defeated party and found it absolutely devoid of statesmen: those who had been its leaders were in obscurity, represented nothing; they had no center of action; and the few who called themselves *pipiolos* exerted no power against the government except a kind of *legality* which consisted of memories of the past." No, definitely this party could no longer do anything for Chile; it was necessary to form a party which would truly represent the interests of the nation. "This manner of seeing things," he continued, "made me hope for, even foresee, the appearance of a *progressive* party, a new party, devoid of old resentments and hatreds, with only national interests and with only the principles of true philosophy." Indeed, "in order to contribute to its creation and regenerate the order of things that prevailed at the time, I opposed everything that I found contrary to my principles."

Lastarria, faithful to these principles, would not accept membership in any party that was not in accord with them. "In my writings, which I never denied," he said, "and of which I have never been

[35] See in Alejandro Fuenzalida Grandón, *Lastarria y su tiempo.*

ashamed, I have always considered myself a liberal, never a *pipiolo* nor a representative of any party." . . . In that way I was always happy and I never sacrificed my principles or the independence of my judgment or any party interests. I preferred to be called a coward a thousand times rather than to be considered a criminal or a blind proselyte." Like Erasmus in the Renaissance, Lastarria withdrew from the opposing parties. "The only thing that I saw," he said, "was two exhausted parties, without any system, which did not represent the national interest, which had nothing of grandeur, wounding each other in a combat without any patriotic results, and up to a certain point puerile and extremely dangerous.

"Should I join any one of the contending parties?" continued the Chilean thinker. "I preferred to live through a difficult epoch alone and to bear in silence the threats of some, the reproaches of others, and the insults of all." His idea for a new progressive party having failed, persecuted, he withdrew to his books and his studies. There was another way, although slower, to carry out the reform—the way of education. "Finding myself exposed to being ruined forever by persecutions of the government, which at that time did not pardon its adversaries, I thought it was useless to keep up an unequal fight: I thought it better to devote myself to study and to the *education* of youth, because only in this field was I permitted to satisfy my ambition to be useful to my country. I gave up politics and withdrew to the schools."

Absolutism of the Parties in Hispanic America

FRANCISCO BILBAO, more pessimistic about the formation of an authentically progressive party, found the root of this failure in the mind of the Hispanic American, who, regardless of his political party, was unable to act politically except in an absolute way. His mentality, molded by the standards of Roman Catholicism, could not adapt itself, without previous education, to the standards of republicanism. "Civilized man," Bilbao said, alluding to Sarmiento, "demands the extermination of the Indians and the gauchos." Dictatorship lurked behind every principle; by means of forms the parties attempted to save what could not be saved. "The *pelucones*, the conservatives, the reds, the liberals, the democrats, the unitarians, the federals, all had courted dictatorship. With the best intentions the parties had proclaimed dictatorship to establish public welfare. . . . That is to say, *despotism* to guarantee *liberty*. A terrible and logical contradiction! Catholicism produces despotism; a republic, liberalism. . . . And both movements found themselves in the monstrous consequence that was called *dictatorship to establish liberty*."

The evil was in the mind, in the education, in the training received. "A republican is a man of beliefs, and brings to politics the character, temperament, and logic of Catholic infallibility. Every force looks upon itself as a power, every power authority, every authority infallible, and every infallibility declares itself logically incapable of error, and every infallibility adores itself and established its legitimacy. Deviation is no longer possible." According to this tragic logic, any opposition was impossible: "Opposition is an offense, despotism is sacred, and obedience a duty." And this was valid for all the political parties, regardless of their principles or programs. "Civilized men say, 'Look at those barbarians—the people.' And now do you want institutions? No. Force, strong power, and dictatorship are necessary." Civilized men asked, "Do you want to give liberty to these bandits?" "If they should ever gain control of the government, everything would be lost; liberty would be impossible." And in this way, "they are deprived of liberty or it disappears for the benefit of liberty." In opposition to this attitude of civilized men, "the masses, disinherited, trampled upon like animals, seek *caudillos*. It is the dictatorship of vengeance and the guarantee of their way of being. The *civilized* parties sought dictatorship to combat, dominate, and civilize the masses. It was the dictatorship of the privileged classes."

Dictatorship, always dictatorship! Both sides sought it to defend their group interests. "The *civilized* parties seek a *provisional dictatorship* to assure their victory over other parties. It is the dictatorship of competition and of rivalry." They could not conceive of order without dictatorships. "The conservative party comes into power. How could they be conservative without a dictatorship? . . . A liberal party comes into power. How can they reform without a dictatorship? . . . If the Federal party is conservative, then the unitarians attack it in the name of reforms. And both of them call upon dictatorship to defend themselves and maintain themselves in power."

73

All of this takes place because the reforms do not stem from reason. Rationalism does not direct these efforts. The United States again serves as an example of a true reform movement, "because their reform is a continual movement of life based upon the sovereignty of reason in every man." The origin of this difference lies in their respective mentalities. "In non-Catholic and free countries man is sovereign and respects the sovereignty of his fellow-man. There are no infallibles who come to power, and all men have faith in the law which guarantees their rights and faith in the vote of all men, which cannot contravene their rights. If there is error, there is no imposition, and they expect the infallible progress of conviction. Such is the politics of a people whose vote cannot be forced or ridiculed. Law is religion, and the religion of *free examination* produces the religion of the law." Loyalty plays a principal role here, because "loyalty in politics becomes as necessary and is as useful as honesty in commerce."

In this kind of politics there are neither winners nor losers; there is only a single group of men elected to administer the affairs of the city. This would be an administration that another group could have tomorrow if it is to the best interests of that administration. Both groups only offer their services to society, and it is society which accepts the services of both. Both groups seek only to serve society to the best of their ability. "But in Catholic countries," said Bilbao, "there is a fantastic and real terror when the opposition party wins, because we know and we believe, or foresee rightly, that it is a defeat without hope; it is the enthronement of something infallible and incapable of committing a wrong, something that establishes itself with the inflexibility of vengeance. This is why there are so many revolutions and so much servility."

Bilbao's pessimism is evident in his bitter statement, "We were born under dictators, we were reared surrounded by them, and dictatorships follow us to the grave." It seems that the Hispanic Americans can do nothing to escape them. In spite of all their efforts, they always recur. Each political formula is only a justification for a new dictatorship. Catholicism, he said, denies liberal principles and institutions, "with the infallible word of councils and popes; but the progress of the period has consisted of using the same arms, of occupying position, in accepting the language and terminology of liberty, and in using suffrage, the press, education, and the schools to the discredit of suffrage . . . and in educating slaves of the church and not citizens of the state." The most that was done was to substitute one church for another, one fanaticism for another fanaticism, one despotsim for another. What was needed was school to teach faith in law. "The school and the spirit and the text and everything that is taught there is only the domain of the enemy of liberty, all of this authorized by those whom we call civilized." There is only one way, there exists only one remedy for such a great evil: intellectual emancipation. The time for us to gain our intellectual emancipation has come. The United States has already won theirs "because they are free in spirit."[36]

Education as a Solution

EDUCATION could offer the only solution, as has already been seen. The evil, the cause of the failure of liberalism in Hispanic America, lay in the lack of vision or the lack of time that the liberators had, for they were more occupied with the immediate success of politics and relegated education to a secondary place. "If the education of the people had begun then," said Echeverría, "if there had been taught from that time on in the schools what liberty, equality, and fraternity were, would not the generation educated in these doctrines, who later in their maturity have had a powerful influence in the triumph of order and of law, have paralyzed the action of anarchists and of tyrants? . . . Those who have worked and are still working for their country, those who are troubled and who are in despair, seeing no end to their troubles, how is it that it has never occurred to them to resort to the only recourse that could remedy these evils, the education of youth oriented toward democracy?" The liberators offered only liberty, but not the means to enjoy it. "Liberty alone," said Echeverría, "divides; it does not unite." It is necessary to educate for liberty, fraternity, and living together. "Order and union arise from fraternity."[37]

[36] *La América en peligro.*
[37] *Manual de enseñanza.*

Lastarria, recalling Simón Rodríguez, Bolívar's tutor, spoke of education as the basis of the political regeneration of Hispanic America. "We thought," Lastarria said, "that instruction in government was the basis of the regeneration, because, without that, it was neither possible to recognize and respect individual and social rights which constitute liberty, nor was it possible to have precise ideas on political organization, on its forms and practices, in order to be able to distinguish those that were opposed to the forces favorable to a democratic republic."[38] Bilbao thought it was necessary to continue the revolution of independence by revolutionizing men's attitudes through education. "To try to continue the results of the revolution is to attempt to carry on another revolution; that is to say, the *revolution* of the unity of *past beliefs* which have not disappeared from the popular mind. . . . Education, which is the way to revolutionize and complete revolutions, receives in this period every development possible." Education invades Spanish beliefs and defeats them by defeating the Hispanic Americans. Education effects true independence by teaching us what true liberty is. "To change the beliefs of the common people and substitute for them a philosophical education is to give them an individual conscience. It is to affirm the revolution." Indeed, "to affirm the revolution is to enthrone liberty."

It was not possible to expect the people to know what to do with something that they had never enjoyed in their lives. The Chilean *guaso*, said Bilbao, "knows only what his parents taught him, and this for him is the end of his intellectual endeavor. He rejects anything else. As a result, there arises the traditional spirit of the men on horseback who spend their lives wandering or going around and around in a circle. The beliefs of our *guasos* are Catholic and Spanish . . . and from them arises the antiliberal reaction." Hence it was necessary to approach the people and educate them. This would be the true revolution. Pure theorists could do nothing for the people, much less for their liberty. It was necessary to teach truth to the people. It was not an easy task, but "truth was advancing on its way, from the state in which we are. . . . Let us doubt, let us suffer, let us carry the weight of transitory epochs, but let us not retrogress to rest under the monument which is collapsing. . . . Let us not separate the people

[38] *Estudios literarios.*

from ourselves any more than they are already separated from us. Let us educate them in the idea of individuality, of the right of equality and of honor."[39]

VI. NORTH AMERICA AS A MODEL

The Two Americas

IN THE PREVIOUS SECTIONS the feeling of the Hispanic Americans towards the North Americans has already been anticipated. It is a feeling of great admiration, derived from the negative attitude which the Hispanic Americans have toward their own historical and cultural situation. North America was, for them, the incarnation of the spirit of modernity, the incarnation of the liberal spirit which they were attempting to create in Hispanic America, a spirit which is part of the character of North Americans simply because they belong to the Anglo-Saxon race. Their institutions were only a natural consequence of the Anglo-Saxon spirit as it developed in the New World. Without England and the United States, it was asserted, there would be no liberty in the world. A country without Englishmen, said Alberdi, is like a forest without birds. "It is my conviction that without England and the United States, liberty would disappear in this century."[40]

In America two opposing political ideologies, democracy and monarchy, had been established. These two ideologies had struggled against each other in Europe until the one representing progress had triumphed. They were native to the races that colonized America, the Anglo-Saxon and the Hispanic. From them there arose two Americas, an America of progress and an America of backwardness. "Freedom of thought, as an inborn right, as the right of rights," said Bilbao, "characterizes the origin and development of society in the United States. A restricted freedom of thought, free investigation limited to exterior things, to politics, administration, etc. . . . was the mutilated freedom proclaimed by the revolutionaries of the South." Political freedom of the Hispanic Americans was not accompanied by freedom of conscience, hence the disorders and the dic-

[39] *Sociabilidad chilena.*
[40] *Manual de enseñanza.*

tatorships. But such different attitudes correspond, said the Chilean thinker, to different mental attitudes: that of North Americans to a sentiment which was found even in their religious attitude. "This means that the North was Protestant," as opposed to the South, which was "Catholic." The man of the North does not accept dogma; on the contrary, his religion is based on free examination. "The man of the North . . . is priest, church, sovereign in dogma, and there is no pontificate that can dominate his reason." From this attitude opposing all dogma there results also his opposition to any kind of despotism. He who does not accept religious despotism likewise will not accept political despotism. *"From his sovereignty over dogma,"* said Bilbao, "there arises his sovereignty in politics." This is what has been lacking in South America, for if it had had the religious independence which North America had, it would also have had its liberal and democratic institutions.

As a result of that same religious independence there arose that feeling of respect for one's fellow-man which was so greatly lacking in Hispanic America. The North American could, because of it, recognize in his fellow-men the rights which he enjoyed. From "this there arises that tolerance, that enlivening discussion, that practical liberty." For this same reason the United States, in contrast to Spanish America, did not have to "carry on a religious revolution to establish freedom of thought. . . . The religion of *free examination* was to be the dogmatic basis of political liberty. The man who is free to accept dogma is necessarily free to form his laws. Despotism is impossible."[41]

"Two opposing principles," said Lastarria, "had therefore become established in the vast American continent: the democratic principle, and with it the liberal system, which forms the basis of Anglo-American social organization, and the principle of monarchy, and with it the ruinous system of force which constituted the life of the Spanish colonies." Two Americas, and with them two forms of government, two forms of social organization and liberty.

"In the North, the people were sovereign in fact and in law, and made the law and administered their interests by means of their representatives. In Spanish America the people did not exist, society was

[41] *El evangelio americano.*

of no consequence; here the people lived only for the glory and benefit of their sovereign, an absolute and natural master." Only one nation, continued Lastarria, "had understood its lofty objectives and wanted to put them into effect: that glorious nation, that nation that was the sum total of the rights and privileges of all humanity was in North America."

In South America, in Latin America, men had to struggle against the past in order to be free. They had to seek models beyond their own cultural sphere. "In this America," said Lastarria, "an entire world renounced its past, tore up its laws, condemned its social organization: from Mexico to Cape Horn a single resounding echo proclaimed the sovereignty of the people, the sovereignty of law, the sovereignty of reason." This America had to realize by its own effort what North America had received as its heritage. The struggle in South America was still more difficult since the new spirit was alien to the social, political, and mental reality within which it must be realized. South America had to turn against itself, against what it was, in order to be able, thus, to become what it wished to be. In this internal struggle the forces of the past had greater advantage. Depending upon the negative forces of Europe, on the one hand, "and on the other upon the clergy who convert religion into a political instrument, the aristocracy had at its disposal powerful influences and wealth to use the revolution for its own benefit, to strip democracy of all the advantages won, and pass in this way over the new spirit and suffocate it."[42]

Alberdi, speaking of the omnipotence of the state, also pointed out the difference between the two Americas. "In the societies of Greco-Roman origin, in both worlds," he declared, "the individual, rather than free, is the slave of the state." The freedom of the state is in no way the freedom of its individuals. "The state is free, so far as it is not subject to an alien power; but the individual lacks liberty so far as he depends upon the state in an all-inclusive and absolute way. The state is free so far as it absorbs and monopolizes the freedom of all its subjects, but its subjects are not free because the government holds all their freedoms." On the other hand, in North America, "the

[42] *Historia constitucional del medio siglo* (Santiago de Chile, 1853).

79

rights of man balanced the rights of the state, and if the state was free from an alien power, the individual was none the less so in regard to the state."[43]

Simón Rodríguez (1771–1854), Bolívar's tutor, also noted the differences existing between the two Americas. "The soil of the United States," he said, "is sown with liberal ideas—cultivated by skillful hands in every spot—protected by an atmosphere of freedom that all its citizens breathe; the soil, having been abandoned to its own course, is incapable of adulterating its own production. The president is the fruit of the land; each citizen, when he speaks without affectation says 'I'; in South America, even the most educated with a slip of the tongue says my 'master'; in the United States public office is virtually advisory—it is considered a responsibility—those who seek it seek a way of displaying their patriotism and . . . their cognizance of their responsibility sustains their patriotism. Among the descendants of the Spaniards, public office is sought for the title or the income just as it had been done by their ancestors; there they want to serve; here they want social prestige. The Hispanic Americans sacrificed everything, including their freedom, for the sake of power or for simple social prestige, no matter how insignificant it was. "In the United States (and this comes to them from the English)," said Simón Rodríguez, "the president, the cabinet members, and all the magistrates are called by their names . . . while we renounce our names for a title; and just as the Capuchins take the name of the city where they were born, the holders of public office forget their families and assume the title of 'Mr. Minister,' 'Mr. Treasurer,' 'Mr. Doorman.' "[44]

Progress as Liberty and Individual Effort

"To EXPECT everything from the State"—this is indeed one of the greatest evils inherited from Spain. It has been the source of all types of servitude. The man who cannot attain his well-being by using his own efforts will never be able to achieve his freedom. Hispanic Americans are different from the North Americans in this also. "If just one youth," said Alberdi, "instead of arguing about the honor of receiv-

[43] *La omnipotencia del estado es la negación de la libertad individual*, 1880.
[44] In J. A. Cova, *Don Simón Rodríguez, maestro y filósofo revolucionario.*

ing a salary as an employee or agent or salaried servant of the state, would prefer to remain master of himself in the management of his farm or rural property, the country from then on would be on the road to greatness, liberty, and true progress." Countries have made progress when their individual citizens are really free. "The North Americans owe the opulence which distinguishes them," Alberdi continued, "to individual freedom, which is freedom *par excellence.*" True greatness is the result of a constructive egotism. Men who desire an authentic well-being do not get entangled in words, nor are they the slaves of ideas which they do not understand, or of false representations. Hence nations like the United States are more a product of egotism than of patriotism. In these countries the fatherland is but a symbol of personal well-being. By working out their own greatness, these people have contributed to forging the greatness of their own country.

Hence there arose two concepts of liberty understood in very different ways in each of the Americas. "The North Americans do not sing of liberty," said Alberdi, "but they practice it in silence. . . . Liberty for them is not a deity; it is an ordinary tool like a bar or a hammer." Liberty is not a word but a fact. Those who love their own well-being above all else, love liberty; and those who have been able to create it with their own hands love this well-being. The great Hispanic-American liberators, he continued, such as San Martín, Bolívar, Sucre, and others, understood liberty in the Spanish way, reducing it to political freedom opposed to Spain, instead of the freedom of the individuals who formed the Hispanic-American society. "Washington and his contemporaries were not in that situation, but in an opposite one. They understood individual freedom better than the independence of their country."

Thus their own greatness would necessarily create the greatness of their country. This was especially interesting to the nations of Latin origin, said Alberdi. "Future destinies will owe their salvation to individualism; they will never be saved if they expect someone to save them by patriotism." Our evil was Spain, its concept of liberty and of state. "The Spanish crown did not found the American colonies to create wealth and power in the colonies, but to create trade and power for the crown itself. . . . Hispanic-American society will be saved and assured of liberty and progress in its future when intelligent egoism and not egotistic patriotism is called to establish republicanism in South America."[45]

From self-government, from this capacity to attain their own well-being came all the North American progress and power, the result of their own efforts. "Yankee civilization," said Sarmiento, "was the work of the plow and the primer; South American civilization was destroyed by the cross and the sword. There they learned to work and to read, here we learned to idle and to pray." While the North American revolution was fought in defense of the rights set forth in the Constitution, the Hispanic American sought to substitute a creole despotism for Spanish despotism. "There a select nucleus of the white race struggles to defend its rights; here the *mestizos* stir up disorderly uprisings without a clear concept of their aspirations. ... Spanish feudalism continues in American *caudillismo*." The North American colonizers organized the economic life of the country, preparing in this way their political and economic independence, while the Hispanic-American colonizers exploited it for the benefit of the mother country. "There the conquering race introduced the virtue of work; here it restricted itself to vegetate in bureaucracy and parasitism."[46]

Francisco Bilbao, dazzled by the people whose model the Hispanic Americans tended to follow to secure their own complete freedom, said: "Those Puritans, or their descendants, have given the world the most beautiful of constitutions, directing the destinies of the greatest, the richest, the wisest, and the freest of nations. That nation is today in history what Greece was to civilization, the luminary of the world, the world of the time, the most positive revelation of divinity, in philosophy, in art, and in politics. That nation has given us this word: *self-government*, as the Greeks gave us *autonomy;* and what is better, they practice what they preach; they put into effect what they think, and they create whatever is necessary for the moral and material perfection of the human species." All their greatness has resulted from this: "There is not a nation that reads more, that prints more, that has a greater number of schools and daily news-

[45] *La omnipotencia del estado.*
[46] *Conflicto y armonía de la razas.*

papers. Today it is the first nation in agriculture, in industry, and in navigation. It is the first nation in war. It has revolutionized naval warfare." Bilbao considered the United States first in all the arts, philosophy, literature, history, politics, and law. "It is the nation," he said, "that makes more discoveries, that invents machines, that transforms nature most rapidly to its own benefit. It is the nation possessed of the *demos*, of the daemon of perfection in every realm. It is a creative nation, and is creative because it is a sovereign nation, because its sovereignty is omnipresent in the individual, in the association, and in the nation." And all of this is due to their capacity for individual liberty: "Their free individual and political life and all of its marvels depend upon the sovereignty of the individual and upon the rational basis for this sovereignty: freedom of thought. . . . What a contrast with South America," he exclaimed, "with what was Spanish America!"[47]

The Anglicizing of Hispanic America

FOR SARMIENTO, as has already been seen, the origin of the incapabilities of Hispanic America was in the race. He believed that the failure of colonization in this America was due to the inferiority of the Spanish race. The Hispanic-American nations tried in vain to copy the constitutions of France or the United States, but they behaved like descendants of a race incapable of democracy. In the North, he said, a pure European race has created a European society; in the South a Euro-African race has mixed with the indigenous to form a conglomerate in which all its defects are concentrated. According to Sarmiento, North American superiority is derived from its ability to remain racially uncontaminated, from its ability not to mix with any inferior race. The Anglo-Saxon groups settled in North America in accordance with their religious ideas or according to certain qualities which distinguish them. Massachusetts was founded by the Puritans; Pennsylvania by the Quaker, Penn; and Virginia by the nobles, from whom was derived the acceptance of slavery in that state. From the Puritans there arose that rejection of any racial mixing with the indigenous. The Puritans, he continued, resorted directly to the Bible; they learned from Moses not to mix with the natives, in con-

47 *El evangelio americano.*

trast to the Spaniards, who immediately mixed with the indigenous population of the New World.

"The North American is, then," said the Argentine scholar, "the Anglo-Saxon free from all mixture with races inferior in energy." The North American has been able, because of this, to preserve "his political traditions, without their becoming degraded with the adoption of racial ineptitudes for governing." When the Pilgrims began their march toward the west, toward America, "old England was the only free nation." But in America they founded a still freer England. "New England is still freer than the land that it left with its kings and secular traditions." This New England was worthy of the great heritage it received, for it was able to increase it. It was the heir of an England that was granting greater liberties to its subjects during the same period that Spain was setting up the Inquisition. In "an epoch," said Sarmiento, "when the rights of defense and guarantees against arbitrary procedures were being suppressed in Spain, men in England won the writ of habeas corpus from Charles II, a king as Catholic as the Catholic kings of Spain. Under this writ nobody could be kept in prison without an order from a competent judge."

It was the new England, North America, which much serve as a model for Hispanic America if it truly desired to be abreast of the times and progress. No nation can now teach us anything except North America, said Sarmiento. "Let us expect nothing from Europe, for it has no connection with our races. Something may come to us from the United States, whence we received our institutions." What was there that we could learn from North America? Its capacity to remain a pure race. "The Anglo-Saxons," declared Sarmiento, "did not admit the indigenous races either as members or as servants in their social constitution." This was the basis of their success, in contrast to the Spanish colonization, "which was carried on like a monopoly of its own race, a race which still had not emerged from the Middle Ages when it came to America . . . and it absorbed into its blood stream a servile prehistoric race."

Sarmiento, with great pessimism regarding the Hispanic-American race, remarked: "Let us recognize the tree by its fruits; they are bad, sometimes bitter, never plentiful. . . . South America is remaining behind and will lose its providential mission as a branch of modern civilization. Let us not detain the United States in its march forward; for that is what some definitely propose. Let us overtake the United States. Let us be America as the sea is the Ocean. Let us be United States."[48] To be United States meant destroying everything that Sarmiento considered the cause of all the evils of Hispanic America. It was necessary to uproot everything Hispanic in order to be like the United States. How could this be done? We have already recognized one way: education; but this was not enough. The other was by means of immigration. It was necessary to have men from other countries; to be precise, from those that were capable of remedying the evil that was caused by the Spanish mixing with inferior races. European immigrants, this indeed was one of the solutions! It was these immigrants who had made North America great.

"The dignity and the future position of the Spanish race in the Atlantic," said Sarmiento, "require that it appear before all nations as a united people who will one day rival in power and progress the Anglo-Saxon race of the North." The immigration from the excess population of old nations to new ones has the same effect as steam applied to industry: It increases their strength a hundred fold and produces in one day the work of a century. "The United States has been enlarged and populated in this way, and this is the way we must grow; and for us an influx of Europeans is more necessary than for the North Americans."[49] What kind of immigration did Sarmiento, Alberdi, and the men who desired the renovation of Hispanic America prefer? The Anglo-Saxon. They had this immigration in mind when they and Alberdi said: "In order to attract those peoples to our midst, it will be necessary to allow them to bring their religion, and not force them to leave their altars on the doorsteps of the republic." Hence the necessity of establishing, before anything else, freedom of religion, freedom in religious matters. Alberdi had also said: Do we want habits of order and industry to prevail in our America? Let's populate it with people in whom those habits are deeply rooted. They are contagious; the American artisan will soon develop

[48] *Argirópolis.*
[49] *Ibid.*

85

alongside the European artisan. The United States is great because it does not despise the European; quite the "contrary, it attracts him, not with open arms, but skillfully, and assimilates him into its population."[50]

In any case it will be necessary to balance Hispanic Americans with new European blood. On one occasion, Sarmiento, with France in mind, said, "The immigration of the Río de la Plata will be Latin. . . . France represents the civilized world . . . and France ought to realize that the Río de la Plata will be for the Latin races what the United States is for the Anglo-Saxons."

At any rate, a healthful European immigration was urgent. We need this more than the United States does, said Sarmiento. "The United States is the descendant of industrious, manufacturing, and navigating England, and it has in its national traditions, in its education, and in its racial tendencies, elements of development, wealth, and civilization that would be sufficient for them without foreign aid." On the other hand, "we need to mix with the population of countries more advanced than ours so that they can give us their arts, their industries, their activity, and their attitude toward work."

Many feared Europe; they feared that it would regain its colonies in America. But this danger would not exist if Hispanic America became as strong as the United States. Indeed, said Sarmiento, "the way to populate, to enrich our country, and to make it strong against Europe is to make the position of foreigners secure, to attract them to our land, to smooth the way for them to settle, and to make them love the country, so that in turn they will bring others with the news of their well-being and the advantages of their position. . . . The more Europeans who come to the country, the more this country will resemble Europe, until the day will arrive when it will be superior in wealth, population, and industry, a thing that has already taken place in the United States." The model was always the United States. The only desirable immigrants were those from Europe who would do in South America what they had done in North America. "Call yourselves the United States of South America," said Sarmiento, "and the feeling of human dignity and a noble emulation will conspire

[50] *Acción de Europa en América.*

to prevent an offense to the name which is associated with great ideas!"[51]

VII. TOWARD A HISPANIC-AMERICAN SOLUTION

A Return to Hispanic-American Reality

IN SPITE of all its defects, the only reality upon which the Hispanic American could rely was his own. The differences, said Alberdi, come from the race and several centuries of different education. The Argentine thinker had great admiration for the Anglo-Saxons, but he knew that this admiration was not going to change Hispanic-American reality. "To try to anglicize the Spanish race," he said "is to disregard nature. . . . Although," he added, "we must indeed open wide the doors to that noble Anglo-Saxon race."[52] Those doors must be the doors of immigration. But the real, the pressing thing was to rely upon existing material and to exert upon it the necessary efforts for its regeneration. This was to be done by the means of which we are already aware: education.

Of course, this did not mean that they disregarded the relationship which Hispanic America had with the universal. Quite the contrary. It was the awareness of this relationship which assured them of a triumphant future. Just as in other countries progress, modernity, had vanquished the forces of darkness, it would also triumph in Hispanic America. But in their eagerness to accelerate this triumph, the Hispanic Americans began to analyze Hispanic-American reality, finding in it very special obstacles characteristic of their environment. These obstacles became more evident when the two Americas were compared. "Our revolution," said Alberdi, "is the product of the development of the human spirit, and has as its end this very development. It is a fact derived from other facts, and it must produce other new facts." In this sense the Hispanic-American revolution was regarded as a phase of the revolution of the spirit of progress in the world. But there was something more. "All peoples," continued Alberdi, "necessarily develop, but each one develops in its own way, because development operates according to certain constant laws,

[51] *Argirópolis.*
[52] *Estudios políticos.*

87

within a strict subordination to the conditions of time and space. And since these conditions never occur in exactly the same manner, it follows that there are no two nations that develop alike. This individual mode of progress constitutes the civilization of each nation."

Alberdi went on to say that each nation "has and must have its own civilization, because each civilization is derived from the combinations of the universal law of development within that nation's individual condition of time and space." This is what Hispanic America did not do. We, he said, have not subordinated our action to the conditions proper to our age and our country; we have not attained the special civilization which should come as a normal result of our national mode of being. This has been a great error in Hispanic America. Alberdi found in this error the cause of all the errors repeated since independence. To continue the life begun in independence, he said, "is not to do what France and the United States are doing, but what our dual law and the dual law of our land orders us to do: to follow the natural development is to acquire a civilization of our own, although imperfect, and not to copy foreign civilizations, although they may be more advanced."

Is this a contradiction of the desire to make Hispanic America a country similar to the United States? No, quite the contrary; the type of development to which Alberdi referred was in the model. The United States represented the maximum development of the universal spirit of progress, but in accordance with that nation's own characteristics. Something similar was desired for Hispanic America: that Hispanic America be in the South what the United States is in the North, that it be a country abreast of universal progress, but with its own characteristics, that is, in accordance with that reality which its citizens could not eliminate. It was not possible to make Anglo-Saxons of the Hispanic Americans, but it would be possible, at least, to educate them in such a way that they would be abreast of those people. The reality was present; it was necessary to consider it; after all, this was the attitude that the Anglo-Saxon people took. They were realists, positivists.

In keeping with this thesis Alberdi proposed to carry out the following projects: first, to investigate "the philosophical elements of human civilization"—that is, the universal; second, to make a study "of the forms that those elements should receive under the particular influences of our age and our environment." Concerning the first investigation, Alberdi said, "It is necessary to heed European intelligence, for it is better trained and versed in philosophical and human things than we. As for the second, there is no need to consult anybody concerning it, nothing but our reason and our own observation."[53] Such was the true path by which Hispanic America was to be incorporated into universal progress. Victorino Lastarria summed this attitude by saying, "We must be original; we have within our society all the elements to be so."[54]

A Reaction against Europe

WITHIN the universal panorama of culture the Hispanic Americans were aware of their lack of progress by comparison with European progress. The greatest exponents of progress were the Anglo-Saxon people, and among these, the United States. In Europe there were still despotisms and a lack of unity. France of the revolution often became a despotic France, an enemy of progress, Simón Rodríguez said, "Europe is *ignorant*, not in literature, not in science, not in art, not in industries, but in politics." In the Old World "a brilliant veil covers a most horrible picture of misery and vices. The great work of Europe was done without any plan, it was fabricated piecemeal, the improvements have been *accumulated*, not *arranged*; art is more brilliant in its workmanship than in its finished product. The most sublime things are confused with the most despicable to form a contrast . . . beautiful for the perfection of the parts, but unpleasant for the impropriety of the whole. It is a pity to see so much talent fruitlessly employed in reforming, works so well planned, producing little or no effect."

Nothing can be expected from Europe, continued Rodríguez, in politics or in morality. "Europe will never reform its morality as it remodels its buildings; modern cities are models of good taste and comfort, but the inhabitants are always the same. They know more

[53] *Discurso pronunciado el día de la apertura del Salón Literario*, 1837.
[54] *Discurso pronunciado en la Sociedad Literaria*, 1842.

than before, but they do not function any better—they deserve praises for the first without meriting criticism for the second."[55] Simón Bolívar's tutor came to the conclusion that Hispanic America had nothing to learn from Europe, either in political organization or in moral education. Sarmiento had the same attitude toward Europe, except that his attitude was based on racial differences. "Let us expect nothing from Europe," he said, "for it has nothing in common with our races." The only place whence something of value could come was the United States. "We can learn something from the United States, from which all our institutions were derived."[56]

Esteban Echeverría also took as his point of departure the difference between the American and European circumstances to affirm that Hispanic America could learn nothing from Europe in regard to politics. "Of what importance to us are the solutions of European philosophy and politics," he asked, "for they do not lead to the objectives which we are seeking? Do we live by chance in that world? ... Does there remain something useful for the country, for the instruction of the people, from all those theories that have no root at all in their life? What program for the future would we present which might satisfy the needs of the country without a complete understanding of their mode of existence as a people?" And he added: "In science we can follow Europe, but not in politics: our world of observation is here, we can touch it, we can feel, it pulsates, we can observe it, study its organism and its condition of life; and Europe can help us little in that."

Let us look to our own reality, however negative it may be, seemed to be the positive attitude of this generation. They knew that it was bad; but they also knew that only they could reform it by taking that reality into account. Echeverría felt that Hispanic-American social problems were not so complicated that they needed a foreign solution. On the contrary, these foreign solutions brought about complications and anarchy. "It has always seemed to us," Echeverría said, "that our social problems are in themselves so simple that it is unnecessary to resort to European philosophy to solve them. It would be sufficient to deduce from the knowledge of the conditions of exist-

[55] See Cova, *Don Simón Rodríguez.*
[56] *Argirópolis.*

ence in our country a few bases or rules for a criterion in order to be able to march freely down the path of true progress. . . . To appeal to the authority of European thinkers is to introduce anarchy, confusion, and the muddling of the solution of our affairs." The anarchy of the parties has, for Echeverría, its origin in this anarchy of ideas, anarchy that is tragically expressed in Hispanic-American society. "Cannot each one invoke a different authority with opposing principles?" he asked. "Has not this been done since the beginning of the revolution? We have never understood each other, and will we never understand each other in this new tower of Babel?" These words anticipate the thesis of the positivists on the unity of minds necessary to establish order. "What will the people learn," he continued, "what will they utilize? How will they see the light of truth in that maze of arguments which are hurled in their faces during the struggle by the writers of opposition parties?"[57]

This did not mean that it was a question of discarding everything that came from Europe regarding politics or social philosophy. No, they would accept anything that had a sense of progress, that is, anything which represented an advance in universal progress within which Hispanic America sought to find a place. Indeed, said Echeverría, "we will consider *progressive* only those doctrines which, while looking to the future, attempt to give us an impetus to the gradual development of class equality, and which will always be in the vanguard of the human spirit." Echeverría considered progress from the standpoint of a socialistic idea peculiar to him which we shall analyze later. "We shall ask for enlightenment from European intelligence," he said, "but with certain conditions."[58]

Among the European ideas which he rejected was the idea of free instruction. This rejection seemed contradictory to the desire for liberty of the generation to which Echeverría belonged. But such was not the case. We have already seen that he sought to reform his society, but according to the principles of liberalism and democracy. Education should be concentrated on the realization of this dual principle. Liberty, pure and simple, without a principle or ordering objective, would only be anarchy. "Free instruction," he said, "is good

[57] *Dogma socialista.*
[58] *Dogma socialista de la Asociación de Mayo.*

91

perhaps in Europe or in countries where secular beliefs and traditions rooted in society maintained its moral equilibrium; free instruction, often promoted by the negligence of our leaders, can sow discord and confusion among us incessantly, and to this free instruction we must attribute in great measure the physical and moral anarchy which has devoured us and which has rendered thirty-four years of revolution unproductive."[59] All education in Hispanic America must have a democratic principle. In another place, referring to the type of knowledge that the Hispanic American possessed, Echeverría came to the conclusion that it was only an acquired knowledge, scarcely enough to solve his problems. "All the knowledge and enlightenment that we possess does not belong to us; it is a fund, if you please, but it does not constitute a real source of wealth, acquired by the sweat of our brow, but a fund which we owe to foreign generosity. It is a garment made of different pieces and different colors which scarcely covers our wretched nakedness."[60]

The rejection of Europe in general and France in particular, in the field of politics and morality, would be accentuated by the French invasion of Mexico. Europe at that time could less than ever be a model or lend assistance to Hispanic America in the solution of its problems. The Chileans, Lastarria and Bilbao, reacted most violently against Europe under these circumstances. The American spirit—that is, the Hispanic-American spirit—became steadfast in their minds. They would also differ from some of the Argentines as to *mestizaje* or the racial problem in general. This idea, said Lastarria, originated in Europe, since it permitted her to justify her violent actions in Hispanic America. European absolutism tried to subdue America again, but this time in the name of a false idea of civilization or racial supremacy. "Have we not seen newspapers founded and books written," said Lastarria, "to propagate the ridiculous theory that the Latin race is by nature different from and has characteristics opposite to those of the Germanic race, and therefore its interests and its happiness force it to seek progress under the protection of absolute governments, because the parliamentary form of government would not

[59] *Mayo y la enseñanza popular en la Plata.*

[60] *Discurso de introducción a una serie de lecturas pronunciadas en el Salón Literario en 1837.*

be within its grasp? Why that falsehood? We Americans know indeed that the fundamental principles of European monarchy—the social, political, religious, and moral basis of Europe—is a Latin principle, that is, pagan, anti-Christian, the principle of absolute unity of power which destroys the individual by abolishing his rights; but we also know that today there does not exist nor can there exist either a Latin or a Germanic race."

These races have been modified. Indeed, why did they persist in this idea? Why did they persist in saying that the Hispanic-American people belong to the Latin race, and hence could only be governed by means of despotism. Lastarria replied: "What they sought with that absurd idea is to make us *Latins* in politics, morality, and religion; that is, to do away with our personality in favor of the unity of an absolute power that will dominate our conscience, our thought, and our will, and with it all the individual rights which we won in our revolution; that is why they invented the theory of races."[61] In reality Lastarria thought that the Latin race in all its purity no longer existed in Hispanic America any more than it existed in Europe. All the evils suffered by the Latin race in this America might be traced to the intellectual heritage it received from Spain, but once this heritage was modified by education, the evil need no longer exist. Only those who were interested in imposing authoritative governments upon Hispanic America could insist to the contrary. The interested party in this case, as Lastarria noted, was again Europe. The French invasion of Mexico served as an example. The conclusions which Lastarria drew from this fact were positive for Hispanic America and negative for Europe. So far as political ideas in Hispanic America were concerned, Europe lagged behind. The European desire for reconquest was but a sign of a state of backwardness. At the same time, the Mexican, Gabino Barreda, noted the same thing: Europe was the expression of backwardness within the march of the positive spirit.[62]

Francisco Bilbao asked: "And why should we South Americans go around begging for European attention, approval, and support. And in Europe, why have we chosen the most enslaved and the most

[61] *La América* (Buenos Aires, 1856 and 1867).
[62] See my work *Positivismo en México*.

93

garrulous of all nations to serve as a model for us in a decadent literature, in despotic politics, in a factual philosophy, in the religion of success, and in the great hypocrisy of covering all the crimes and assaults with the word *civilization?* A lie! France has never been free. France has never been liberated. France has never practiced liberty. France has never suffered for the liberty of the world." Our forefathers believed that they owed all their ideas to France, but they were in error. "We must destroy this error and free ourselves from spiritual subservience to France." France, in the name of civilization, destroys and commits perjury among the nations of America and the world. "If France is not the responsible one, then, what nation is it that permits a bandit to spread slaughter in the world? The doctrine of civilization has established in the spirit of mankind that species of French absolutism or pontificate. The origin of the theory is Germanic; but the French have used it to their benefit and justification." How has France justified her aggressions? "The German philosophy demonstrated that all the work of centuries . . . had its definitive incarnation in the Germanic peoples. What does Cousin do? He accepts the theory, but he substitutes France for Germany. In this way France became the incarnation of the spirit." And since civilization always triumphed, according to this thesis, the attack on Mexico "is the most grandiose and resounding sign of civilization."[63]

"France, whom we have loved so much, what has she done," asked Bilbao, "[but] betray and bombard Mexico. Mexico had finally arrived at the supreme moment of its regeneration: you submerge it again in the horrors of war in an alliance with priests and traitors, and you place upon the ruins of Puebla the farce of an empire. England, oh, England! What is the nation of powdered wigs and rapacious lords doing in India? Blood and exploitation, despotism and conquest. It also appeared for a moment in Mexico and offered three ships to Maximillian. . . . Away with what you call European civilization. Europe cannot civilize itself, and yet it wants to civilize us. Europe with its social and political action, with its dogma, its morality, its diplomacy, its institutions and doctrines, is the very opposite of America. . . . There monarchy, feudalism, theocracy, castes, and ruling families; here democracy. In Europe the practice of conquest;

[63] *La América en peligro,* 1862.

in America, its abolition. . . . In Europe all the superstitions, all the fanaticisms, all the institutions of error, all the miseries and anachronisms of history accumulated among peoples made servile and fanatical for glory and power; in America the purification of history, the religion of justice which permeates."[64] Speaking of America's future, Bilbao said: "Today America is entering into the mechanism of the world movement. . . . The Mexican victory will be the signal of a new era. The Thermopylaes of America are in Puebla." And speaking again of the model which seemed permanent, he said: "An Alliance with the United States, free of slavery, will give us the domination of civilization. . . . Civilization today is America and the Republic."[65] In this way, America must be sufficient unto herself.

Hispanic America and North America

WITHIN the American continent Hispanic America has a reality which makes it entirely different from the Anglo-Saxon America. Hence it was necessary to give special attention to this reality. "Spanish America," said Simón Rodríguez, "cannot imitate the United States, for they are unlike except that they both have a form of government with the same name: republic." Rodríguez believed that certain circumstances existing in Hispanic America made it quite distinct from Anglo-Saxon America. Although these circumstances were more negative than positive, they were peculiar to Hispanic America; therefore, in order to resolve Hispanic-American problems, it was necessary to resort to a solution which was peculiar to her. "Our America," concluded Rodríguez, "should imitate . . . neither Europe, which has no practical skill in politics and is corrupt in its customs and defective in its entirety, nor the United States, whose circumstances are entirely different. . . . Our America must be *original*."[66]

What is Hispanic American, what is peculiar to this part of America, is not necessarily inferior to what is European or North American, if we consider its own product and its reality. To believe otherwise would be only an echo of that heritage which we received from Spain, the heritage of scorn. "Only in Spanish America," said Rod-

---

[64] *El evangelio americano*, 1864.

[65] *La América en peligro*.

[66] See Cova, *Don Simón Rodríguez*.

ríguez, "is a man's merit doubted solely because he is American. The colonists took this example from the mother country, for nowhere else is the talent of a Spaniard held in less regard than in Spain." An outstanding example was the liberator Bolívar, whose person and work were defended by his tutor against the calumny and defamation of which he was the object on the part of the Hispanic Americans themselves, whom he helped to liberate. "Let the peoples recognize their *true defenders*," he said, "in those who sustain the attacks which the cause suffers; let them see in the principles of Bolívar the principles of *general security* and in his person the master column of the republican system. . . . Bolívar deserves to be defended; Americans must consider him as a father, charged with the treasure of their rights, fighting alone against millions of enemies and seeking aid from the very ones he is defending."

Bolívar is for his tutor the original model of what the South American should be; hence his vigorous defense. Bolívar, in spite of his faults, is the greatest expression of liberty to which all Hispanic Americans have aspired, an idea of liberty peculiar to this America, but no more valid than the idea that other peoples have had of the same liberty. "The man of South America," proclaimed Rodríguez, "is Bolívar. His enemies persisted in making him odious and despicable, and they influence the opinion of those who do not know him. If they are permitted to discredit the prototype, no one will want to imitate him, and if the leaders of the new republics do not imitate Bolívar, *the cause of liberty is lost*." Led by his desire to re-evaluate a Hispanic-American symbol, Rodríguez compared Bolívar to two other men symbolic of liberty in North America and Europe: Washington and Napoleon.

The three revolutionary heroes are different, but that does not mean that any one is superior or inferior to the others. "A parallel between Washington, Napoleon, and Bolívar," he said, "with the purpose of elevating one alone would be impertinent. It would be a difficult task, in three so dissimilar revolutions, to make the facts correspond exactly in order to establish rank among the three men of the century. All that should be said, on behalf of the talent that has earned them such a justifiable reputation, is that any one of the three, in his own circumstances, would have distinguished himself in the same way, because all would have done the same thing." Only different circumstances make these heroes different. "The theater," he said, "makes action more spectacular, but not any more meritorious; different people, places, and environment have undoubtedly influenced the procedures." Likewise, Europe, North America, and Hispanic America are different because of their circumstances, but each has its own merit. Europe, the United States, and Hispanic America "differ among themselves as much as the heroes which they have produced resemble each other," concluded Rodríguez. "History will distinguish one from another only by their names."[67]

Hispanic America also had its values—not all of them negative. On the one hand, the achievement of political independence and, on the other, the action leading to the realization of the intellectual emancipation of Hispanic America have been an expression of these values. Andrés Bello spoke of that spirit of sacrifice and love for freedom of the home which the Hispanic Americans had inherited from Spain. The Hispanic Americans had great faults, but they also possessed great virtues. The problem had to be resolved by emphasizing the good qualities and remedying the faults so far as possible. If one carefully analyzed such faults, he would find them likewise in the most exemplary nations of history. North America, with all its great qualities, possessed certain defects, in view of which Hispanic America could high-light certain of its virtues which otherwise would have remained hidden.

Francisco Bilbao also called attention to the differences which made it possible to emphasize the qualities peculiar to Hispanic America. The growth of the United States commanded his interest because of its proximity to Hispanic America. He knew that it would try to extend its dominating influence over weak Hispanic America. The United States, he said, is extending its claws more and more every day "in that hunt which it has undertaken against the south. . . . Yesterday it was Texas, then it was the north of Mexico . . . and then Panama." To counteract this danger, he visualized a Pan-American congress to bring about unity of Indian-Spanish America. His dream was vain.

In his book, *El Evangelio Americano,* he showed that, in spite of

[67] *Defensa de Bolívar.*

its great faults, Spanish America also has positive values in comparison with North America, whose defects become evident in spite of its good qualities. Speaking of the United States, he said, "Free thought, self-government, moral freedom, and a land open to immigration were the reasons for its growth and its glory. . . . This was a heroic moment in its annals. Everything increased: wealth, population, power, and liberty." This was the North America that was admired by South America. But, he added, "by scorning traditions and systems and creating a spirit which devours time and space, it has succeeded in forming a nation and a unique genius"; and "by looking at themselves and finding themselves so great, they have fallen into the temptation of Titan, convinced that they were the arbiters of the earth and even the possessors of Olympus."

The United States, a great and powerful nation, "did not abolish slavery in its states nor preserve the heroic Indian races nor become the champions of the universal cause, but rather the champions of American self-interest and of Anglo-Saxon individualism." Therefore, said Bilbao, "they rushed toward the south." Not everything about it, then, was beneficial or positive for Hispanic America. The Chilean thinker said of the United States, "We shall not scorn, but rather we shall absorb, everything worthwhile in North American spirit and life." The North has positive values; it has liberty; it came into being with liberty. On the other hand, in the South slavery came with theocratic Spain. However, in spite of this heritage, in South America "there was the word, there was light in the depths of suffering, and we broke the sepulchral stone, and we buried those centuries in the sepulcher which were destined for us." Then, immediately, "we had to organize everything. We had to consecrate the sovereignty of the people in the very midst of theocratic education." But in spite of all the obstacles and difficulties, "we, a poor people, eliminated slavery from all the republics of the South," said Bilbao reproachfully; "you, a happy and rich people, have not done so. We have and still are incorporating the primitive races into our nations, as in Peru, where almost the entire nation is Indian, because we believe that these primitive races are our blood and our flesh, and you jesuitically exterminated them. . . . We do not see in the world nor in the pleasures of the world the ultimate objective of mankind; the Negro, the Indian, the disinherited, the unfortunate, and the weak find among us the respect due the title and dignity of the human being. . . . Observe then," he concluded, "what the republicans of South America are attempting to place in the balance beside North American pride, wealth, and power."[68]

Toward an Original Culture

HISPANIC AMERICA, Simón Rodríguez had said, "must be original." There was much to learn from Europe and North America, but there was also much to learn from Spanish America. The problems of Hispanic Americans could be solved only by focusing their attention on their own reality, that is, by understanding it. The idea of an original culture for this America began to develop in the minds of Hispanic-American scholars. It was not a question of going from one state of dependency to another. Quite the contrary; they sought the intellectual emancipation of Hispanic America so that it could attain its own fulfillment.

On May 3, 1842, upon the organization of the Literary Society of Santiago, Chile, Victorino Lastarria delivered a historic address on the necessity for a national culture. He proposed to the Chilean writers that they read the great classics of the Castilian tongue, for, said he, they would find in them the source of that rich language which we speak. In addition to these classics, they were also to read the works of the great French literary figures who serve as a creative stimulus because of the wealth of new visions which French literature embodies. But they were not to subjugate themselves to Castilian or French literature. "Let us establish, then," he said, "our nascent literature on the independence and the freedom of the spirit, let us scorn that mean criticism which attempts to dominate everything— its dictates generally serve only to shackle the mind; let us shake off those bonds and let our fancy soar, for nature is boundless. Do not forget, however, that liberty does not exist in license; this is the most dangerous pitfall: liberty is not prone to dwell except where there is truth and moderation.

[68] *El evangelio americano.*

"I must tell you," he added, "that you should read the works of the most eminent French writers of the day, not in order to copy and translate them unwisely into your works, but rather so that you may saturate yourselves in the philosophical tone which characterizes their literature." It is not a matter of imitating or copying, but simply of utilizing what can serve the development of a distinct Hispanic-American literature. Imitating or copying "would only keep our literature alive with a borrowed existence, always dependent upon the exotic, the very thing that would be less suitable to us. . . . No, gentlemen," said Lastarria, "but we much be original; we have within our own society all the elements to be so, all the elements to make our literature an authentic expression of our nationality."

This was the most urgent need of Hispanic-American people. Their true independence depended upon understanding this necessity. "There are no people on the face of the earth," said Lastarria, "who have a more imperative need to be original in literature than the Americans, for all their variations are peculiar to them, and they have nothing in common with the things that constitute the originality of the Old World." The nature of America, "the moral and social necessities of our people, their interests, their customs, and their sentiments" are the materials for a literature that seeks to be original. "Begin, then, to take advantage of such abundant wealth and to fulfill your mission usefully and progressively; write for the people, enlighten them by battling their vices and encouraging their virtues, by recollecting their heroic deeds, by encouraging them to venerate their religion and their institutions; so you will tighten the bonds which unite them, you will teach them to love their fatherland, and you will accustom them to regard their liberty and their social existence as one. This is the only path which you should follow to consummate the great task of making our literature national, useful, and progressive."[69]

And in 1865, having recently felt the impact of the French invasion in Mexico, Lastarria again defended the same thesis on the necessity of a literature, but he now broadened it to include an American culture. Europe, he admitted, has certain values; but these, in

[69] *Discurso de 1842*, previously cited.

order to be positive, must be assimilated into our culture. In America there has arisen a new social and political concept which has little or nothing to do with Europe: democracy. Only with these ideas in mind, therefore, should we accept European cultural values. "This does not deny the progress achieved by European science, nor does it attempt to erase it to begin anew that arduous and long struggle which intelligence has waged in the Old World in order to arrive at the place it now occupies." No, quite the contrary, it is necessary to make use of European science, to take advantage of it, but to adapt it, "without forgetting that we are, above all Americans—that is, democrats—and therefore obliged to develop here European ways of life, which have conditions diametrically opposed to ours. . . . So, then, when we utilize European science in the American sense, we shall indeed make a contribution to our regeneration."[70]

Andrés Bello, in an address delivered in 1848 at the University of Santiago, Chile, also spoke of the necessity of an American science. "Shall we continue to be condemned to repeat servilely the lessons of European science without venturing to discuss them," he asked, "to improve upon them with local application, and to give them a stamp of our own nationality?" If we were to do so, he answered, we would betray the spirit of this very science "which prescribes careful and extensive examination and observation, free discussion, and conscientious conviction." Only a lack of means can justify conceding a vote of confidence to this science, at least for the time being. But it is not to be so in all fields, in all branches of science. There exist some branches of science which require local investigation, such as history. "Could Chilean history be written better elsewhere than in Chile?" And he added, "There are few sciences which can be taught effectively without the necessity of adapting them to our physical nature and our social conditions."

But that is not all, continued Bello. "The Old World desires . . . the collaboration of the New; and it not only desires it, it provokes it and requires it. . . . European science seeks data from us; shall we have not even enough zeal and application to gather it for them?" But this is not the only task for America; it is not enough. "Will not

[70] *La América.*

the American republics play a greater role in the progress of the sciences," he asked, "will not they have a greater part in the realm of the accomplishments of human understanding than the African tribes or the islands of Oceania?" The Americans are capable of contributing their experiences in the different fields of science—in the natural sciences as well as the political, literary and moral—whenever they use as a point of departure the experience of the American reality which is accessible to them. "I could elaborate these considerations a great deal more by applying them to politics, to the moral man, to poetry, and to all kinds of literary composition, because either it is not true that literature is the reflection of the life of a people, or one must admit that each nation, except those submerged in barbarism, is called upon to portray itself in a literature of its own and to impose upon that literature certain forms."[71]

In another work, published the same year, Andrés Bello returned to the same theme when he spoke of the *Autonomía cultural de América*. It is a kind of destiny, he said, that some cultures subjugate others. "Europe has already influenced us more than it should. While we are taking advantage of European enlightenment, we should, at the same time, imitate its independence of thought. . . . Young Chileans! Learn to judge for yourselves; aspire to independence of thought. Drink from the fountains, at least from the streams nearest to them. . . . Inquire into each civilization as revealed in its works; ask each historian for his sources. That is the first philosophy that we must learn from Europe." From Europe we must learn the European's capacity to study his own reality.

"Our civilization," he concluded, "will also be judged by its works; and if they see us servilely copying European civilization, even that which is not applicable, what will a Michelet, a Guizot think of us? They will say: 'America still has not shaken off its chains; it is following blindly in our footsteps; there is not an original thought in her works, nothing original, nothing indigenous; she copies the forms of our philosophy without absorbing its spirit. Her civilization is an exotic plant which still does not take its nourishment from the soil which sustains it.' " Faithful to this spirit, Bello defended the basic

[71] *"Discurso en el aniversario de la humanidad,"* *Anales de la Universidad* (Santiago de Chile, 1848).

reality of Hispanic America which its reformers had futilely tried
to deny: Spain.

Toward an American Philosophy

Juan Bautista Alberdi, continuing the same line of thought of
those men previously quoted, declared, in his now famous classic on
American philosophy, "There is no universal philosophy, because
there is no universal solution to the problems which form its basis.
Each country, each epoch, each philosopher has had his own individual philosophy, which has grown more or less, which has lasted more
or less, because each country, each epoch, and each school has come
forward with different solutions to the problems of the human spirit."
Hence we can speak of an Oriental, Greek, Roman, German, French,
or English philosophy; "it therefore follows that there must be an
American philosophy."

Taking this view as a point of departure, Alberdi draws certain
practical conclusions. All philosophies have something of truth and
something of falsehood. It is necessary, therefore, to resort to those
which have something we can use to confront our American reality.
"The rule of our time," he said, "is not to be killed by any system;
in philosophy tolerance is the law of our time. . . . Within the possibility of being incomplete, for the purpose of being useful, we shall
concern ourselves only with the philosophy of the nineteenth century,
and from this philosophy itself we shall exclude everything that is
least contemporary and least applicable to the social necessities of our
countries, whose means of satisfaction must furnish us with the material of our philosophy." Thus we shall have to approach the great
European philosophers of the nineteenth century, such as Kant, Hegel, Stuart, Cousin, Jouffroy, and others. But so far as northern Europe is concerned, Germany and Scotland, we need study very little:
"Nothing could be less appropriate for initiating the young South
American mind into the problems of philosophy than the spirit and
forms of northern European thought." Americans should look to
France for enlightenment, for it belongs to southern Europe. "We,
who are also southerners by origin and location, rightly belong to
their intelligent initiative." Moreover, German and Scottish philosophies are assimilated intelligently into French philosophy.

He considered all this with American reality in mind. America must be the point of departure in every selection instrumental in solving its problems from a philosophical point of view. "Obviously we are going to study philosophy; but we will do so in order that this study, ordinarily fruitless, will bring us some advantage; we will study, as we have said, not philosophy for itself, not philosophy applied to the mechanism of sensations, not philosophy applied to the abstract theory of human sciences, but philosophy applied to objects of more immediate interest for us—in short, political philosophy, the philosophy of our industry and wealth, the philosophy of our literature, the philosophy of our religion and our history." It is necessary to investigate the motive of conduct and progress of everything in American reality. Alberdi desired a philosophy for the American people, not a universal one—a concrete philosophy derived from our reality, not an abstract philosophy drawn from the universal. Every philosophy, he said, has "arisen from the most imperative needs of each period and of each country." And so it shall arise in America.

North America offers us an example of this mode of philosophizing or understanding philosophy. "Pure abstraction," he said, "metaphysics for itself alone, will not take root in America. And the United States of North America has shown us that it is not true that a previous philosophical development is indispensable in order to attain political and social development. . . . They have established a new social order, and it did not arise from metaphysics. There is not a country in the world less metaphysical than the United States, and there is not a country that has contributed greater material for speculation to the philosophical nations with their admirable practical advancement." Hence Alberdi arrives at the only possible conclusion: "We must formulate a philosophy based on our needs. And these needs, the problems which they pose, are those relative to liberty and the rights and privileges in the social and political order. Therefore American philosophy must be essentially political and social in its objectives, ardent and prophetic in its instincts, synthetic and organic in its method, positive and realistic in its procedures, republican in its spirit and destiny. . . . We have mentioned American philosophy, and it is imperative to demonstrate that it can exist. A complete philosophy is one which solves problems of interest to all humanity. A contemporary philosophy solves problems of interest for the moment. American philosophy will solve the problem of American destiny."

Philosophy, according to Alberdi, is universal on the one hand and particular on the other. In its fundamental elements it interests humanity, it is universal; but in its application it interests nations, it is national and temporal. It is in this local, particular aspect that it must be of special interest to all nations. It must interest them to know their *raison d'être*, their progress, and their happiness. "And it is only because their individual happiness is a part of the happiness of mankind in general" that man is interested in the universality of philosophical solutions. "But his point of departure and his progress is always his nationality." Philosophy is universal so far as it is concerned with the nature of its objects, procedures, means, and objectives. Wherever man philosophizes, he observes, forms concepts, reasons, infers, and draws conclusions. It is only from this point of view that there can be a philosophy. But there is no philosophy from the point of view of the observed, the concept, reason, inference, and especially conclusions; that is, the reality itself. That is something local. Its problems are not, then, the problems of any one area, and therefore neither are its solutions. "Philosophy becomes localized because of the instantaneous and local character of the problems which are of special interest to a nation, and it gives to these problems the forms of its solutions. . . . The philosophy of a nation is the series of solutions which have been given to the problems concerning its general destiny. Our philosophy will be, then, a series of solutions given to the problems of interest to national destinies."

According to these ideas, what should America's philosophy be? What is the philosophy most suitable for American youth to study? "A philosophy," declared Alberdi, "which because of its brief and concise teaching, will not waste the time that might be more advantageously used in studies of a more productive and useful application, and which because of its basis will serve only to introduce it into the spirit and tendency which dominate the development of institutions and government of the century in which we live and, above all, of the continent which we inhabit."[72] In other words, it must be a philosophy of our time and space, an American philosophy.

These men, beset by the urgencies of the time and with a multitude of problems to solve, could accept only a practical philosophy, a philosophy that would attack the problems which their reality posed. Historical relativism became clearly evident as a natural consequence of their desire for intellectual independence. This relativism was to lead them, consequently, to the acceptance of positivism.

VIII. APPRENTICESHIP IN FOREIGN SOURCES

The Cuban Process Toward Independence

As a result of historical circumstances, Cuba observed from the sidelines the rest of Hispanic America which from the moment of its independence was engaged in a bloody struggle to destroy Spanish tutelage and heritage. In 1898, Cuba became the last of the Spanish colonies in America to attain its independence. Meanwhile, she continued to observe closely the experiences of her sister republics in Hispanic America, at times trying to imitate them and at others seeking immediate help from them.

Cuba's expectations were profoundly reflected in the work of her scholars, who observed and learned. Forced to wait, these men began to attempt to realize in Cuba something already initiated in Hispanic America as a second phase of independence: intellectual emancipation. They aspired to political independence, but with prior preparation for intellectual independence. They won over and educated Cubans to the cause of liberty. Education preceded arms; the teacher preceded the soldier. José Agustín Caballero (1765–1835), Félix Varela (1788–1853), José Antonio Saco (1797–1879), José de la Luz y Caballero (1800–62), and Enrique José Varona (1849–1933) had hoped and struggled for the freedom of the island, preparing the Cubans mentally for its achievement. José Martí became the synthesis of these desires.

[72] *Ideas para presidir a la confección del curso de filosofía contemporánea en el Colegio de Humanidades* (Montevideo, 1840); collected in *Antología* by José Gaos and in Arturo Ardao's book, *La filosofía pre-universitaria en el Uruguay.*

The Cuban thinkers knew, or had learned, that political emancipation was insufficient, for if it was to be really worth while, it could be considered only as a function of a more complete emancipation, intellectual emancipation. The Cubans considered themselves sons of Spain, but they also considered themselves Cubans, that is, sons of a country and an environment different from the Spanish. At first they did not attempt to break with Spain; they sought only that these differences should be recognized. Father José Augstín Caballero in 1810 before the famous Cortes of Cádiz, presented a project in the name of Cuba in which he said: "Those who clamor for reforms do not aspire to establish a state with its complete juridical independent organization; they only want Spain to recognize the personality of the colony. They believe that there will be a more tranquil and prosperous co-existence if the mother country decentralizes its governmental status."[73] As for political organization, they sought a provisional council of the republic that would collaborate with the governor-general of the island.

The personality of the colony, Cuba's own personality, is what the Cubans wanted recognized. In 1822, Father Varela made such a request of the mother country. He asked for the island's independence in internal affairs and broader collaboration on the problems dealing with the community of Hispanic nations, such as was the practice in the British Empire. It must be thus, he said, given "the profound differences which exist between Spain and its overseas possessions in such things as climate, population, economic status, customs, and ideas." It was true that Spain had dictated certain laws especially for the colonies, but these, said Varela, "once they have crossed the great ocean, become weak and even disappear, and are replaced by the will of man, which is so much more terrible when it becomes complacent in its first attempts to exercise arbitrary power or to enjoy an ancient and consolidated impunity."[74]

Independence and Heritage

José Antonio Saco, like the other Cuban thinkers, desired Cuban

[73] Medardo Vitier, *Las ideas en Cuba* (Habana, 1938).
[74] *Ibid.*

independence. He realized that this independence was not to be gained by violence alone. The struggle for independence would be futile if Cuba's colonial heritage had not undergone a prior transformation. Saco was opposed to the existing regime; he struggled against it and tried to reform it; but he was also opposed to revolution. There was another way: annexation by the United States. This Saco also rejected because the people were not yet prepared for it, since, given their heritage, annexation would only mean a change in masters. He feared the race and the Spanish heritage. A subjugated people who had never exercised the rights of freedom would be an easy prey to another nation. In addition, there was little white population in Cuba. "Oh," he said in a letter, "if Cuba had today two or more million whites, how gladly would I see her pass into the hands of our neighbors! Then, however great the immigration of North Americans, we would absorb them and, increasing and prospering to the astonishment of nations, Cuba would always be Cuban."[75] But it was not possible; an enslaved race predominated in Cuba, a race which could only expect to be enslaved again by the nation which annexed it. Cuba would never be a country with the same rights as those of the states of the North American Union; it would only come to be a North American colony. He, like another Cuban political figure, feared that the enslaved sons of free Spaniards could only be slaves.

Saco, like the other great Hispanic-American thinkers of his time, realized the faults inherited from the autocratic mother country, faults due to a bad political and economic education. This was one of the reasons why he fought the system of representatives to the Cortes. This system was inadequate because of the lack of knowledge that the Peninsular deputies had of American reality, the inadequate number of deputies from the Antilles, and the distance between them and the mother country; furthermore, "no matter how painful it was, it was necessary to tell the truth," he said. "I firmly believe that among the deputies overseas, whether they live in the Peninsula or whether they come from the Antilles, there will be some who will never betray the interest of the country which honors them with its confidence; but our nature is weak, and weakened still more by the detestable political education which we have received in Cuba and Puerto

[75] *Ibid.*

Rico. I also believe that there are others who, forgetting their duties, will turn their position into a steppingstone for the advancement of their personal interests." This is the education of corruption or seduction in politics. "One could, indeed, reply to this," he added, "by saying that the same thing would happen with the people appointed to the Cuban or Puerto Rican legislature; but there is an enormous difference between coming as a deputy to Spain and being a deputy to the legislature of those islands. . . . A minister has infinitely more means of seducing or of corrupting than a high-ranking executive of the islands."

In the field of economics there was also an evil inherited from the mother country and from the social organization that she had given to the Antilles; this made it impossible for the Antillians to achieve the industrial progress that characterized the great new nations. "By an ill-fated upheaval of social ideas," said Saco, "occupations which were the strongest support of the States were considered among us as degrading." This led young men to avoid these occupations and to seek only those considered honorable. "The trade of shoemaker, tailor, carpenter, blacksmith, mason, and other occupations which are highly regarded in the most civilized nations of the earth are considered base in Cuba; and so lamentable is this false opinion that this fatal stigma extends to almost all our professions." Those professions considered degrading were therefore abandoned to the Negroes: "Destined only for menial labor, all these trades were assigned exclusively to them, as fitting to their social status; and the master, who from the very beginning was used to treating the slave with scorn, very soon began to look upon the slaves' occupations in the same way. . . . In such a deplorable situation, it could no longer be expected that any white Cuban would devote himself to the crafts, since by the mere act of practicing them, it appeared that he was renouncing his class privileges." Consequently the occupations in crafts and industry were abandoned to the Negroes, while the whites dedicated themselves to literary careers or to other occupations considered more honorable. "Once this barrier had been established, each race was obliged to move in a limited sphere, since the whites could not break it because public opinion forbade it, and neither could the Negroes and mulattoes because laws and customs prohibited it."

The legislative efforts of the mother country to stimulate the industrialization of her colonies were futile under these conditions. The evil lay in the habits and customs of the countries; laws could accomplish nothing in this respect, only a different kind of education. "When the law clashes with the ideas of honor or of infamy which nations have conceived and combats these ideas only with the arms of authority, those ideas unfortunately always prevail. Law, in such chaos, should proceed with caution toward its objective down winding paths; and by using indirect means, it should keep undermining public opinion until the day arrives when it can deliver a decisive blow."

What course should we follow? "The revolution of ideas," education. "The heads of families should be the ones primarily charged with this, since the lessons which they give to their children are almost always their model of conduct. . . . It is true that there are heads of families who plant haughty ideas in the hearts of their children, but it is also true that there are other parents who inspire their children with good ideas; and if they do not exercise them, it is because they do not find a helpful hand to give them the necessary support." When these parents see the expediency of turning a lazy son into a hardworking man, they will then become the most interested in such a reform. They will thus be able to convert themselves into an impenetrable mass which will protect them from the attacks of insolence.

It is not a question, Saco added, of making artisans of the rich; but only of preventing them from degrading the artisans and insulting them with their foolish pride. What was desired was that "they not corrupt the hearts of their children by giving them barbarous and antipatriotic sentiments which some day might be fatal to them, because the rich man, nurtured from infancy with such haughty ideas, if he should become poverty stricken, as frequently happens, is then condemned to live in misery, for he considers contemptible many occupations by which he could earn his living." The evils of this false education are still evident in the mother country and in America. Saco begged the Cubans to learn from outside sources. "Today, right today," he said, "what pitiful examples the revolutions of Spain and America present before our very eyes!"[76]

The Cubans wanted their independence, but without haste. The

[76] *Memoria sobre la vagancia en la Isla de Cuba, 1832.*

Antilles were not yet prepared to attain independence in its fullest sense. They must first be educated; the first struggle must take place on the field of education. All their efforts should be concentrated on this field. In the meantime, in the political field, they sought from the mother country only a greater respect for their problems and conditions. They sought a political organization which, without breaking the ties with the mother country and their collaboration with her, would permit them to concentrate on problems that were peculiar to the Antilles.

Saco was opposed to assimilation of the Antilles by Spain since this was incompatible with the special laws which were being discussed for the colonies. He sought equality, such as England and her colonies understood it. "I am an enemy of assimilation between the Antilles and Spain," he said. "I am a decided partisan of equality because with equality all the evils of assimilation are removed at once and all the benefits of liberty in the broadest sense are attained, by making it possible to establish all the differences which the special conditions of the Antilles require. The English colonies are the best governed in the world; nevertheless, no man in his right mind would commit the absurdity of saying that they are absorbed by the mother country, for in the strict sense of the word there exists between the mother country and the colonies only a similarity of institutions." There is no hurry to form an independent state. First it is desirable to change people; their habits and their customs must change. The Cubans did not want to follow the same course as the rest of Hispanic America; they did not want revolution and violence. Circumstances had not permitted the Cubans to follow such a course, but these same circumstances allowed them to learn from the experiences of their other sister nations. José Antonio Saco wrote in a letter: "This, my friend, is certainly not the path of popularity, and even though it is very gratifying to the soul, there are cases, as you know, in which, in order to be a good citizen, it is necessary to sacrifice it on the altars of the fatherland." Independence won by violence was considered, therefore, as contrary and prejudicial to "the true interests of Cuba." But, "even though Cuba cannot be independent today, she can be within twenty, thirty, or forty years."[77]

[77] Vitier, *Las ideas en Cuba.*

Education for Freedom

José de la Luz y Caballero was responsible for preparing the Cubans for achieving their independence through education. He likewise was not a partisan of violence; he hoped for a Cuba that could attain its freedom through progress. "He really never dreamed," said one of his disciples, "of disturbing the people's minds by preparing them for immediate and destructive action; he longed, on the contrary, to enlighten them with the truth and to settle them in virtue, but nevertheless in the end he did perturb them." Through his teaching he "sowed everywhere sublime and fertile germs of morality and virile grandeur which would develop in their souls and logically bring about a profound disagreement between their reality and their principles and, later, an aspiration to harmony."[78]

What was the basis of this education? It was freedom of thought in opposition to all ideological dogmatism. If the Cubans were successful in learning to think freely, they would also be successful in the field of politics. Political independence was to be derived from freedom of thought. Luz y Caballero taught the Cubans to reject all dogmatism, at the same time that he taught them to desire the political freedom of their country. He educated men for the liberty which in the very near future they were to demand in full. One of his biographers and friends said of him: "It has been said, to the amazement of all who knew Luz intimately, that he taught his students to hate Spain and that the present revolution in Cuba is due to him." But such was not the case, he added; the teacher's motto was, "Neither war nor conspiracy of any kind." "He wanted progress, and progress to the greatest degree possible; but he wanted to achieve it as it had been achieved in England, without any shocks, violence, upheavals, or bloodshed."[79]

A Spaniard, Marcelino Menéndez Pelayo, referred to Luz as an enemy of Spain, as a separatist and agitator: "Don José de la Luz y Caballero, skillful director of secondary schools, a great propagandist of sophistry and separatism among the youth of Cuba where they

[78] Manuel Sanguily, *José de la Luz y Caballero*, in *Obras Completas*.

[79] José Ignacio Rodríguez, *Vida de José de la Luz y Caballero* (Nueva York, 1874).

venerate him as their Confucius. .... He indoctrinated the minds of an entire generation against Spain, and he created in the Colegio del Salvador an institution of future workers and champions of the jungle."[80] In truth, the leaders of the independence were to come from its classrooms, but Luz had never spoken to them of war or of violence. Violence came only when the Cubans, eager for their freedom, realized that there was no other way, when they saw that an evolution similar to that of the English colonies was impossible. Facing Spain, and in spite of all they had learned from the experiences of the Hispanic-American republics which had attained their independence previously, they found that there was no other way than the one that they were to take at the opportune time.

Luz y Caballero attempted, above all, to free the Cubans from the evil habits which the mother country had imposed upon them. Hence he proposed "to open new careers to the youth of our country condemned to consecrate itself exclusively to law, to medicine, or to idleness; to spread scientific knowledge, to perfect the manufacture of our products, and to profit from our natural resources; to facilitate the acquisition of knowledge for every enterprise which depends on physical and mathematical sciences and to contribute to the advancement of the liberal and mechanical arts." The education of Cuban youth must be focused on Cuba's own reality. "How can I know what my duty is," asked the Cuban teacher, "if I do not know what the events and circumstances require? Is it not on the demands of circumstances that order and harmony in the moral world are based? ... What? Does not human nature have laws as all nature does? ... The law of duty, then, far from opposing the principle of the greatest utility, finds in it its greatest support. .... The one is precept; the other is theory."[81]

First there is reality; then come ideas. Reality precedes moral duty, and it is within this reality that this duty was to become valid. Luz y Caballero also held this same idea when he argued that the study of physics should precede the study of logic. "To begin with physics," he said, "or in general with the natural sciences is to begin at the be-

[80] *Historia de los heterodoxos españoles*, note to Book VIII, Ch. III.

[81] José de la Luz y Caballero, "*Communicados*," *Diario de la Marina*, Sept. 13, 1838.

ginning; man is by nature drawn to the contemplation of external objects by the countless number of sensations that strike his senses: he is therefore by necessity a naturalist before he is an ideologist; he must first begin with the exterior before he studies the interior: man cannot know his interior world except through a knowledge of the exterior." To go from nature to ideology is to go from the known world to the unknown, from the reality that is given to us to the reality that we have to attain. This is the reason, said the Cuban teacher, that the method of the natural sciences has been applied to the moral sciences. "The ideologists and the psychologists have dealt with them in sciences of observation and, if it is possible, of experience." Logic should also have reality as its basis. "Who can deny the importance of logic," he asked, "or, rather, of philosophical studies? It must not be a logic of pure rules taken blindly or based on the words of a teacher, but rather a logic which rests firmly on the spirit of observation.... Man must observe before drawing conclusions; he must receive impressions before reflecting upon them; he must first walk before he can explain walking."[82]

Among Luz y Caballero's disciples such ideas were reflected in a positive sense for Cuban reality and in a negative sense against all ideology or political power foreign to Cuban reality. The man who asked youth to cast off all ideological authority was also asking youth to rid itself of all authority alien to its reality, including political. "It is necessary," he said, "to have reason strongly fortified in order to cast off the yoke of authority in any form in which it appears. And what more terrible form than the words of a teacher for the weak understanding of his disciples? One owes respect to teachers, but not faith.... My aim has been to demolish authority and at the same time to stop presumption."[83] To demolish authority, to shake the yoke of authority in whatever form it might appear—this was Luz y Caballero's formula in his educational campaign for Cuban liberty. From intellectual independence Cubans would move easily to political independence.

Cuban reality was to be the touchstone for any philosophy or ideology that sought to take root in Cuba. This was a reality with its own

[82] "*Documentos para su vida*" *Revista de Cuba*, Vol. V (Habana, 1878–83).
[83] *Ibid.*

rights and destiny; any philosophy or ideology that might conflict or hinder in any way these rights and this destiny should be cast aside. First there must be reality, and then ideologies. Luz y Caballero was faithful to this maxim. He taught the Cuban youth nothing contrary to the demands of their reality. During a stay in Germany he had become familiar with the idealistic philosophy of Schelling, Fichte, Kant, and Hegel; but, in spite of his knowledge of the works of these men, he never spoke of them to his young disciples. "No one better than I," he said, "could without danger have gathered such an abundant harvest from Germany, and even though I have gained some recognition for having introduced into the country the idealism of that country which I adore, I have come to the conclusion in all conscience that it could harm rather than benefit our country."[84] Cuban reality was above any vanity or dilettantism. Luz y Caballero could accept no philosophy which would in any way justify an authority alien to his country's reality nor any idea of conformity with any forms alien to it. He could not say with Hegel, "If reality does not adapt itself to ideas, so much the worse for reality"; quite the contrary: so much the worse for ideas if they could not be adapted to reality.

The Struggle for Intellectual Independence

In 1839 the influence of the eclectic philosopher Victor Cousin began to be felt in Cuba. This influence became more widespread as it won followers among Cuban youth. Luz y Caballero noted immediately the possibilities and consequences that such a philosophy might have in the development of the new Cuban generations. He soon realized the negative consequences of this philosophy relative to that ideal which was so acceptable to him: intellectual independence, and, in the not far distant future, the political independence of his country. This philosophy presented history as the visible government of God, whence came the belief that everything was as it should be and that everything was in its place. This is the way historical reality was because it should be this way and no other. Cuba, governed despotically by the captains-general, living off slavery and slave trade, with a white population governed by the saber and a black population gov-

---

[84] Enrique Piñeyro, *Hombres y glorias de América* (Paris, 1903).

erned by the lash, was the best of all regimes, an expression of divine government, and, therefore, good. All historical facts, the good as well as the bad, could be justified. As far as Cuba was concerned, the only justifiable historical facts were purely negative, the evils that she suffered. Luz y Caballero reacted, saying, "The practical consequences of such a philosophical system would necessarily be harmful to the political progress of the world, and especially to the island of Cuba, where, because of the existence of slavery and ultraconservative and reactionary political institutions, the enervating action of eclecticism, as a system, would be felt more strongly."

Luz y Caballero did not hesitate; one must attack the evil at its root and give battle publicly to Cousin's eclecticism. It was not a matter of making an exhibition or of simple explanations in order to display erudition. "It would have been a mistake for me," he said, "to have undertaken . . . a task of simple explanation; the works of this celebrated psychologist are plagued with errors and contradictions. . . . There was another motive for having given this turn to the refutation—a feeling of patriotism has governed this undertaking." There was a struggle for patriotism in defense of Cuban reality and rights. The ideological struggle must precede the armed struggle which was soon to take place. Luz y Caballero fought against an ideological absolutism just as his disciples were later to struggle against a political absolutism. He fought for intellectual freedom with the same patriotism that the Cubans were later to display in their struggle for political freedom. The Cuban teacher was guided by neither pride nor scorn, but by the desire for truth, a truth which must be valid for Cuba. "Neither expression of pride in regard to my own poor strength, nor . . . scorn from M. Cousin. There is nothing here but the frank manifestation of a candid soul which neither knows how nor desires to disguise truth, even if it works to his sorrow." Merely to refute was not difficult, but it was not a question simply of refuting, but of something more important; it was a matter of showing those who were dazzled by the doctrine, those who had not seen its errors and damaging effects, the evils that it could cause. "Every sentiment," he said, "gives way in me to our country's need."

Luz y Caballero wished to teach the youth of his time to struggle against and discredit the sophisms which might disorient them. "Having realized the inefficacy of pointing out general rules to expose the sophism, we have attempted to teach youth a practical way to recognize these sophisms and to discredit them, so that, trained in the procedure with the example that is here given them, without fear of certain refutation, they may apply a similar scrutiny to them and convince themselves how easy it is to expose and shatter the paralogism, however disguised or tempting it may appear to them." If Cuban youth is to have a philosophy of its own, a philosophy of its reality, it will have to begin by confronting those philosophies which, although alien to this reality, attempt to dominate it. "It is my intention," declared Luz y Caballero, "that Cuban youth continue casting off the yoke of literary authority, for without this prior step there is no hope of establishing and acclimatizing a true philosophical school in our beloved country." This meant, of course, a philosophical school that took Cuban reality as its point of departure. "Let everybody understand," he added, "that it is more trouble than pleasure for me to impugn M. Cousin, yielding thereby to an imperative necessity which harasses the youth of my country."

Luz y Caballero did not look upon the polemic as a simple academic problem which must be elucidated; it involved something more—there was enveloped in it a political problem which would necessarily affect the idea of a nation that was taking form in the island. He was fully aware of the ideological roots of Cousin's eclecticism, an obliging philosophy popular with the government of the Restoration in France. Cousin's eclecticism was only a "political affair under the guise of philosophy, nothing more!" To a malleable philosophy which could easily justify a reality contradictory to Cuban ideals of liberty, it was necessary to oppose a philosophy which would destroy it and at the same time defend such ideals. "Cuban youth already has," he said, "its *Complete Course in Sophistry;* but it will also have, although not so completely, a sufficient spirit of national fight to uncover and destroy the nets with which certain individuals in the guise of friendship attempt to enmesh it. The truth, however, is that these men are the greatest enemies of youth's soul." For this reason, "I have adopted severe forms intentionally and with an essentially patriotic idea in mind ... that of discrediting from all points those doctrines which are poisonous to our beloved Cuban youth."

Summarizing Luz y Caballero's polemic against Cousin's eclecticism, represented in Cuba by Manuel González and José Zacarías González del Valle, one could say that it was a defense of realism, in the sense already indicated, and an offense against the idealism which tried to superimpose itself upon this reality. Cousin's followers accused Luz y Caballero of being a materialist; hence, in one of the passages of the polemic, he said: "I am hoping that they will demonstrate to me that from Locke's proposition that 'all our knowledge is derived from experience,' that from this very naïve principle, *materialism* necessarily results." But, even if that were so, if that were reality, the true reality, reality must impose itself. "I will go further," he added, "that if materialism is derived inevitably from this, then all men must necessarily be materialists, because that is such obvious truth that we must of necessity yield to the evidence." It is of no importance that the consequences are unfavorable to certain plans; the important thing is always the truth. "One might argue that that is a prejudicial truth, and it might be abused." With this idea, only harm can be done to morality and religion, added Luz y Caballero, since fear in the face of a reality that must be taken into account is cowardly instilled. "If one of the two principles held as truth turns out to be nothing but an apparent truth, let it fall before real truth." Its touchstone would always have to be reality; there was no other solution for the Cuban teacher.

Religion itself cannot escape this reality, for reality imposes certain limits upon religion. Independent of what his idea of God's reality may be, man's idea is limited by the reality within which he finds himself. "Man extracts his idea of God from the world, so that if man had no sense of the finite, he would not be able to rise to the infinite; therefore, there is no rigorous absolute for human conception. . . . Man sees God in the world itself, even though God is different from the world, because in the world he sees a plan, order, and harmony . . . then by means of observation, he comes to the idea of God." For this reason men have different ideas about God, according to the reality which serves them as a point of departure. "For example: polytheism and monotheism, idolatry in its various forms, and true religion; as our knowledge of nature, so is our idea of God always subject to nature."

Reality always occupies the first plane; but Cousin's eclecticism upset this order by trying to superimpose upon it ideas which in the final analysis were only empty and meaningless words. With Cousin's eclecticism, said Luz y Caballero, "the prejudicial tendencies of scholasticism" come to life again, "words again occupy the seat of science reserved only for objects." Instead of a step forward, it was a step backward. "Cuban youth fell again into the weaknesses from which other teachers had already freed it. Some eminent men rejoice in that involved philosophy and in that rubbish, and by precept and example those tactics are rendered acceptable to youth and we return to the weaknesses from which we have recovered with so much effort and trouble."

Luz y Caballero had entered the polemic for patriotic reasons. The Cuban teacher saw clearly the danger that the work of his predecessors, Caballero, Varela, and Saco, ran if the Cuban took his eyes off his reality. In the world of pure ideas Cuba had nothing to do; it was a world alien to the reality in which there was neither a past nor a future. Cuba's progress would cease, she would have no future whatever, and without that she would not have the liberty she so much desired. "To consider only the first effects, without searching for the causes," he said, "or to compare with later effects previous or contemporary ones, is to stagnate by one's own will; it is to contravene the invariable law of human progress, it is to protect against progress itself, it is to deny the past and close the doors to the future." One must know one's reality in order to confront it and transform it; if Cuba is to be transformed, the Cubans will have to recognize her as their reality. Luz y Caballero, without saying this directly, since he had already done so when he expounded his patriotic reasons, expressed the above idea in the following words: "One must surround nature in order to dominate it: if we go blindly ahead, trying to *divine* instead of *observe*, it will escape us completely." He was also aware of the practical role of the philosopher in the natural as well as the social field: "To overcome the difficulties that nature and society present," he said, "is the first task of the philosopher." The philosopher must help man to overcome his difficulties, and to do so, he must confront his reality, however difficult it may be. He should not reject his reality in any way; he should, on the contrary, know it and attack it, when necessary, with all the means within his reach. "Do not fear those timid philosophers," said the Cuban teacher, "for neither comparative physiology, nor phrenology, nor any true form which knowledge may take can destroy the foundations of human responsibility, resting upon facts as ineluctable as our own existence, resting, I say, upon the same sensitivity and reason common to every race."

A morality which does not take this reality into consideration would be ineffective. "How effective," he asked, "can our advice be ... if we are content to recommend what exalts man without indicating to him the means of attaining it? ... The moralists do that." This, he added, is a powerful motive for destroying the psychological doctrines that serve them as a point of departure. Since they destroy man instead of perfecting him, they attempt to eliminate the study of his corporeal functions, or "they oppose the study of morality in relation to the physical."

No, the Cubans definitely could not follow Cousin's philosophical school. They could not follow the doctrine of a "man so essentially conciliatory and yielding as the head of the eclectic school. . . . We differ on every point from this school . . . ; they, limited by their conscience, not only disregard humanity, but place themselves in the impossible position of not being able to cure its weaknesses or to improve its virtues. . . . We, on the other hand, attempt to rise above ourselves, to confront the world and our fellow-men with the intermediary of the senses." It was a matter of two irreconcilable points of view: "M. Cousin's scientific basis is to admit everything and combine everything." Luz y Caballero knew well enough what this could mean for the Cubans; for this reason his own motto was, "Explain everything and admit nothing without consideration and reason." No conciliations, no compromising situations.

In the name of patriotism and for the good of his country, Luz y Caballero attacked Cousin's metaphysics. It was a battle for the intellectual emancipation of the youth who would soon fight for the political emancipation of the Island. Without this battle, youth would run the risk of becoming conciliatory and compromising with a reality which once recognized could be changed if it were attacked. Luz y Caballero summarized the reasons for his polemic by saying: "But let us go on to another point more advantageous for Cuban youth, whose benefit is the only motive of our pen. I want to mention the tactics of the metaphysicists, who expound their nonsense in order to prevent anybody from attacking them easily; and it is to be assumed that since the subject matter they deal with is obscure by its very nature, it is not possible to give it greater clarity, nor will it ever be within the reach of any but a few privileged intellects. So it is that poor youths, some out of modesty and respect for the great men who expounded their doctrines in such a way, conform and become resigned, attributing this failure to their lack of ability; and others, out of pure vanity and in order not to be counted among the inept, hasten to join the chosen few. . . . Another incalculable harm that the metaphysical ideas work on youth is to inspire a great scorn for any investigation of the physical order. . . . At one and the same time they corrupt the understanding and the taste of youth, giving it a sterile and unproductive nourishment when there is so much grain to gather in the broad fields of science."[85]

All education should be based upon this reality, upon the direct experience of this reality. Luz y Caballero as well as Varcla, Saco, and Caballero foresaw the consequences of such an education. Masters of their reality, the Cubans claimed it for themselves; and conscious of this reality, they rebelled against the injustices which they had suffered. Attentive to this reality, they learned to direct it and orient it, to transform it with all the means within their reach, even including arms when there was no other way. Cuba, with more time at its disposal, began her emancipation in a different manner from that in which other countries of Hispanic America had begun theirs.

IX. TOWARD THE PHILOSOPHY OF A NEW ORDER

The Ideal for a New Hispanic America

WHAT was the ideal sought in this struggle for the intellectual emancipation of Hispanic America? Sarmiento summed it up in these few words: "It was a question of being a *gaucho* or of not being a *gaucho*,

[85] *Impugnación al examen de Cousin sobre el Ensayo del Entendimiento de Locke* (Habana, 1840). Reprinted under the title *La Polémica Filosófica*, in the *Biblioteca de Autores Cubanos*, Universidad de la Habana, 1948.

of wearing a poncho or a frock coat, of riding in a cart or on a train, of going barefoot or wearing shoes, of going to the local bar or to school." Or in other words, it was a question of being a man with a colonial mentality or a man with a modern mentality. The dilemma was between the past and the future: to continues as a slave to old habits or to take openly the road to progress; to remain in a world of the past or to be like the great nations that represented occidental progress, the United States and England.

Juan Bautista Alberdi sought an education for Argentina that would make this ideal of progress possible. No more secondary schools of moral sciences; what was needed were secondary schools of the exact sciences. "I do not intend," he said, "that morality should be forgotten. I know that without it industry is impossible; but facts prove that man arrives sooner at a sense of morality by practicing the industrious and productive habits of wholesome ideas than by abstract instruction." Hispanic America no longer needs lawyers or theologians; it needs geologists or naturalists. "Her progress will come with roads, artesian wells, and immigration, and not with agitating or servile newspapers, or with sermons or legends." Let the clergy keep hands off the education of our lawyers, statesmen, businessmen, soldiers and sailors. "Can the clergy," he asked, "motivate our youth to the industrial and mercantile undertakings which ought to distinguish the South American man? Can our youth get from the clergy that strong desire for activity and enterprise which will make him the Hispanic-American Yankee? . . . The English language, as the language of liberty, industry, and order, should be required more than Latin." For, he added, "how can we follow the example and the civilizing action of the Anglo-Saxon race without a knowledge of its language?" We shall have to increase our schools of commerce and industry. "Our youth must be educated for the industrial life; and to accomplish that, it must be taught the arts and sciences associated with industry. Our South American man must be educated to overcome the great and overwhelming enemy of our progress: great empty spaces, material backwardness, and the brutish and primitive nature of our continent."[86]

[86] *Bases y puntos de partida para la organización política de la República Argentina*, 1852.

In Mexico, at the other end of Hispanic America, José Luis Mora said: "Let us dismiss especially the error that a form of government is a talisman to which the prosperity of empires is linked. Let us replace this false idea with the truth that the fate of men is improved by spreading morality and industry." Industry also meant for the Mexican the ideal of an independent Mexico occupying a position abreast of progress. Like the Argentine, he felt that it was necessary to reform education by preparing citizens to be sufficient unto themselves, so that they might create with their hands their own well-being. The mania for government employment was one of the nefarious forms of the Spanish heritage which still hindered the march of progress. But this would be eliminated the day the Mexicans recognized the fruits of personal effort, when they learned to be sufficient unto themselves and stopped being slaves of the groups which made the state an instrument to serve their limited interests. Education should be, then, oriented toward the development of men devoted to the only source of personal well-being and liberty: industry. "There is certainly nothing more prejudicial to the industriousness of man than the desire for or the holding of public office, for these are considered and are, in effect, a way of subsisting without hard work, and of living, as is commonly said, a life of ease. The government employee, even the one most burdened with duties, works infinitely less than the artisan or the most leisurely laborer." Since his salary is almost always fixed, "without any increase or decrease, he lacks the real stimulation which impels man to work; that is, the advancement of his fortune and the increase of his pleasures." These men, said Mora, "are not only enemies of work but also the destroyers of industry. . . . Free enterprise has given employment, dignity, and patriotism to many who previously did not enjoy them."[87]

Industry as a Basis for a New Social Order

WEALTH derived from industry was considered the best means for ending the anarchy which beset the Hispanic-American countries. It was therefore necessary to point the efforts of the Hispanic Americans toward this field. "Work," said Mora, "industry, and wealth make men truly and solidly virtuous." Both anarchy and despotism arose

[87] José María Luis Mora, *"Empleomanía," Ensayos, ideas y retratos.*

123

from the incapacity of the Hispanic American to free himself from the state. Work, industry, and wealth are the things which, by making the individual "absolutely free from other things, produce that firmness and noble strength of character which resist the oppressor and make illusory all attempts at corruption. A man who is accustomed to living and maintaining himself without having to debase himself before any power, or beg from that power his subsistence will certainly never support its distorted points of view, its disorganized plans, or its tyranny."[88] Then the state would be what it is in all nations where progress encourages its achievement: a faithful guardian of the individual's interests, a protector of the rewards obtained by these licit means of enrichment. Such was the order that was to replace the despotic colonial order and the anarchy of the groups struggling for the rights to impose this despotism.

Alberdi looked upon "industry as the only means of guiding youth to order." Order which led to progress was to be found in those nations in which industry was the source of wealth. "When England saw Europe ablaze in civil war," Alberdi said, "England did not influence its youth towards mysticism for salvation; it raised a temple to industry and made a cult of it, which forced the demagogues to be humiliated by their madness. . . . Industry was the calming force *par excellence*. It led, by means of a state of well-being and wealth, to order and, through order, to liberty. Examples of this were England and the United States." Hence, he concluded, "Instruction in America should direct its aims towards industry."

In previous passages we have seen that Alberdi, when comparing Hispanic America with Anglo-Saxon countries, found that the latter converted their egoism into an instrument in the service of the grandeur of the nation. While individuals progress by attaining the maximum benefits from their efforts, maximum comfort, the nation continues to express the progress and well-being of its citizens. Industry is likewise a great medium of moralization, said Alberdi. "While facilitating the means for earning a living, it also prevents crime, generally the direct result of misery and idleness. In vain will you fill the minds of youth with abstract notions on religion; if you allow it to be idle and poor, unless you lead it into monastic beggary, it will be dragged into corruption by its desire for the com-

[88] *Ibid.*

124

forts which it cannot obtain because of lack of means." Such youth will be corrupted, without ceasing at the same time to be fanatical. He again uses the example of the Anglo-Saxon countries: "England and the United States have attained a religious morality through industry, while Spain has not been able to develop industry and liberty through simple devotion. Spain's fault has never been lack of religion; but religion was unable to lift it out of povetry, corruption, and despotism."[89] Wealth which originated from industry was the best means for establishing a new moral and social order.

Nevertheless, in Chile José Victorino Lastarria, faithful to the liberal spirit which characterized Chilean thought, did not regard industrial wealth as a solution to the problem of intellectual emancipation of the Hispanic-American peoples. He knew that it was not enough. He did not believe that it was sufficient to establish either a true liberal order or an authentic morality. He did not believe in egoism as a source of progress for nations. Individual labor was not enough for its own welfare; it was necessary to help others, to enlighten them. "We had to reject," he said, "the perverse doctrine which held that material progress and the predominance of wealth are the only elements of a political order."[90]

"Everybody believes," said the Chilean thinker, "that he must further his personal interests, that he must engage in any enterprise which will enlarge those interests and which will give to the nation the support which in their concept it needs, *wealth:* high-flown associations were improvised to expand commerce, to unearth the treasures which nature hides in the veins of the Andes, philanthropic societies to protect agriculture and to eliminate the obstacles which hinder its march. Wealth, gentlemen, will give us power and strength, but not individual liberty; it will make Chile worthy of respect and will carry its name all over the globe, but its government will be tottering, and it will be reduced to depending upon bayonets on the one hand and upon great supplies of gold on the other, and it will not be the father of a great social family, but its master; its slaves will only await the occasion to cast off servitude, but if they were its children, they would seek the opportunity to protect their father."

[89] *Bases.*
[90] *Recuerdos literarios.*

125

Wealth and industry were not enough. "Democracy requires still another support, that of *enlightenment*."

Lastarria regarded pure material progress as a danger if it were not accompanied by the education of the people. Pure material progress would not necessarily produce liberal and democratic nations like the Anglo-Saxon ones. Without enlightenment it would only produce a new form of despotism. Theocratic despotism would be replaced by plutocratic despotism. One form of colonialism would follow another: the cross and the sword would be replaced by gold and bayonets. Lasterria saw very clearly what pure material progress in Hispanic America would become if it did not also devote its attention to education. Spain had neglected the enlightenment of her colonies in America, for in their ignorance she had found the best shackles to keep them submissive. "Democracy which is liberty," said Lastarria, "is not legitimate, is is not useful, nor is it beneficial except when the people have reached their maturity, and we are not yet adults. The strength that we should have used in reaching that maturity which is enlightenment was subjugated for three centuries to satisfying the greed of a backward mother country, and later employed in destroying chains and establishing an independent government. It is our lot to go back, to fill the vacuum which our ancestors left us, and to make their work more solid, in order not to leave enemies to overcome and in order to follow with a firm step the path which the century traces for us. . . . We have been fortunate to receive a partial enlightenment; well, then, let us serve the people, let us light their way on their path to social progress."[91]

Philosophy as a Basis for Order

THE DIFFICULTIES in establishing order, the incapacity of individuals to understand each other, had its roots in an uncontrolled imagination which went beyond what reality could offer the individual. Imagination had predominated in Hispanic America to the detriment of reality. Science, thought the Argentines, had turned into political fantasy, and the political fantasies were the sins for which the people, not the politicians, paid. Fantasy had produced theorizers incapable of confronting a given reality. Beyond this reality they had been weav-

[91] *Discurso de 1842 en la Sociedad Chilena.*

ing a web of deceptive illusions and, with them, another web of multiple charms. The *caudillo* imagined worlds which in the final analysis were impossible. Then the *caudillo* was forced to restrain the imagination which he had aroused in the people. Tyranny was always the result of uncontrolled imagination.

It was now time to set up against the tyranny of imagination a philosophical method which would abandon imaginative premises: an experimental method. The purpose of this method was to derive principles from reality itself by restraining the imagination which attempted to escape from reality. Imagination was the source of the ideas of the doctrinarians; the experimental method would necessarily be the source of the ideas of the realists. Ideas of a universal character would no longer be important, but rather the reality in which ideas were to be realized. Esteban Echeverría, in the *Dogma Socialista*, said, "To be great in politics does not mean to be up to the level of world civilization, but up to the level of the needs of the country." Thus the Argentine leader took a position against the doctrinarians who, without any other basis than their own reasoning, had tried to make of Argentina something similar to a body of *a priori* ideas. It was only by using reality as a point of departure that the idea of a new order so zealously sought by these men could be attained.

Unbridled fantasy in each individual produced anarchy; and anarchy, tyranny. Each individual acted in accordance with the principles of his imagination. What was needed was a common reservoir of truths to serve as a basis for understanding, and with understanding, order. The new generation which took over after the war of independence devoted itself to the task of constructing or finding this common source of beliefs. Esteban Echeverría said: "One of the many obstacles which today stand in the way of, and for a long time will stand in the way of, the reorganization of our society is the anarchy which reigns in all our hearts and minds and the lack of a set of *common beliefs* capable of forming, strengthening, and infusing the public mind with an irresistible superiority." The peace which Hispanic-American countries sought so eagerly was possible only by discovering this fund of common beliefs. "In order to emerge from this chaos," said Echeverría, "we need a light to guide us, a belief to encourage us, a religion to console us, a moral basis, a *common criterion* of truth to serve as a basis of the labor of every mind and for the reorganization of the country and society." It was necessary to establish a body of principles which would be the expression of the common interests of all and of each individual. "We desire," he said, "to formulate a system of common beliefs and clear principles to serve as a guide on the path that we have taken."[92]

Also seeking a common fund of truths which would make a new order possible, the Mexican José Luis Mora demanded an education which would rid the mind of false chimeras, the source of all misunderstanding and disorder. "It is important not only to restrain the unruly, but also to have a wise doctrine to rid the mind of chimerical projects and fallacious whims, a doctrine that will free the minds of people from turbulent desires which cause them to approach the good with scorn and then to follow devotedly an imaginary improvement." The chimera can be only a part of personal liberty, but it must never be elevated to a social doctrine. The individual as such can imagine and desire what he wants, but as a social entity, he must search for a common fund of truths, that is, elements of social comprehension. This is the mission of the state and of politics.

This common fund of truths was to be formulated by means of persuasion. There was to be no violence whatsoever. Violence only engenders violence. "The effects of force," said Mora, "are rapid but passing; those of persuasion are slow but sure." Education, either by leading or allowing itself to be led, must be oriented toward the formation of this common fund of truths. But there could be no better fund than that formulated with the objective of experience. In the fancy, in fantasy, man is completely free and can easily be in disagreement with others. Before an experienced reality, the evidence of that reality will be indisputable. On the other hand, imagination can separate experience if the experience is legitimate. This common fund of truth should therefore be based upon experience. This was beginning to be called the field of positivism. Mora would substitute a practical education based upon positive experience for an education based upon a purely theoretical philosophy.

"Theory," he said, "necessarily consists of certain knowledge suit-

[92] *Dogma socialista de la Asociacion de Mayo.*

able only for the adornment of the understanding and it is taken for granted that this knowledge has no practical application . . . ; practice necessarily consists of a method of procedure established years and centuries before in specific cases and circumstances; it is not questioned, nor is it believed susceptible to improvements or advancements." An education of this kind, "instead of creating in young men the spirit of investigation and of doubt which always leads to and approaches more or less the understanding of truth, inspires in them the habit of dogmatism and disputation which leads them away from truth in purely human knowledge." A spirit of investigation must be formed in youth if a permanent order was to be established; that is, a positive order based on pure reality.

This was the task that fell to the generation following independence. Among the new emancipators there was noted already a spirit which had been alien to Hispanic Americans: the practical spirit, the positive spirit. In 1833, José Luis Mora was already speaking of *positivism*, in opposition to the purely theoretical. The men of his generation who had attempted to reform the mentality of the Mexicans are looked upon as men of positivism. Mora said, "The positivists were called to execute special forms of education," since the old education falsified and destroyed "all the convictions that make a *positivist* of a man."[93] They began to consider the possibility of establishing a philosophy which, by replacing the official philosophy of the colony, would make the formation of a new order possible. They felt a real need for something to which they could give the name of positivism. Soon these men came into contact with the philosophy they so desired, the philosophy called positivism.

The Discovery of Positivism

Sarmiento, Alberdi, Lasterria, and other members of this Hispanic-American generation accepted positivism readily. As soon as its influence began to be felt in Hispanic America, they recognized it as the philosophy whose principles they had upheld without any previous direct contact with the movement. Sarmiento, in a letter written to Francisco P. Moreno in reply to the analysis that the latter had made of his work *Conflictos y armonía de las razas en América*

[93] See my work *Positivismo en México*.

(1833), recognized the relationship of his thought to Spencer's positivistic philosophy. "You are indeed following Spencer's evolutionary ideas," he said, "which I have proclaimed openly in social matters, leaving to you and to Ameghino the Darwinian ideas, if you are convinced of them." As for me, he added, "I have neither the pretention nor the right to be a Darwinist. I agree with Spencer because we think the same way." Sarmiento considered Spencer's way of thinking as his own. The philosophy which best expressed the desires of Sarmiento's generation was Spencer's evolutionary positivism.

In 1833, José Victorino Lastarria wrote in *La Época:* "If I am enthusiastic about Comte, I am in good company, with M. Littré, who in his book on this philosopher considers him among the great, and I can say with him that I owe my philosophical existence, that is, a doctrine, to him, for if in my first writings I found an experimental criterion . . . it is true that I did not have a philosophical doctrine until after availing myself of M. Comte's objective method." Lastarria believed that, without any knowledge of positivism, he had nonetheless followed Comte in his method. In *Recuerdos literarios,* published in 1878, he recalled that his interpretation of the *Influencia social de la Conquista,* which he had presented as a memorial address at the University of Chile in 1844, was inspired by a spirit similar to that which had moved Comte to his interpretation of history. This interpretation failed because it was too extemporaneous. Andrés Bello had attacked it in the name of faith and tradition, and the Argentines in exile had attacked it in the name of historical fatalism.

"The failure of 1844," Lastarria recalled, "we much confess, caught us unawares. In truth, we were not familiar with any writer at all who had thought as we did; and even though at that time Auguste Comte was concluding the publication of his *Cours de Phiposophie Positive,* we had neither the remotest notice of the name of this illustrious philosopher nor of his book nor of his system of history, *which was the same as ours;* nor do we believe that there was anyone in Chile at that time who knew about him, even though today our attention is drawn to the fact that the editor of *El Mercurio* ended his criticism by giving us a bit of advice in which, through a kind of presentiment, he classified us in the future positivistic school when he said: 'Continue in the positivistic bent which you have given to your studies, and do not be intimidated by discouragement.' " This generation was to know positivism later, but their spirit was already predisposed to recognize it as their doctrine. Lastarria commented, "We could not gain a thorough knowledge of Auguste Comte's *Philosophie Positive* until 1868." Before they began their study of Comte's work, these men had read about it in the writings of Littré on French philosophy. "In this reading," said Lastarria, "we went from surprise to surprise; it was a revelation for us." A generation of Americans living in the "virginal forests and the high mountains of the New World without libraries or teachers," in a world of "prodigious wealth that is not available to nor helps those who study," came to historical conclusions similar to those which the French teacher in cultured Europe had reached. "Had we not begun at exactly the same time that Auguste Comte was preparing his work, at a time when the press was beginning to publish his immortal work which did not reach Chile until years later"—asked Lastarria—"had we not begun with the same concepts on which to establish in America a philosophy of history?" Comte, like the Spanish American thinkers, had looked upon "history," said Lastarria, "as a natural phenomenon, taking mankind as the material for this phenomenon and his aptitudes as its strength. In this way he departed from Herder's and Vico's theological concepts and the metaphysics of the German philosophers in order to establish sociological laws and to discover the interrelationships of events and to correlate them with the mental state of the epoch in which they occurred." But this discovery, he added, "did not reach us until twenty-eight years after we had begun with the same concept to formulate a similar doctrine."[94] Positivism thus was already in the minds of the Hispanic-American thinkers, and when they discovered it, they readily assimilated it.

[94] Lastarria, *Recuerdos literarios.*

The New Order

I. POSITIVISM AS A LIBERAL PHILOSOPHY

Against Historical Fatalism

THE CHILEAN philosophers were characterized by their spirit of lofty liberalism. The freedom of the individual—that is, his capacity to decide his own destiny—was of paramount importance to them. They were opposed to all historical fatalism in which the individual did not count as a free entity. Lastarria felt that this was the spirit that should be inculcated in the Hispanic Americans. All forms of historical fatalism had only one purpose, to serve as instruments for certain strong nations to dominate the weak. The strong nations, eager to exploit the wealth of the weaker nations, supported theories which justified the subordinate role of weaker ones. These same theories justified the Spanish conquest and the preservation of the social forms imposed by Spain. They were the justification for all kinds of conservatism.

Lastarria, recalling his polemics with Andrés Bello, said: "We would not accept Herder's theory, nor any other that was based on the supposition of a fatal and necessary evolution of humanity without any inclusion of man's liberty, nor would we agree with Bello that Herder had given history all its dignity, discovering in it the designs of providence; for we would not believe that the human species on earth was condemned by divine providence to realize a certain destiny apart from its own activity and freedom." Lastarria believed in the philosophy of history; he believed that it should be studied and that it should be written, but from the point of view of

135

the capability of the individual to determine his own course. "Before 1868," he continued, "the author of these *Recuerdos* did not know that Kant had considered history a natural phenomenon. . . . But, reading in 1840 the *Scienza nuova* of Vico and then Herder's *Ideen zur Philosophie der Geschichte der Menscheit*, we had rebelled against the theories of both men precisely because they were founded upon a supernatural concept of history. Both of them, using as a point of departure the supposition that mankind is governed in his historical evolution by providential laws, build their system by omitting entirely the conditions that constitute the freedom of human nature."[1] Lastarria was opposed to what he called the theological concept of history, since it was by means of this concept that all responsibility was eliminated, along with progress and freedom. And a science which thus discards what is essential to humanity cannot be the science of humanity, he concluded.

The philosophy of history was a science, but in order to be so it must be based on principles other than those held by Vico and Herder. Lastarria said, "We argued in this way: If there is a philosophy in history, and if, consequently, history is a science, it is also necessary that the events which shape human evolution should not be supernatural phenomena subject to laws of fate or providence, for in such a case history can only be the object of a body of truths which form the nucleus of a doctrine, for each historian will understand or interpret those laws according to his own ideas and will determine what is truth according to his own way of thinking." The assumptions should be otherwise. "In order for there to be a science in history one must believe that human events are natural phenomena linked to each other and dependent upon human action and will; consequently, in order to discover the body of truths which because of their connection with a single object, humanity, form a body of doctrine or philosophy of history, it is necessary to investigate the relationship which those events have to each other and to man's activity, that is, to all his faculties." Such was the emphasis that Lastarria in 1844 gave to his investigation on the social influence of the Conquest, and the method which years later he thought he recognized in Comtian positivism.

[1] Lastarria, *Recuerdos literarios*.

For men like Lastarria who hoped to emancipate the Hispanic Americans intellectually, to accept the idea of fatalism in history would have been to deny their ideal. Neither Vico's, Herder's, nor Hegel's ideas could be accepted in the conception of a philosophy of history for the nations of Hispanic America. "I do not believe in historical fatalism, as some thinkers conceive it," said Lastarria. "We did not accept the theory of the historical school of Hegel, which assumes that all social events are the work of the idea or of the spirit." Quite the contrary. To start from another point of view would lead them to the justification of their great desire. "In our system by using as a point of departure the principle that mankind is capable of self-perfection and that the faculty of directing and promoting his development is given to him alone, provided he is essentially free and therefore responsible, we concluded by recognizing that it is also his duty to correct the experience of his predecessors in order to assure his future." In other words, it is the Hispanic American's duty to correct his past, to remake it, to realize that series of values which Spain had been incapable of realizing in the colony. "We must construct our democratic civilization, and to do so, we must determine what part of the old must be destroyed."

Fatalism in history was nothing more than the expression of the individual's irresponsibility, the easiest justification for his errors and his inability to correct his negative experiences. "In order to appraise events, we did not have a subjective metaphysical or theological system, like Hegel, Vico, Herder, or Michelet, but an *experimental criterion*, based on human nature, on its laws of liberty and perfectibility, and consequently we did not not run the risk of forming a judgment for each case, nor much less did we fall into the fatal error of disregarding human responsibility, of excusing crime, of vindicating or glorifying a man or an event because the one had acted or the other had taken place according to the circumstances of the time, or of obeying a certain prevailing way of thinking." Historical fatalism was nothing more than a defensive weapon in the hands of those who were still trying to justify the Spain of the Conquest. "This doctrine which justifies everything," added Lastarria, "was the one the president of the university [Bello] employed to refute our position, and it is also the one that has induced several of our historians to defend and even to admire sixteenth-century Spain for her conquests and her regime in America" by holding that her crimes were those of the time and not her own, "by agreeing with the historical school of absolution and applause which eliminates the duty of pointing out to new generations what they are to condemn and remedy in the civilization which they have received from their forebears."[2]

Lastarria and Comtism

THE CHILEAN thinker had found a justification of his former theses in the positivist philosophy of Auguste Comte, but not in all of Comtian philosophy. In fact, the points of departure were diverse and even antagonistic. While Comte used society as a point of departure, Lastarria used the individual. He accepted the Comtian law of the three stages of the evolution of the mind, for he saw in them the relationships of coexistence and causality which can explain history; but he departed from Comte in that he considered human liberty the determining factor in social actions. Lastarria thought that, in order to know the laws which moral progress obeys, it was necessary to take observation as a guide. Observation—that is, resorting to experience —drew him to positivism. Positivism had also given him a theoretical basis for his desire for Hispanic-American progress. In positivism he had found that "the movement of humanity in all spheres of its activity is characterized by a forward march, accelerated or restrained, circular or arched, rectilinear or truncated, but always a march."[3] He had also found a justification for the sense of responsibility which the people of Hispanic America needed so much. "Each generation is responsible for its deeds," said Lastarria, "because it is the duty of each one to complete the experiences of its predecessors." In other words, it is the duty of Hispanic America to complete the experiences of its colonial past by not living contentedly in its shadow, "without blindly accepting the errors and crimes of their forebears." This is what "Auguste Comte expressed with profound wisdom" when he said that "during its time each age is the point of departure and the support of the following age, by verifying the past and preparing for the future and including both in a hereditary solidarity."

[2] *Ibid.*
[3] *Miscelánea histórica y literaria*, Vol. II (1868).

But this same liberalism, his belief in the capacity of the individual to control his own destiny, led Lastarria to reject that part of Comte's philosophy in which society dominates the individual: the religion of humanity. Comte's method itself "gave me the necessary strength to reject the final philosophy that this thinker adopted when the subjective method dominated his mind." This was now the work of a madman; Lastarria could not follow this aspect of the French philosopher. "Auguste Comte," he said, "after having studied human progress and having understood its laws in all truth, failed when he attempted to formulate the new synthesis into an absurd religion and a political system that is repugnant to good sense because it has as its bases faith and spiritual power." It was distasteful to Lastarria that a philosophy which used as its point of departure the observation of reality should terminate in the despotism of a new belief and in a political order no less despotic. Comtian positivism paid homage to the most reactionary of political systems, a system in which, in the name of a hypothetical progress, liberty was restrained and a new order as despotic as the theological one was established. Individual liberty was dethroned and despotism was enthroned. Religious positivism, said Lastarria, by attempting to give all its influence to social power, arrived at the conclusion that "the concept of right should disappear from the political realm, just as the concept of cause should disappear from the philosophical realm, and that human law is as absurd as it is immoral." The Chilean thinker was completely opposed to this thesis; he believed that the omnipotent rights which certain states abrogate should be distributed among individuals.

Lastarria could not accept this part of Comte's theory, for to do so would have meant the negation of all his struggles. He accepted from Comte the scientific fundamentals of social organization, but he opposed his ideas on the purpose of the state. He could not agree with the Auguste Comte who in 1851 defended Napoleon III's *coup d'état* as a "felicitous crisis which has put an end to a parliamentary republic and instituted a dictatorial republic." Nor could he agree with the Comte who said that the Czar of Russia "was the only statesman of Christianity." Lastarria stood for liberty; the work of many years and a no less long history of struggles and sacrifices in favor of the parliamentary form of government and of all the social institutions that were an expression of the freedom of the individual made him oppose this aspect of Comte's positivism. In his work *Lecciones de política positiva*, Lastarria considers liberty the final aim of all society.

Lastarria and Stuart Mill

THE STATE was for Lastarria an instrument to serve the ends of individual freedom and not the end product of this freedom. The mission of the state, he said, "is to represent the principle of right in society, in its foreign relations by using force when it is necessary to defend that right, as well as in internal matters to facilitate the conditions of its existence and development for society as a whole and for each of its members." Only when the state limited its actions in this manner was peace a fact. "When the state limits its action in this way, internal peace is a result and not an end of the state, as Humboldt holds; and if some time it does change, the state does not need to go beyond the limits of the law."[4] Establishing that the mission of the state was to protect national independence and maintain internal peace did not mean, the Chilean thinker said, limiting its action, but orienting it towards the ends that were proper to it by eliminating the pretexts of those who, in the name of other purposes, defended an absolute system. To preserve national independence, "have not all individual rights as well as all the active faculties of society always been sacrificed to construct a strong power which can preserve and defend those two supreme ends?" Lastarria was therefore opposed to tyrannies established to secure liberty. He did not accept a form of government based on a disregard for rights which it was supposed to protect. He accepted the state as a defender of national sovereignty on the exterior and of order in the interior, but in both cases as defender of individual rights. The law must set the limits of the state in the exercise of this obligation, which must never go beyond those limits.

Hence Lastarria's opposition to the English positivist John Stuart Mill. For Mill, said Lastarria, the individual was master of himself, his body and his soul. And this was a sovereignty which no outside element had the right to seize. Nevertheless, he himself held that

[4] *La América.*

the state could intervene to prevent one individual from harming another. Here individual sovereignty disappeared before the power of the state, since the state was the only agency that could adjudge the damage and the one that had the power to find it wherever it chose to see it. "Such a concept of liberty is so false that there is no one in America who does not recognize its absurdity."

Furthermore, added Lastarria, Mill did not have a clear idea of liberty. "For him liberty is only the ultimate result of the protection of the individual against all tyrannies whether they come from the state or society," but Mill "assumed the existence of a government irreproachable in its organization." Mill believed that danger existed only "in the oppression of the minorities or the individual by the majorities; hence it is proposed to seek the point at which the rivalry between society and the individual begins." This point was the redeeming principle, and he "finds in it his own protection, the only thing that authorizes men individually and collectively to intervene in the freedom of action which belongs to their fellow-men." Beginning with the principle of utility, he seeks the instances in which this intervention in the field of individual freedom is justified, when the actions of one individual alter the interests of another—that is, when an individual commits a deed harmful to others by acting or not acting when it is necessary. The individual is therefore responsible for all his acts and omissions, for what he does and what he fails to do. "But of what does this utility consist; who defines and qualifies it? . . . Does it consist of the good for the greatest number, as Bentham said, or is it based on the permanent interest of man as a progressive being, as Mill says?" But, "what is that good, what are those interests?" Here, said Lastarria, was Mill's error; he lacked a definite criterion for limiting the freedom of the individual. Who qualifies? Who defines? "Have there ever been vaguer words in political language more susceptible to serving despotism as well as liberty? . . .

"If Mill had understood that liberty is only the use of right, as we Americans understand it practically," said Lastarria, "if he had noted that right is everything that is characterized by a voluntary condition of our existence and development, if he had seen that the end of man consists only of the development of all his physical, moral, and intellectual faculties, he would have saved himself the trouble of searching for the bases of his theories in the system of utility and the multitude of its contradictory exceptions. . . . He would have recognized that the state has no other end than the enforcement of right, and is therefore limited by justice, whether it is constituted in a monarchy, in an oligarchy, or in a popular government."

Mill's error originated in his desire to reconcile progress with order. He did not recognize the contradiction that was implicit in theory. Lastarria perceived this contradiction and the origin and hidden aims of the theory. "His error," he said, "was in believing that *order* and *progress* are truly the social and political aims of every government; but he did not realize that such an error was a French invention, by which an attempt was made to defend the doctrine of the unity of the state, that is, the Latin monarchy, which in the name of order and progress destroys and sacrifices individual rights, the freedom of society." Lastarria discovered the Latin roots of a series of political and social principles which formed Hispanic America and from which it must free itself. Stuart Mill, an Anglo-Saxon, fell into the trap of the spirit of absolutism; but not so the Hispanic American, Lastarria, who knew very well the pitfalls of this spirit. Order, like "the permanence of the institutions, which owes its existence to obedience and love of society," said the Chilean teacher, "and the progress, advancement, and improvement of society are not and cannot be the political ends of the state. . . . they are, on the contrary, the pure results of a harmony which exists when the state is limited to representing the principle of right and to furnishing the conditions for its existence and development to each and every one of the spheres of social activity."

Stuart Mill, said Lastarria, in order to distinguish a good government from a bad one in the midst of a great complexity of interests, found it necessary to indicate "the essential qualities which a government must have to favor each one of those interests." This was an extremely dangerous thesis, which makes the state intervene under the pretext of favoring these interests. "Nothing is more fatal than to assume that the government can and must prescribe laws for morality, education, thought, and industry . . . by necessarily possessing special knowledge in each one of those fields." On the contrary, the individual must be allowed freedom in all his actions, thus limiting those of the state. . . . The true role of the state is to allow complete freedom to each one of those elements, because the state has no other function regarding them than to facilitate their existence and development.

The English philosopher allowed himself to be "carried along by his arbitrary theories to the point of assuming that a representative government can be established only among a people who can obey and who are capable of doing whatever is necessary to maintain it." And the author thought "that governments are made by men, that one can choose among the various forms of government the one that is best for the people." This was his error. "The form of government is not chosen, and, even though it does not spring forth like a work of nature according to Mill's expression, it does spring from social circumstances independent of the will of those who believe that they are choosing it of their own will." According to Mill's thesis, those who govern are those who choose the kind of government that is best for the people. In Hispanic America such a thesis would be fatal, since it would not comply with the circumstances which determine the forms of government, but it would, on the contrary, depend upon what those who govern consider most prudent and useful for the development of the nation. This idea was responsible for the vacillation of the emancipators concerning the kind of government that was most suitable for our countries. They believed that the form could be chosen in accordance with a special logic, without realizing that circumstances had already determined what that form was, independent of the fact that, according to this logic, the people were not prepared mentally. Thus Lastarria defended the right of Hispanic America to change to a republican form of government. Circumstances themselves had determined the form of government that was compatible with Hispanic America, once it had freed itself from colonial absolutism. This was what the leaders of Hispanic-American emancipation had not been able to see clearly, and this was the source of many of their mistakes. They had lacked confidence in the capability of the people without realizing that the people would adapt themselves only to the circumstances that were given to them, to the circumstances of a society moving towards modern social forms.

"The wisest men of the Hispanic-American revolution," said Lastarria, "also thought that since our republics were not like those of

Athens . . . or like that of the United States, we could not establish
a republic; but the unity of the absolute state was shattered, and in
its place there arose individual rights on the broad basis of social and
political equality." The principle of authority had disappeared from
the state, from religion, and from morality. Nevertheless, in spite
of that, the opposite took place, a republic arose. "Individuality recovered its rights only to be converted into selfishness and ambition
and to elevate the rule of passions; religious fanaticism gave way to
disbelief." This was the only thing that they were able to see. The
anarchy which followed the colonial order was looked upon as the
inability of the Hispanic-American people to attain a new order. They
did not see in it what Lastarria saw clearly, that it was a necessary
stage through which they must pass from a system of absolute government to a liberal or republican form of government. The Chilean
thinker realized this because he believed in progress, which is what
leads to the so-called stage of self-determination in the individual.
This was in keeping with his positivism. He knew that, independent
of the desires of man, independent of what his will desires, society
progresses by following the path that will lead it to full liberty.
Selfishness, ambition, the rule of passions, and disbelief were but
forms that appear in one of the stages of the march of Hispanic
America toward republicanism. These forms were the instruments
with which the old colonial order had been crushed; they were necessary evils. "It was not enough to defeat the armies of the king," said
Lastarria, "it was necessary to defeat the old society in order to create the new; and then . . . the republican form came as a logical and
necessary result."[5] The representative republican form of government was established in America because it had risen from its own
environment. It was the form proper to its social and political development. In this way Lastarria made clear his firm belief in the
realization of the ideal which he regarded so highly: Hispanic-American republicanism. Hispanic America, as well as Anglo-Saxon America, would realize the form of government proper to its conditions.
Vacillations would finally cease, for the Hispanic Americans were convinced of what was suitable for our nations, and the only thing left
to do was to assist in its prompt realization.

[5] *Ibid.*

II. THE ORTHODOX AND THE HETERODOX

Positivism in the Intellectual Life of Chile

LASTARRIA had recognized positivism in 1868; the parallel between it and his ideas had surprised him, causing him to join the movement. Henceforth positivism would play an integral part in the intellectual life of the Chilean republic. It was totally or partially accepted or it was simply rejected, but in any case it was always present, provoking comment and discussion. A new generation that put several of these philosophical principles into practice grew up around these comments and discussions. One group was inclined toward accepting the Comtian philosophy *in toto*. This was the orthodox group represented by the Lagarrigue brothers: Jorge (1854–94), Juan Enrique (1852–1927), and Luis (1864–?). Another group followed the line of thought of their teacher Lastarria, accepting from Comtism only those aspects which did not impair the liberal ideal. This group was brilliantly represented by Valentín Letelier (1852–1919).

The Academy of Belles Lettres was one of the cultural institutions which disseminated positivism by means of explanation and criticism. The purposes of this academy were expressed clearly in the first of its principles: "The aim of the Academy of Belles Lettres is to cultivate literary art as an expression of philosophical truth by adopting as a rule of composition and criticism, in scientific works, conformity to facts demonstrated in scientific fashion by science, and in sociological works and works of literature, fidelity to the development of human nature."[6] Lastarria had succeeded in grouping together in this academy the old liberal fighters who, for different reasons, had separated from one another and were following diverse courses. Diego Barros Arana, Miguel Luis Amunátegui, Benjamín Vicuña Mackenna, and others were among the signers of the by-laws. In the inaugural address delivered by Lastarria on April 26, he said: "We have come here from different schools of thought, forgetting the causes which kept us separated, which led us far, very far, from the pathway which, in better days, we had cleared together." The development that had made them forget their old quarrels was the triumph of ultramontanism in this period of Chilean politics and education. This genera-

[6] Lastarria, *Recuerdos literarios*.

tion's ideal of intellectual emancipation was in grave danger. The reaction became evident in the founding of the Academy of Belles Lettres. The Academy was only a continuation of the work to which Lastarria's generation had been dedicated since 1842. It was the continuation of the struggle for the independence of the spirit which the Chilean thinker made clear when he said, "The study of sciences and of letters in democratic nations, such as the American nations, can absolutely have no other foundation than the *freedom of the spirit* to investigate truth, a freedom which constitutes one of the most precious rights of man, those rights or liberties which make up the essence and substance of democracy, because, without affirming or practicing them, it cannot exist in any nation."

One year later, on April 12, 1874, during the first anniversary celebration of the academy, Lastarria recalled the reasons for founding it. "A foreign movement," he said, "was operating at the beginning of 1873, drawing everyone's attention toward public instruction. It was thought that public instruction was in danger of being dominated by interests and even by political whims which tended to make the situation worse, by changing into disastrous slavery the legal dependence in which we live today." But, he added, this movement did not seem to lead anywhere, not because of its inherent weaknesses, but because of "the lack of flexibility and habits of individual liberty and, more than that, because of the deeply rooted custom of abandoning to the ruling powers the direction of social activity even in affairs that by their very nature can only be ruled by this activity." It was then that a group of men questioned "if it would not be possible to organize at least a modest center in which sciences and letters could find the freedom that, in the lofty regions of intelligence, would guarantee the free development of their principles and doctrines and protect them from sectarian interests, and political whims. A great number of men of letters began immediately to prove that this was possible with their voluntary and unselfish adherence to the principles of the new institution."[7] But in 1881, Lastarria himself closed the academy, which had been disintegrating little by little. Nevertheless, those eight years were enough for it to leave its mark on Chilean cultural life.

In the Academy of Belles Lettres a large number of young men

[7] *Ibid.*

found an answer and a stimulus to their anxieties. Lastarria spoke proudly of the interest which the youth of that time showed in the work of the academy by coming to it and collaborating in its cultural task. Valentín Letelier and the brothers Jorge and Juan Enrique Lagarrigue belonged to that group of young men who participated enthusiastically in the activities of the academy. On November 13, 1875, a Cuban orator by the name of Zambrana gave a number of lectures in the academy criticizing positivistic philosophy. On the twentieth of the same month Jorge Lagarrigue delivered a lecture in the same academy in which he brilliantly refuted the Cuban orator. Lastarria said of this cultural event: "The attack on positivistic philosophy brought to our attention some of the objections of the experimental school to certain conclusions of the great French philosopher [Comte], without denying or rejecting the bases and the criterion of the positivistic philosophy; and he [Zambrana] moreover attempted to cast doubt on this philosophy with the malicious recriminations which the metaphysicists and theologians have directed against it, thus neglecting one of the first conditions of tolerance, which consists of respecting and not doing violence to other people's opinions, using against them, when they are erroneous, only means of persuasion; for they [recriminations] will always be ineffective if they are invested with violence or embellished with scorn from which truth flees. But the defenders of the philosophy which guides our studies rejected and explained those attacks by demonstrating the advantage of the scientific or positivistic method, which can be applied to the examination of all material and moral phenomena without falling into the two essential difficulties of metaphysics, materialism and idealism."[8]

A few months before, on July 18, Jorge Lagarrigue had read in the academy an article on positivistic philosophy. "Lastarria and many other members of the academy," Lagarrigue recalled, "shook my hand as I stepped down from the rostrum." Eduardo de la Barra, secretary of the academy, "told me that whenever I wanted, I could become a member of the academy; but I told him that I was too young."[9] That same year Valentín Letelier also delivered a lecture in the same cultural institution. It was likewise in the Academy of

[8] *Ibid.*
[9] *Trozos del Diario íntimo.*

147

Belles Lettres that Victorino Lastarria's work, *Lecciones de Política Positiva,* originated; these lectures were given as a course and published in 1874.

At the same time that the academy was functioning, a number of young men led by Jorge Lagarrigue were meeting in a group called the Society of Enlightenment, founded in 1872 by Arnoldo Montt, who died two years later leaving Lagarrigue in charge. As a result of Lagarrigue's influence, this group read and commented on the works of the positivists, especially Comte and Littré. The young Chilean positivist, in a letter written to a friend and preserved in his *Diario,* set forth the relationship between positivistic philosophy and the Society of Enlightenment. "In the first half of 1872," he said, "I completely lost my religious faith. Certain books, science, the continual discussions which I had with many believers, and my own long meditations convinced me of the falsehood of divine revelation. But what was left for me in exchange for faith? Nothing but pure skepticism. My soul sought something more. It was then that the thought of founding a society occurred to me. Several young men who had lost their religious faith proposed the founding of this society to seek a means of finding the truth to which human intelligence always aspires." Two years passed and the society progressed, but skepticism remained. "I did not know for what cause to work, to what end to direct my continual efforts. . . . Finally, at the beginning of 1874, I discovered the positivist doctrine; I studied it, and I meditated on it, and it enlightened my mind; it encouraged me to work, and it gave me complete confidence in the future. Because of it I now dedicate myself entirely to working in our society. I now have a purpose in life: to contribute in some way to the progress of our country and to all humanity. The means for it will be the diffusion of positivistic knowledge." A society, he added, will not be strong nor will it last long if it does not have a doctrine or group of principles recognized by all its members. "It is then necessary, if we wish to have a long life, to establish some fundamental principles, without accepting which one cannot be a member of our society. . . . I believe," he concluded, "that these bonds cannot be other than the principles of the philosophy of humanity."

Jorge Lagarrigue, in an address to the Society of Enlightenment on March 31, said: "The feeling for humanity possesses more and more strongly all those minds that are interested in the destiny of civilization. This same feeling brings us here . . . we all have the same faith, faith in the progress of humanity. We have all assumed as one of the most compelling of duties that of contributing to the great work of civilization. And since we have learned that the sciences are the powerful forces which lead nations down the path of progress, our first duty is to cultivate them with enthusiastic devotion, in order to spread, immediately, their beneficent seed among our beloved compatriots. To enlighten our minds with the light of truth and to spread it among the people immediately: this is our dual and sacred duty. Workers for progress, we must never be fainthearted in our activities; arduous if you wish, but prolific in brilliant results. The Society of Enlightenment presents a vast field in which we can carry on our activity, and an altar on which to render a beneficial cult to our true god, Humanity."[10] These words anticipated Chilean orthodox positivism.

But another of these young men of whom we have spoken also belonged to this society, Valentín Letelier (1852–1919). Here he, too, found the doctrine that he needed to orient his course of action. But, like the old teacher Lastarria, he rejected the Comtian theology, the religion of humanitarianism, the despotic bases of positivism, and everything else that stood for the denial of the liberal spirit of which he felt himself an heir. While Lagarrigue finally rejected Littré, who was opposed to the religious Comte, Letelier accepted from Comtism only what Littré regarded as positive. Heterodox positivism appeared in Chile with Valentín Letelier. The history of the Chilean republic would soon offer an opportunity for the expression of two theses on the same national problem. The orthodox and the heterodox would present their respective decisions and their respective points of view.

The Orthodox Chileans

ON JANUARY 3, 1875, Jorge Lagarrigue wrote in his *Diario:* "I have been writing the first page of the translation which I intend to make of two lessons of Auguste Comte's *Cours de philosophie positive*

[10] *Ibid.*

preceded by a preface by Emilio Littré. . . . I am doing this work because I believe it my duty to propagate that philosophy which has enlightened my mind and because I believe that positivism is the final point toward which societies move in their constant march of progress. The sciences, almost all having arrived at a truly positive state, prepare the way." In this manner the young Chilean philosopher oriented his future thoughts and actions. He had lost faith in the Roman Catholic religion, but he would soon find faith in another religion. On May 1, 1874, he had written with great glee in the same *Diario:* "Yesterday was one of the great days of my life. I received two great works from Europe: The *Philosophie positive* of Auguste Comte and the *History of Civilization in England* by Thomas Buckle."

His position was not unknown to Lastarria. "A few months ago," said Lagarrigue, "a book entitled *Lecciones de Política Positiva* was published by José Victorino Lastarria. In the first part he treated the social question as a preliminary to the political question with which he dealt in the second part. Lastarria was forced to suspend the lectures which he was giving in the Academy of Belles Lettres because almost no one came to hear him; and his book, even up to the time at which I am writing, has still not merited the honor of a criticism. It appeared on our intellectual horizon without producing even the slightest reaction, the slightest sensation. An icy indifference has accompanied its appearance." Against this indifference Jorge Lagarrigue arose. It was an indifference which he felt was contrary to truth. "I want to serve my country," he said, "by combating error, by spreading and defending truth. I believe that I can do this by propagating the great doctrines of positivistic philosophy." The day that Lagarrigue refuted the opinions of the Cuban Zambrana against positive philosophy the greatest honor and stimulation that he received were the congratulations of and a visit from Lastarria. "Mr. Lastarria," he said, "has told me that tomorrow he will pay me a visit, for he wishes to congratulate me personally. . . . Tomorrow I shall have at my side, in my home, the first thinker of my country, for whom I have so much respect and admiration. My happiness and my emotion are indescribable! How much I wish that the aged Littré could see for just one moment everything that is taking place in our isolated country! How happy and content he would be!" Henceforth the young thinker devoted himself enthusiastically to reading and re-reading the works of Comte, Littré, and all the great positivists. "On Sunday, January 30, 1876," he wrote, "I received a reward greater than I deserved. I received a letter from M. Littré, my great teacher."

Finally, on March 29, 1876, Jorge Lagarrigue, once his parents gave permission, left for Europe on his way to Paris, the cradle of positivism. On May 26 he had his first interview with Littré: "I have seen, I have talked with one of the most notable teachers of the nineteenth century, a man who has been my true teacher, my second father." He also met Pierre Lafitte, who, in contrast to Littré, was an adherent of Comte's religion of humanity. At his suggestion he read *Politique positive* by the French philosopher. Lagarrigue felt more and more attracted by this aspect of positivistic philosophy. "I must confess it," he said, "a great struggle is taking place in my mind; it is therefore indispensable from every point of view for me to study the French *Système politique positive*. I have always been inclined toward the religion of humanity." Little by little this idea was overcoming his various objections. "Although I accept Comte's religious idea," he said, "I am still far from accepting the religious regime that he proposes and still much less his political system, which seems to be contrary to modern tendencies." Lafitte's courses increased the pressure that would direct the young Chilean positivist. On March 17, 1877, he wrote: "Every day I am more and more inclined toward positivistic religion."

Juan Enrique Lagarrigue, from Chile, began to inquire about the reason for his brother's silence in regard to Littré. "Enrique asked me if my silence in regard to M. Littré is due to the fact that I have become a positivist." In fact, on July 27, 1877, he wrote: "Now that I have begun to study Positive Religion, I feel inclined toward it, and my old teacher is losing some of his philosophical importance for me. M. Littré, as a philosopher, seems very insignificant to me when compared to the gigantic figure of Auguste Comte. . . . I have not yet embraced the religion of humanity, but it appears that the trend of my ideas will lead me toward it: the word 'religion' no longer frightens me." He later wrote to his brother Enrique as follows: "When one leaves Catholicism and enters a revolutionary or negativistic period, one has a deep estrangement from everything that has the name of religion, worship, priesthood . . . and it is understandable how I have spent so much time on the last page of the *Cours de philosophie positive.*"

But he soon began to compare Littré's school with Lafitte. "The first, limited to the intellectual side of Comte's doctrine, is unable to produce either a true union or the slightest organization among its followers. . . . In the second, which has a priesthood, a recognized leader, M. Lafitte, there is the most perfect union and agreement among its partisans. . . . If Auguste Comte's doctrine is to play the same social role in the future, as I believe it will, that religious beliefs have in the past, its progress and action will be due principally to Auguste Comte's complete school, and its partisans will be the true representatives of positivism." Lagarrigue was already opposed to Littré's thesis, according to which Auguste Comte's *Politique positive* was alien to his system, outside the unity of his philosophy. Lagarrigue maintained the unity of the Comtian work. In *Cours de philosophie positive,* he said, there were already the germs of his religion of humanity. As for the cult, he considered it a necessity which only a fear of the ridiculous could hinder.

In Paris he also met several Hispanic-American and Brazilian positivists. In his *Diario* he tells about his meeting with Gabino Barreda—who had returned to Europe after putting into effect the educational reform in Mexico—and his realization that Barreda's positivism was only intellectual. "There had been to see Lafitte," said Lagarrigue, "a Mexican, Barreda, who became acquainted with positivism through his compatriot Contreras, a direct disciple of Comte. But it appears that his positivism is only intellectual."[11] The friendship which arose between Lagarrigue and the Brazilian Miguel Lemos was important in the development of his work. "Yesterday I met Lemos from Brazil. He already accepts the religion of humanity, and he has only a few doubts about certain points of positivism." A short time afterwards he met another of the future disciples of humanity in Brazil, Teixeira Mendes. Together the Chilean and the Brazilians accepted little by little Comte's religious philoso-

[11] See my work *Positivismo en México.*

phy until they became the most orthodox followers of his doctrines. Teixeira Mendes first, and later Miguel Lemos, returned to Brazil in 1881, where they began their apostleship on behalf of the religion of humanity. Lemos, with Lafitte's authorization, established the positivistic apostleship and the first church in Rio de Janeiro. In 1883, Jorge Lagarrigue, within a short time after his return to Chile, also established the positivistic apostleship of Chile.

The orthodoxy of the Ibero-Americans soon clashed with the recognized head of the Comtian church, Pierre Lafitte. The disciple of the French philosopher, who had initiated them into the religion of humanity, soon became to them a sophist and opportunist unfaithful to the master's doctrine. The first clash took place in Paris in 1881, for it was in that year that the French government sent an expedition to Tunis to secure its colonial empire. The Positivist Society of France and of England demanded that a protest in the name of humanity be made, for they recalled Comte's opposition to all forms of colonial politics and that in 1854 he had sought the return of Gibraltar to Spain. Lagarrigue gave the following account in his *Diario:* "On Wednesday [June 13, 1881] the discussion on the question of Tunis continued. Robinet, Laporte, and Dubuisson firmly demanded that a protest be made against this violation of morality in the name of politics. Lafitte, because of inertia and temporizing too much with the government leaders, is opposed to any such declaration."

Another motive was a disciplinary act of Miguel Lemos in Brazil, who expelled from the bosom of the Brazilian church one of its members, Joaquim Ribeiro de Mendoça, a slaveowner who insisted on holding responsible political positions. Comte had decreed that positivists could not hold slaves or occupy responsible political posts as long as a peaceful and industrial regime called a sociocracy had not been established. Lemos futilely appealed to Lafitte's authority to make the dissident Brazilian obey the regulation until, acting upon his own, he expelled him. Lafitte begged him to be prudent and not to take what Comte had said so literally, and to distinguish between what was unalterable and what was circumstantial.

Lagarrigue also referred to this affair when he wrote: "On Sunday night [March 1, 1882], after leaving M. Robinet's home, I again discussed this matter with M. Lafitte. He praised Lemos highly, but he was reluctant to censure O. directly. And since I convinced him that this positivist had disavowed his own authority when he disavowed that of Lemos, who had consecrated him, he told me that right here there were many people who supported positivism who did not recognize his authority as absolute. And he added that if he rejected them, he himself would have to withdraw from the leadership of the positivists." That attitude on the part of the head of the positivistic church soon openly changed the attitude of its disciples in America. "When I heard this," added Lagarrigue, "I had nothing more to say. Since M. Lafitte had no proper sacerdotal authority, much less could he support another's. This only confirms our belief that positivism lacks a true universal head, and that the second great priest of humanity has not arisen yet. It is sad to admit it, but it is true."

And there was still something more. In February of 1883, Lagarrigue wrote to Lemos that Lafitte was disposed to accept a position that the prime minister of France, Gambetta, had offered him: a lectureship in sociology at the Polytechnical School. Lemos answered, "The day that M. Lafitte carries his defection to the point of becoming a simple official professor, we will break with him without hesitation." On September 9, 1883, the schism took place. Miguel Lemos broke with Lafitte. In February, 1884, Jorge Lagarrigue followed him. The European positivist centers continued faithful to Lafitte. The Western group, as they called the Americans, pulled away. Comtian orthodoxy was transferred to America.[12]

From 1884 until 1894, the year of his death, Jorge Lagarrigue remained in Paris spreading positivistic propaganda and defending what he considered to be the orthodoxy of his teacher, Auguste Comte. But he had left in Chile a propagandist for the school, an apostle, his older brother, Juan Enrique. They had both been initiated into the positivistic philosophy, but Juan Enrique became more and more determined not to accept the religious aspects of the school. From Paris, Jorge Lagarrigue wrote letter after letter to attract his brother

[12] This problem is explained in O Apostolado Positivista no Brazil, Circular anual, by Miguel Lemos (Rio de Janeiro, Iglesia Positivista del Brasil). See also works cited in note 7 of the introduction. Jorge Lagarrigue, Le faux et le vrai Positivisme.

to the bosom of the Comtian church. On April 25, 1877, Enrique wrote to his brother: "Fundamentally I believe, like you, that there is no other way. Indeed, in order to organize that religion more formally, all revealed religions will have to disappear."

But Juan Enrique did not seem to decide on this course. "In his last letter," Jorge wrote, "Enrique still does not appear to have decided to accept religious positivism. How hard it is to make a conversion! . . . Enrique was always opposed to religious positivism, and I was always trying to convert him. . . .Enrique was always disputing Comte's ideas. I almost despair of converting him while I am in Paris." "You persist in rejecting positivistic ideas," he wrote to him. "I can tell you nothing in that respect, except my feeling when I see that you did not recognize the grandeur and the truth of the new doctrine. But when you tell me that your way of seeing the solution of the human problem is still vague and nevertheless add, 'Let me be a writer who expounds his ideas with a certain tranquility,' I can't help speaking to you in all frankness and pointing out to you the grave duties that are incumbent upon a thinker. At this moment of grave intellectual and moral anarchy it is an unforgivable error to expound new ideas when one is not sufficiently prepared for the difficult studies of sociology and morality. I tell you, Enrique, you can never solve a social problem, nor should you attempt it. It isn't that you do not have the intellectual ability, but rather that you have not strengthened it in the study of positivistic sciences. And since you do not have it, how can you describe laws in sociology, in which the positivistic sciences have played such an important role?"

Nevertheless, it all seemed futile. Jorge Lagarrigue almost despaired of being able to convince his brother, at least as long as he did not have the opportunity to see him personally. "Enrique," wrote Jorge, "was always opposed to our ideas. I no longer expect to change him except when I return to my beloved country. Intellectual pride and vanity stand too much in the way of his being able to understand the Religion of Humanity; it is so true that a certain subordination is the first condition of all intellectual progress." And again in his *Diario*, he commented: "I wrote a few pages to Enrique on the division of the two powers, which he absolutely refuses to admit. And this is the very foundation of positivism. How much power revolutionary pride and preoccupations have!" But, finally, on December 13, 1880, Juan Enrique arrived unexpectedly in Paris to spend a few months with his brother. That was enough. Jorge began to write in his diary: "Enrique has already read the first two volumes of *Politique positive*, and little by little he is beginning to recognize Auguste Comte's immense superiority. He has already discarded his former opinion of Littré. . . . Enrique is becoming more and more of a positivist. He is reading the *Synthèse subjective* and studying mathematics. . . . Yesterday we wrote home; Enrique wrote to Luis Espejo. He told him all his prejudices against the Religion of Humanity have disappeared, and he declared that Comte is the greatest genius humanity has produced." Juan Enrique Lagarrigue returned to Chile on March 1, 1882. He had become an apostle of humanity. He was the very incarnation of positivistic orthodoxy in Chile.

The Apostle of Humanity

JUAN ENRIQUE LAGARRIGUE devoted himself to the difficult task of converting men to the religion of humanity, but he did not limit himself to preaching to his fellow-countrymen. As a good apostle of humanity, his work recognized no frontiers. He flooded America and Europe with letters addressed to anyone who, because of his work or his power, had served or could serve the cause of human felicity. Lagarrigue began to correspond with the Spanish writer Juan Valera, whom he tried in vain to convert. He wrote to Countess Pardo Bazán for the same purpose; Theodore Roosevelt, Kaiser Wilhelm II, Clemençeau, the king and queen of England, prime ministers, Ghandi, Leo Tolstoi, and many great figures received his invitations, advice, or protests. He made many pleas for peace. There was no international crime that did not receive the protest of this apostle, nor any meeting on behalf of peace that did not receive his suggestions. In 1893 he wrote to Wilhelm II: "Allow me to beg you respectfully, in the name of humanity, to return Alsace-Lorraine to France. This will be the decisive act for cementing universal peace." And after the war with Spain over Cuba and the Philippines, he wrote to President McKinley of the United States: "Unfortunately the United States has allowed itself to be carried along to the point of injuring mankind. This deplorable mistake will not fail to have its influence on the sad affairs of South Africa and China. The purer the precedents of a nation, the greater the consequences of its evil examples. After the war with Spain, a shadow fell upon the fine colonial tradition of the venerable Penn, confirmed in the independence of the United States by the immortal triumvirate of Washington, Jefferson, and Franklin."[13]

His protests were not confined to foreign lands only; in his own country he protested the seizure of the provinces of Tacna and Arica from Peru after the war between Peru and Chile in 1883, and he pleaded for giving Bolivia an outlet to the sea, which that country had lost in the same war. "If Chile wants to follow the path of progress," wrote Lagarrigue, "a path that includes both happiness and glory, she must return Tacna and Arica to Peru, and she must do it spontaneously. . . . I hope that you can be persuaded, fellow citizens, that true national grandeur can only be attained along with the highest virtue. . . . If Chile decides to hand over what morally does not belong to her, she will feel purified to the depths of her being and capable of raising herself to her most glorious destiny."[14]

Juan Enrique Lagarrigue signed many pamphlets and circulars which were distributed to any person who in any way might be attracted to the religion adopted by the orthodox positivists of Chile. In these writings one can see how this Hispanic American approached many of the problems presented to him. In contrast to the Mexican positivists, the Chilean approached the social problems of his period, like socialism, and judged them with sympathy and understanding. He was always able to find in Comte justification for his opinions. Lagarrigue condemned the Chilean government's proposed law against strikes which set a prison term or a fine of from one hundred to one thousand *pesos* as the penalty for striking. "Such a proposal," said Lagarrigue, "seems incredible in a republican form of government. The unquestionable right of the proletariat to go on strike in order to obtain an increase in salaries is categorically denied in it. . . . This is unheard of and it turns the proletariat immediately into slaves.

---

[13] These letters were published by the Apostolado de la Religión de la Humanidad in Santiago de Chile. Collected in *Intervenciones religiosas en favor de la paz.*

[14] *Sobre Tacna y Arica* (Santiago de Chile, 1909); and in *Intervenciones religiosas en favor de la paz.*

... When a normal regime is established ... the priesthood of humanity will be the mediator in the conflicts between the proletariat and the patricians. Meanwhile, strikes are the only defense that the proletariat has, and this defense should in no way be taken away from them."[15] And in another place he refers specifically to socialism as one of the aims of positivism, although it is opposed to community ownership. He said: "Among the many problems which positivism can solve is that of socialism originating in the aspiration of the proletariat to improve its sad condition. This aspiration cannot be more legitimate." But, he added, community ownership is an erroneous solution. "Positivism rejects all examination of the prime acquisition of capital, for it would only lead to upsetting the social order, and positivism limits itself to demanding a good example." Origin is not important; what is important is the use that is made of this wealth. Positivism "preserves the separation of management and labor; but it considers management as mere administrators of human capital, morally responsible for its use."[16]

The wealthy are not, therefore, the owners of their possessions; they are simply the guardians of the wealth which belongs to humanity, and humanity should demand an accounting of the use that is made of this wealth. There is no division of classes; there is merely a division of occupation. Money, which in Mexico is considered a sign of superiority, even moral superiority,[17] was regarded by Lagarrigue as an instrument that could be used in the service of established cordial relationship among men. The principle of this cordial relationship was altruism. "The fatal anarchy which has invaded everything," he said, "and which threatens to dissolve homes and countries and to change the world into a horrible field of bloody discord will be dispelled by the sacred breath of the altruistic doctrine, and our altruistic doctrine and our existence will assume on the earth the most beautiful conditions of virtue, harmony, and felicity. Whites, yellows, and blacks, plebians and patricians, once united, will work together zealously in the great task of human progress, and our planet will be changed more and more into the holy mansion of glorious peace."

[15] Juan Enrique Lagarrigue, *Sobre el proyecto de ley contra las huelgas.*
[16] *La religión de la humanidad.*
[17] See my work *Apogeo y decadencia del positivismo en México.*

Following Comte, he supported a conservatism which represented an assimilation of the past, without break. "The past must be the basis of all future progress.... Today it is said that we must do everything again without keeping anything which our ancestors have left us." And then he added: "From the sociological point of view, such a proposal is tantamount to trying to build without a foundation. In fact, in the social organism as well as in the individual organism, there exists no real improvement without evolution, and, for progressive development, a future which does not have its roots in the past is a vain illusion, capable only of nullifying efforts and producing disorders which stray from the philosophical path of universal well-being." Lagarrigue envisioned a new kind of knight, whom he called a new type of knight of the future; he was to be charged with executing justice among the humble, dispensing kindness to those who suffered. He recognized the imperfection of the present social order which required the intervention of generous men who, with new arms, modern arms such as wealth, could carry out the necessary reforms. "These men," he said, "will be the knights of the normal regime, who, in contrast to those of the Middle Ages who had to resort to the sword, will call upon wealth to protect the weak, since war will definitely be replaced by peace."[18]

Chilean Heterodoxy

IN VICTORINO LASTARRIA's famous inaugural address at the Academy of Belles Lettres, he altered Auguste Comte's motto, "Order and Progress": "It is unquestionable," he said, "that our association has as its purpose the satisfaction of a social need. This is proved beyond doubt by the fact that all of us have accepted, fearlessly and openly, the first principle of our institution, which, upon the establishment of the cultivation of literary art as its objective, adopted as a rule of writing and criticism, in scientific works, conformity with facts demonstrated in a positive way by science, and in sociological and literary works, conformity with the laws of human nature, which are *Liberty and Progress*."[19] A few years earlier, in Mexico, another

[18] *En servicio de la doctrina altruista.*
[19] *Recuerdos literarios.*

positivist, Gabino Barreda, had made a similar change, substituting *Love, Order,* and *Progress* for *Liberty, Order,* and *Progress.*[20] Barreda thus justified his association with the Mexican Liberal party, which came into power after the defeat of the conservatives; as for Lastarria, he justified the ideal which he had always followed. Their divergence from positivism was implicit in this change of Comte's motto. Comte established progress, but within the limits of order; Lastarria, progress, but within the limits of liberty. Comte was a new conservative, Lastarria 100 per cent liberal. The Chilean leader's positivism was to be passed on to Valentín Letelier.

Letelier acquired his positivism in the Academy of Belles Lettres and in the Society of Enlightenment. He also belonged to that group of young men of whom Jorge Lagarrigue spoke in his *Diario.* In this *Diario,* Lagarrigue frequently mentioned his friend Valentín Letelier and his interest in learning about positivistic philosophy. In 1875, Lagarrigue wrote: ". . . on Monday of the past week, I received from Copiapó a letter from Valentín Letelier, who has been appointed professor of literature and philosophy in the *Lycée* of that city. He appears eager to study positivistic philosophy." In France, Lagarrigue corresponded with Letelier trying to attract him to the religion of humanity. "I received a letter from Letelier," Lagarrigue recounts; "it is an answer to the one I wrote him. He tells me that he will be pleased to correspond with me. By the contents of the letter he appears to be a person favorably disposed toward embracing positivistic religion some time in the future. He confesses that one ought to read Comte's last works before condemning them. He is very insistent upon establishing positivistic morality; he does not know that Comte established the basis."

Nevertheless, Letelier's liberalism took strong roots. The religion of humanity was not convincing to him. Jorge Lagarrigue tried in vain to instruct him; all his efforts failed. Although he succeeded in convincing his brother Juan Enrique, as has been seen, to embrace the positivistic religion on the day that he went to Paris on a visit, his efforts failed with Letelier when he met him in the French capital in 1882. Lagarrigue wrote: "Last night we went to visit Letelier.

[20] See my work *Positivismo en México.*

... I took him Robinet's *Philosophie positive* and the positivistic cult in Brazil and the *Patria Brasilera*. We were there from eight until eleven o'clock discussing positivism. The revolutionary hydra, pride and vanity, by giving him personal infallibility, prevent Letelier's conversion."

Letelier was truly lost for the apostleship of humanity. His heterodoxy was incurable. While the Lagarrigue brothers had succeeded in escaping from the destructive rationalism of Littré who disavowed the best part of the work of the master of positivism, Letelier remained loyal to it. "Now one sees the profound evil that Littré has caused," said Lagarrigue. "He has only given arms to negativism, to the revolution against the great builder Auguste Comte." And he added, full of self-deception: "Everything will have been done to convert Letelier. If he is not converted, it will be because he is not one of those truly elevated persons in whom veneration finally triumphs over personal pride and vanity."

Eighteen years later, in 1900, the other orthodox positivist, Juan Enrique Lagarrigue, acknowledged receipt of Letelier's work *La Evolución en la Historia*. In a letter he said: "Your two-volume work, which you were kind enough to send to us, represents much labor and is very erudite, but I regret that the profound organic spirit of positivism does not substantiate it. The same thing is happening to you that is happening to several contemporary thinkers who, since they did not follow Auguste Comte in his principal work, *Système de philosophie positive*, in which he founded the religion of humanity, have strayed from the path of true intellectual and moral regeneration." All efforts to seek the bases for moral and social reorganization were futile for the positivist orthodoxy because they were already established. Auguste Comte stated them clearly in his great work. To attempt to discover these bases was like trying to discover the Mediterranean. The only results were futile attempts and with them dangerous deviations which were later paid for at a high price, the retarding of human progress. For this reason Lagarrigue ended his letter by saying, "I pray that you will succeed in overcoming the obstacles which prevent you from seeing the moral doctrine in positivism."

Two Attitudes

THE YEAR 1891 was a trying year in Chilean history. The executive power and the legislative bodies were engaged in a violent struggle. The President of the Republic, José Manuel Balmaceda, dissolved Congress, and Congress disavowed the legitimacy of the President. The President, said the two houses of Congress, has renounced "the legitimate authority with which he was invested to assume personal and arbitrary power which has no origin other than his will nor any limits other than those which events can give it." With this struggle an old fight reached a crisis; two sets of ideas were engaged in a mortal struggle: the ideas which the dictator Diego Portales represented and the liberal ideals of José Victorino Lastarria. Behind these ideas were two classes: the conservative or monarchial and the liberal or bourgeois. The ideal of Lastarria and his generation had matured; a new generation had matured; a new generation was arising which required nothing of the old colonial order.

The executive power had been gradually losing the strength given to it by Diego Portales' constitution. In its place the "Parliament," which Lastarria conceived as the maximum expression of liberalism, had been increasing its strength little by little. In 1891 the fight became an armed struggle. Chile, which, in contrast to the other Hispanic-American countries, had been able to avoid revolutions for a period of sixty years, became involved in revolution. The Congress disavowed the government and took up arms against it. The government, on its side, declared that Congress was in rebellion. The army declared that Congress was in rebellion. The army, composed of more Creole and traditional elements, supported the President. The navy, of European background, especially Anglo-Saxon, took the side of Congress. The struggle lasted eight months, and at the end of this time President Balmaceda was forced to resign, only to commit suicide a few days later. The liberal spirit definitely triumphed over the last vestiges of the colonial spirit. After several years Lastarria's ideal had defeated Portales'. The struggle was over. The period of Chilean *bourgeoisie* began with great strength.

Juan Enrique Lagarrigue and Valentín Letelier took different sides in this struggle, corresponding to the respective ideas which they held. Lagarrigue, faithful to Comtian conservatism, was inclined to favor President Balmaceda, while Letelier, faithful to his liberalism, opposed him. Both the orthodox and the heterodox positivists made clear their respective stands on the national problem.

Juan Enrique Lagarrigue, faithful to the letter of Comte, was unable to take the side of parliamentarianism, which the French philosopher had opposed. Comte had applauded Napoleon III's *coup d'état* and was a partisan of all governments capable of establishing the order that leads toward progress. In 1888, Jorge Lagarrigue, while in France, had written a letter and pamphlet entitled *La dictature Républicaine* to George Ernest Boulanger, a hero of the Franco-Prussian War who was accused of aspiring to a dictatorship. This letter and a pamphlet invited him to carry out Comte's ideal, since Lagarrigue considered him the only man capable of putting this idea into effect in France. He said: "Auguste Comte is the first republican who has made fully obvious the absurdity and immorality of the parliamentary system. He is likewise the first who has seen in the light of social science the best form of government befitting France's present situation." Comte's teachings might be summed up in the necessity to "concentrate all the political power in the hands of a single statesman who is directly responsible to the country . . . combined with a truly spiritual liberty. . . . I believe," he added, that because of what Boulanger had done up to now, "you are to be this man so necessary to the salvation of France and of humanity; you are to be the Constantine of our epoch."[21]

To President Balmaceda, Juan Enrique Lagarrigue sent what he called *Propuesta de solución para la actual crisis política*. In this proposal he wrote: "For the present crisis there is, in our opinion, only one worthwhile solution which will assure the glorious future of Chile, and that is that the *Executive Power*, the incarnation today of *order*, should prevail over *Congress*, the very incarnation of *disorder*. . . . In spite of his parliamentary predecessors, the present chief of state has spontaneously tended toward dictatorship by virtue of the directive and responsible situation in which he finds himself

---

[21] *La dictature républicaine d'après Auguste Comte.*

and as a person who has a true public conscience. That evolution in his political judgment, far from debasing him, does him honor and proves in him that capital sociological axiom: man agitates and humanity leads him on; man only passes judgment upon those persistent rebels against social progress." And he added, "However much one declares himself unwisely against republican dictatorship, it is still the best form of government, just as the parliamentary system is the worst." Republican dictatorship, however, should not be confused with tyranny. "A Congress can be more tyrannical than a dictator."

He went on to make history by saying: "Chile's prosperity, in a great part, comes to it from having had a regime that is more dictatorial than parliamentary. Basically it is the chief of state who has made all the laws here." The Congress, when it opposed Balmaceda, in order to appeal to him invoked the abdication of the liberator O'Higgins. This indeed was the worst example to recall! What happened after that abdication? Lagarrigue asked. "The country sank into chaos until the illustrious Portales rescued it." If the renowned O'Higgins had not abdicated, "we would now be closer to a sociocracy." Hence it was necessary for the head of the nation to decide upon a *coup d'état*. "The *coup d'état* could be criticized only if it were contrary to social progress, but in no way could it be criticized when its purpose was to serve social progress without repressing the radically disorganizing tendencies of Congress.

In another pamphlet which he circulated on the same problem, Juan Enrique Lagarrigue said: "I am moved to write only by my interest in my country's moving towards a sociocracy and freeing itself from all revolutionary and metaphysical tendencies." In the present conflict the entire problem is reduced to the following: "Either the parliamentary system or the presidential system triumphs. . . . Which is most suitable for Chile's future? It is clear from all evidence that the presidential system should triumph. Many years ago Auguste Comte, the founder of positivism, declared that the parliamentary system was inept. The presidential system must triumph, or our country will pay the penalty of being led woefully astray instead of advancing. . . . For every Chilean with a strong heart and a clear mind who is not thinking logically, it is undeniable that it is the

Congress which has gone astray today and not the executive power. Public opinion should be on the side of the President."[22]

On the other hand, Valentín Letelier fought dictatorship, and he found the justification for his opposition to it in positivism, although it was no longer in Comtian but in Spencerian positivism. Persecuted, imprisoned, and exiled because of his defense of law, "under the threats of tyranny I supported by my conduct the same doctrines that I had upheld by word in these classrooms under the reign of liberty." Letelier considered the university closely related to the government: In the university, he said, "the professor appears duty bound both to train professional men with a knowledge of law and to educate statesmen with a knowledge of science."[23] Letelier was a worthy successor to Lastarria and his generation. For him education was the basis of the reform to which they aspired. From this point of view it was not possible for him to be on the side of a government unmindful of the liberating objectives of the state, independent of the order which it must necessarily maintain.

Letelier felt that it was the war of the Pacific (1879), the war against Peru and Bolivia, that gave rise to Balmaceda's tyranny. Apparently, he said, Chileans could take pride in the fact that their constitutional order was not changed in that war. "But although juridically there was no change whatsoever in the legal order, a great concentration of powers in the hands of the executive was, in fact, brought about because of the force of events." Society granted him these powers. "The strongest governments are those that depend upon greatest support from the social elements, because there is no prerogative, however exorbitant with which society does not invest them *de facto* when the necessities of its organism so require." War established these necessities. "Therefore the state of war, like other conditions, links triumph to social cohesion, to discipline, to obedience, to the unity of points of view; it tends, even against the desires of those governed and against the will of those who govern, to develop spontaneously the political strength of the governments." Basing his thought upon Spencer, he said: "This principle of political science is perfectly clear when one observes that, in the most backward societies where a state of war is permanent, the governments are auto-

[22] *Dictamen positivista sobre el conflicto entre el Gobierno y el Congreso.*
[23] *La tiranía y la revolución.*

cratic, and that the most liberal governments are the product of *industrial* societies, where war appears from time to time as an accidental phenomenon." Hence, while Comtism considered dictatorship necessary to establish sociocracy, Spencer looked upon dictatorship or tyranny as but a backward form of society which belonged to a warring period, a period that gave way to the industrial.

Letelier continued to draw on Spencer for the conclusions on which he based his opposition to and his criticism of Balmaceda's *coup d'état*. "Inevitably," he said, "most of Peru's conquering army was destined to serve as an instrument of oppression or tyranny in the hands of any bold leader." Every dictatorship, he added, necessarily leads towards illegality. "When a government no longer abides by the law, it becomes a dictatorship; and a dictatorship, even when it is not a lawful institution, can be a justifiable one; but if, in turn, it departs from the law, it becomes a tyranny, and every tyranny is for the same reason unjustifiable." Corruption of systems of government also gives rise to the dependency of the citizens on their governors. "Indeed," he concluded, "the remedy is not in law." The problem is not solved by restricting the vote. That would only perpetrate exploitation, and this is always dangerous. "Even when the majority of the people ordinarily look with indifference upon the exercise of their rights, they will not submit meekly to having the rights snatched away which once have been given to them." Letelier was therefore opposed to every effort that meant a restriction of suffrage as a remedy to avoid any possible dictatorship or attempt similar to Balmaceda's. Spencerian positivism also provided a solution. "In my opinion the remedy consists," he said, "in stimulating *industrial development,* on the one hand, to place each voter in a position of relative independence and, on the other hand, in propagating primary instruction more and more and, especially, instruction in civic matters, in order to educate the judgment of those who one day will be called upon to exercise the right of suffrage." The Chilean thinker, following new philosophies, sought the same remedy for the evils of the Hispanic-American people as the previous generation, the generation of Lastarria and Bilbao, of Sarmiento and Alberdi, or José María Luis Mora and José Luz ÿ Caballero. Their one common objective was education and the creation of wealth through industry.

III. TOWARD A POLITICAL SCIENCE

Is a Science of Politics Possible?

VALENTÍN LETELIER, faithful to Chile's liberal tradition, was more and more deeply occupied by the possibility of a political science adapted to Hispanic-American circumstances or, more specifically, to Chilean circumstances. Letelier, as well as Lastarria, viewed positivism as a rich source for formulating such a science. He viewed it only as a source, not as the solution for the problem. Positivism was nothing more than a good point of departure and the justification for much that had been done in the field of political theory. Hispanic America had its own problems, and therefore it should have its own solutions. Furthermore, positivism used the experience of a given reality as a point of departure, and for the Americans this reality could only be American.

De la ciencia política en Chile was the title of a book which Letelier published in 1886. In it he posed the problem mentioned above concerning the possibilities of a political science in Chile. Comte, Mill, and Bain were the positivistic philosophers used as a basis for approaching this problem, but Auguste Comte exercised the most powerful influence on this work. Politics was for Letelier a phenomenon which must be explained as such. Indeed, every phenomenon, once it had been explained, could be reduced to a definite legality, to a definite science. But could political phenomena be reduced to a definite science? Too many men of the positivistic nineteenth century who asked this question were referring to a kind of natural science. More specifically, they were asking, Could political phenomena be made subject to natural laws?

A phenomenon, Letelier said, can be explained in three different ways: "By attributing it either to a supernatural cause, that is, to one or many gods; or to abstract entities, such as destiny, chance, or fate; or to the property of matter, a law of nature." Hence the explanations are of three kinds: supernatural or theological, subjective or metaphysical, and objective, positivistic, or scientific. Each one of these three types of explanation gave rise to three types of philosophy: theology, metaphysics, and science. Following Comte still more closely, he established that one type of explanation necessarily excludes the others. "Scientific explanations become unnecessary and exclude all theological and metaphysical explanations; and supernatural interventions cease as natural causes are discovered."

He continued to ask, Can political phenomena be made subject to natural laws? Is it possible to explain politics scientifically? For a good positivist like Letelier there was only one kind of science, natural science; hence he thought it necessary to reduce political phenomena to this kind of science. Was that possible? All phenomena, he continued, are grouped in six great classes, each of which is explained by a respective science. There are mathematical phenomena, which are explained by mathematical science; astronomical, by astronomy; physical, by physics; chemical, by chemistry; biological, by biology; and sociological, by sociology. Indeed, as each of these sciences became more complex, it became more difficult to explain it, and since sociology was the newest of these sciences, it presented the greatest difficulties. In its application to politics, he added, "Sociology has not as yet given us any means for discovering the truth and rectifying error, unless it is by means of those painful experiences which nations normally undergo and which are at times resolved by futile upheavals and by revolutions." There was still no science that could put an end to these discrepancies, no science that could reconcile diverse political opinions. "Politics has not succeeded in putting an end to these discrepancies. . . . While scientific discussions will sooner or later bring contenders into agreement, political discussions have only inflamed men's minds, made concord more difficult, and perpetuated divisions which were apparently on the point of disappearing." The problem was, as could be seen, How can individuals in a field which concerns them so greatly be reconciled? Hispanic America already had a long and bloody experience in this reality.

Political Science and History

WHAT was the political experience of our nations? So far as Chile is concerned, Letelier demonstrated how Chileans had attempted to approach political reality from three points of view: the liberal, the reactionary, and the conservative. "The *liberal* school," he said, "believes that society is essentially a malleable and plastic mass, and in order to satisfy its political necessities can be fashioned after purely

imaginary utopias, or at least after feasible but premature ideals."
This was a utopian school, removed from reality. "On the other
hand, the *reactionary* school, basing its thought on the same premise,
completely ignores the change in social conditions brought about by
the modern revolution and dreams of a complete restoration of an
extinct theocratic regime." This school likewise failed to recognize
reality when it ignored the changes that were taking place. "The
conservative school, which approves and even applauds the historical
development of society, of thought, and of institutions, fancied that
institutions, thought, and society would halt once and for all at the
point where they are at present, and they oppose all change and stul-
tify further development of politics and human faculties." Each of
these schools had, in turn, become stultified.

Each one of these schools thus ignored reality, removed from the
reality that was present in time, that is, history; these schools always
attempted to ignore time, by denying it or stopping it in its tracks.
But was it possible for a science of politics to take history into account?
Was it not possible that all science, in order to be a science, must
ignore the historical? "If political science existed," said Letelier,
"there is no doubt that such learned persons as those who lead our
parties would come to an agreement in their arguments, even if they
were not in agreement on the elections." If this science did exist, "its
purpose would be to determine those natural laws by virtue of which
those political phenomena take place." But was there anyone who did
not know that all political policies were the work, not of general and
regular causes, but of a determined will, that of those who govern;
that, as a result, it was not possible to discover among the events of
a given state any principle of causality or coexistence?

Such a science did not seem possible because it would be incompatible with history. "The real, the true, the positive would be that
the great historical personages, who according to reliable sources
were responsible for the events of the past, were not the authors of
these events and that these events developed by virtue of general
causes which we do not know and which work independent of human
will." But it was impossible. Politics is the work of individual wills,
and these wills are the forces of history. A science of politics would
have to ignore history. "The only general principle that can be found

among political events is that they are always the work of those
who rule or, rather, of those who exercise the greatest social influence, whether they are governors, party leaders, or mere republics
etc. . . . This would lead us to conclude that it is history that is opposed to the establishment of a political science." And was it so? Letelier then reversed the problem: Is it not true that a science of historical studies has not been formulated and that this is the cause
of the conflict between history and political science? If a science of
history existed, would not a political science then be possible? The
problem had to be changed. It appeared that historical studies were
opposed to, or at least prevented, the formulation of a political science, said Letelier; since politics is a social phenomenon, it cannot be
formulated into a science as long as history, which studies all social
phenomena as a unit, does not succeed in discovering the general law
of relationship which it is assumed should exist among these phenomena. This has not been possible because up to the present there
has been great superficiality in historical studies. "The inadequacy
with which, in truth, political and military matters are treated (in
spite of the restrictive and meticulous methods which historians use)
is such that statesmen could not infer from these studies a single rule
for government, nor could they derive from them a solution of a
single political problem." Everything appeared here "as a series of
unrelated events, as a series of effects without causes, as an exposition
of phenomena without laws, which are produced spontaneously."
As historical works are generally written, they are presented as "simple and unrelated expositions of particular phenomena, when all abstract science is, on the contrary, an exposition of general laws. . . .
They are, in a word, pure memory studies, while every science is
above all a study of understanding."

What is it that we need? asked Letelier. We need a philosophy
of history, and only a science of politics will make this possible.
Comte and Spencer had already insisted on many occasions that the
lack of unity in and superficiality of historical works were due to the
lack of scientific preparation. A philosophy of history was therefore
necessary in order to build a political theory upon history. Many
efforts had already been made to formulate this philosophy. The
first consideration was to "discover among events some principle of

general causality, which, because it is suitable for explaining all possible events, makes it unnecessary to narrate all events." For every "science, in order to discover an unknown law or to study one already discovered, it is not necessary to examine all the related phenomena. . . . In the same way, social laws, in the event they exist, could be discovered and then studied, without the necessity of knowing all the events of history." But it is reasonable to inquire, "Does some general principle really exist in society which preserves society and causes it to develop and which is suitable to explain all political events?" What had been done up to the present was insufficient. The philosophy of the history of the Bible, Bossuet, Vico, Montesquieu, and Buckle was not enough. "The formulation of a political science is impossible, given the present status of the philosophy of history."

Which Political Theory to Choose?

NEVERTHELESS, in spite of the difficulties in formulating a political theory, it is true that history offered numerous theories. Which was preferable? The choice of a political science is one of the greatest dangers that is encountered. Which of all the existing theories is the true one—Plato's, Aristotle's, Mill's, Rousseau's, Comte's, Spencer's? As for Chile, said Letelier, "the only truly serious work that has been written on politics in this country, Lastarria's *Política positiva*, presents a constitutional plan which very few will think practical and suitable under the present social conditions."

Which theory should be chosen? "Should youth be educated for the reaction, the revolution, the church, or the state, or for one or the other of the opposing parties?" Such education would be futile, for, after all, political parties govern without a political science. Hence, "rather than spread dangerous doctrines, which do not always produce the desired social effects, it behooves us to wait until other nations try them out in order to imitate immediately and with assurance their successful application." In this sense Letelier considered the cultural backwardnes of Hispanic America beneficial. It made her avoid experiments which could produce negative results. By observing Europe's experiments, Hispanic America could avoid Europe's errors and adopt her successes.

As for Chile, he said, the only theory that could have any value

171

whatsoever was Lastarria's. Nevertheless, in the present situation, there were a number of new influences, especially in the books that were being read at that time. And these books were but the index of what the man of the time wanted or what best suited his way of thinking. "In truth," he said, "the studious man does not surround himself with any books except those whose doctrines suit his own thought, so that without hearing him talk or without reading any of his works, one can infer from his daily reading what his fundamental principles are." Guided by this general indication, one can study "in Spencer, Stuart Mill, Comte, Littré, and other great thinkers whose works are found in many private libraries of social science what the status of political science is among us." And this status shows that the most popular doctrine at present is positivism.

Positivistic political science denies that the influence of the will on politics is as decisive as general histories say. On the contrary, it maintains "that all events—the formation and the development of states, institutional changes, revolutions, etc.—are brought about as the result of general causes rather than through the will of those who govern." Here Letelier poses a question that must be answered to save his liberalism, to wit: if all political events are brought about as a result of social forces, what has become of free will? The problem is posed at present under the domination of the sciences in the same terms as under the domination of the ancient philosophies. The immutability which distinguished the absolute causes of ancient philosophies is likewise inherent in natural laws. "In this sense, wherever it may exist, a society must attempt to develop in conformity with a predetermined norm, unless extraneous forces obstruct or alter its development."

Here Letelier's liberalism forced him to oppose a possible determinism. Will, human liberty, should be able to exert some influence on the world of history and politics. A legal order was sought, but not an order that was contrary to the sense of freedom and responsibility. "After all," said Letelier, "social laws, if they exist, must be by their very nature so subject to modification that, while they are still being executed, the *will* of each individual must be able to contribute actively or passively to their fulfillment: conservatives slowing them down, liberals hastening their execution, and reactionaries and revolutionaries agitating it." The hierarchy in the order of reality and sciences pointed out by Comte is for Letelier only a hierarchy in the order of liberty. One goes from the determinant to the indeterminant, from order to liberty. The complexity that is noted in the scale of the different sciences is only the manifestation of a world of liberty which becomes clearly evident in the human realm. "Human liberty," said Letelier, "which lacks free will in the fields of unalterable phenomena, such as mathematics and astronomy, begins to acquire it the moment it is extended into those areas whose phenomena are susceptible to change." In some fields man's will and freedom are more obvious than in others. Faced with certain realities, his will is ineffective, while in other situations it is effective. One cannot, said Letelier, make two and two equal three or prevent the earth from revolving around the sun; but one can, indeed, deflect a ray of light in the physical order; in chemistry, elements can be broken down into their component parts, and in biology, life can be prolonged or terminated. "Analogically, one can in the social order, the most complex and the highest, modify the form, mode, and time of events." This is the reason that political phenomena are assumed to be the "exclusive work of the will. . . . Human action is subject to superior laws and is free only to the degree that it can modify them."

Valentín Letelier thus saved freedom from absolute determinism. Neither was he a partisan of an absolute liberty, which would only be complete anarchy. He very seriously inquired into the existence of a science of politics. In the human realm he was also confronted with a series of determining realities. In this area man attains his greatest freedom, but this freedom is not absolute; human action encounters here certain limitations. "Politics," he said, "is determined in each case by historical antecedents and by social circumstances of which the statesman may perhaps be unaware, but which nonetheless operate in a decisive and undeniable manner." Nevertheless, it appears at times that political events are the results of the whims of some political figure. "But let us begin by noting that on every occasion the men who appear to be arbiters of society are those who place themselves in the service of some social necessity, or at least of some general aspiration, thus becoming simple instruments of that need. Letelier's thesis does not seem to be either absolute determinism or anarchy. "Born, reared and educated in the realm of society, man receives from society the sentiments, the character, the ideas, and the habits which he will follow all his life." This will determine his future conduct, but not to the point of making his freedom impossible. Once liberty was salvaged, then Letelier could talk of a political science, a science which relies upon an area of activity which prevents the individual's freedom, action, and will from being pure anarchy. If it is thus, he said, "if as is inferred from the cases studied, social forces always operate in spite of, or with the concurrence of, the human will . . . , our duty as statesmen and as rational beings is to study them in order to facilitate their development and to avoid futile disturbances."

A Political Science for Statesmen

FROM THE INDUCTION made from society, said Letelier, there has arisen a new science: sociology. The Chilean thinker was here following Comte again. Sociology is divided into static and dynamic sociology. "If events," said Letelier, "are not the work of the will but of society, it is evident that those events which disturb the development of the social order cannot be avoided by means of *repressive laws* but by means of *preventive laws*." Here again appears the liberal who, basing his thought on positivism, is opposed to any despotic action exercised on the individual. The mission of the state is to foresee, and to foresee is to anticipate events, to prevent them from happening if they are inimical to society. The innate tendency of empirical politics to repress the *visible effects* rather than to remove or *neutralize the determining causes* comes precisely from the fact that these relations of causality are so little known and that the studies of social dynamics are so little disseminated. A knowledge of social dynamics can permit those who govern to anticipate events and to turn them to their proper channels. Ordinarily, by virtue of these relationships of antecedent and consequence, an indication of evil appears before the evil itself, and the ruler who recognizes these relationships can prevent or temper its effects.

The ignorance of leaders concerning social dynamics leads them to confuse different events and to attempt to apply ambiguous solutions to them. For example, said Letelier, a turmoil of religious fanatics is not the same as the turmoil of a workingman seeking an increase in salary, and one cannot be suppressed in the same way as the other. "The first may be attributed to intolerance"; the second cannot, because it is but an "unmistakable symptom of new demands initiated by social classes which were, up to that time, peaceful, submissive, and abject." The method of avoiding each of these situations must be different. "In our times, with a blindness less justifiable than that of Greece and Rome in maintaining slavery in that the laws of social causality are better understood, many would like to explain the strikes that are taking place daily in industrial countries by saying that they are capricious, caused by the simple spirit of rebellion which has suddenly possessed the masses."

Such situations could be avoided if those who govern, by taking heed of social dynamics, anticipate the solutions before unrest becomes violence. Inability to prevent these situations leads necessarily to violence when they do appear. "The leader who is inspired by science knows," said Letelier, "in fact, that positivistic politics prefers *preventing* social evils to *repressing* them." Since social phenomena, like natural phenomena, are subject to the law of causality, "they can be much more accurately foreseen and predicted, the better the general causes are known which according to theory produce them. . . . Whoever knows even the rudiments of sociology can foresee with assurance the general course of the mind and societies in future centuries." A politics based on this science could suggest means for putting an end to continual strikes, to the permanent threat of communism, to the periodical crises of nations, and to a chronic state of misery.

As far as Chile is concerned, he said, "There, for example, the agricultural proletariat, submissive, abject, without any idea of morals, without ambition, and without hope of improvement, is a perennial source of criminals. . . . What ought we do to improve it without the danger of awakening in it, as in the European proletariat, the revolutionary spirit?" We must take note of the causes that keep it in such a condition in order to avoid its turning to violence. No more utopias; we must approach reality by studying its causes. "The principal cause of our political corruption, a real stain on our customs, is, without a doubt, the fact that our institutions, dictated as they were by the impulses of a sound but premature idealism, have conferred *de jure* upon the masses the right of a political participation for which they were not and are not yet prepared." These rights were given to the masses before they were prepared to exercise them. Instead of heeding the social and political reality of the country, the Chileans imitated the political and governmental forms of countries whose social reality was different. There was a need for a criterion based on political science, and the absence of this criterion led to frequent mistakes. "Even as late as 1833 the founders of the Republic of Chile committed this error; all of them, liberals as well as conservatives, formulated constitutional plans with their attention less on our social necessities than on what Greece and Rome, France, and the United States had done."

The greatest evils among nations are caused by political idealism, since it blinds their leaders to reality. It allows fantasy to assume the role that belongs to experience. One grave error has been "to believe that such a preconceived principle as liberty, popular sovereignty, religion, authority, justice, or the like, was sufficient to solve all political problems and to satisfy all social needs." Comte, continued Letelier, observed with much acumen, which he lacked when he wrote his *Politique positive,* that the failure of present-day republics to establish stable institutions arises in great part from the fact that they plan them with complete disregard of the social state which they are attempting to set in order. Moved by "absolute ideals, the doctrinarians disregard the social conditions in which they are to operate, they look upon society as an essentially plastic mass malleable to their will, and they struggle to establish arbitrary orders of things, increasing at the same time the disturbances and the confusion of the very revolutionary state that they are trying to organize."

As for Chile, Letelier continued, "The thing that lends more validity to the constitution of 1833[24] is its marked tendency to react against idealistic and imitative politics . . . and to satisfy the primary need of that time, which was to re-establish the order changed by constant stimuli and by the great development that had been necessary, and its tendency to assure the work of our independence." If one heeds science, one learns that in it, "in every case, institutions are

[24] Don Diego Portales is the author of this constitution.

to be dictated for the people," and likewise that it condemns "the disturbing metaphysical tendencies to fit people into institutions, whether they are suitable or not."

The different political schools, without any notion of science, falsified reality and disoriented it. There were several of these schools, said Letelier. There is one, "according to which the purpose of politics was only to maintain the present order; and, guided by this criterion and without any notion of social development, [it] has opposed among contemporary nations the establishment of public liberties and has hindered severely the considerable development which, by means of these liberties, society and the human spirit have acquired." Another school, "without any clear idea of order, attempted to resolve all political problems by the absolute criterion of liberty." This was the liberal school. "While we realize that there is nothing more difficult than to imbue men and societies with a moral sense of order and discipline, the liberal school continues dauntlessly proclaiming as the only solution to all political problems a dogma of an essentially dispersive character, such as absolute liberty."

Letelier continued, as is obvious, faithful to the political ideology of Lastarria and his generation. Lastarria, as will be remembered, opposed the two forms of political parties which he found: the *pelucones* and *pipiolos*, conservatives and liberals. He wanted to form a third party, or perhaps something greater, a third class, and Letelier was one of the most worthy representatives of that class. It was a kind of *bourgeoisie sui generis*, the same type of *bourgeoisie* that had been developing throughout Hispanic America. Letelier, like his teacher before him, pointed out a third course in politics, which was no longer order for the sake of order nor utopian liberty, but an ordered responsible liberty, a liberty based on reality, experience, and science. His liberalism might be called a scientific liberalism, without being, of course, what this same term signified in Mexico. Letelier was opposed to an irresponsible liberalism alien to reality. Liberalism in its absolute sense was useful only to overthrow the old colonial order, but once this mission was carried out, its continuation was contrary to progress. The followers of this liberalism put into motion the forces which succeeded in overthrowing the old institutions but which could not establish new ones. This liberalism, "in the name of freedom in education, opposes the organization of a public service of instruction, preferring to stimulate the diffusion of contradictory systems of antagonistic sects and schools and by thus conspiring to keep society and the national spirit divided, instead of attempting to reconstruct by means of a national system of education the unity of our knowledge." This school, instead of analyzing the causes which could have motivated certain social and political events, was content to apply emergency means to their solution. For the followers of this school, said Letelier, "the cause of strikes, communism, nihilism, etc. was that on such and such an occasion the police did not arrive on time."[25] This school could only fold its arms before the social problems. It was not capable of solving them. It left such an extreme free play to society that it led to anarchy.

But this did not mean, as has already been seen, that Letelier was in any way a follower of despotism. He wanted a responsible liberalism, a liberalism whose limits are set by the responsible individuals who compose society. In a marginal note he said: "We beg our readers not to consider us as supporters of despotism when we proclaim the authoritarianism of the state as the doctrine of contemporary society. The arbitrariness of those in command, whether they are autocrats, kings, or presidents, is always antisocial and therefore always illegal. But the national authoritarianism of the state is a government not essentially *responsible*, and it can be, as it is in the present circumstances, from every angle irreplaceable for the direction of political development." It was an order, but a responsible order; it was also liberty, but a responsible liberty.

Only political science could endow a government with responsibility. This science was not determined by group or individual interests, but by the interests of society. "The science of government, if it exists, can be neither conservative nor liberal, nor radical in the vulgar sense of the word. However varied the applications may be, all science is one throughout the world; and therefore names which correspond to local parties whose mission is to pursue purposes of the moment are not proper to political science." This science will endow society with a true instrument for peace and order, without implying

[25] Compare this attitude with that of the Mexican positivists. See my work *Apogeo y decadencia del positivismo en México*.

restrictions on individual liberty. "Just as there is not a liberal mathematics, a radical, or a conservative mathematics," said Letelier, "but only a single science of numbers which serves all parties, so there is not nor can there be but one political science whose general principles serve all as a standard and guide."

IV. DECEPTION AND DESTRUCTION
The Great Defeat

PERU, like the other Hispanic-American nations, followed the path of anarchy and dictatorship. During short periods of tranquility, such as those of General Ramón Castilla's government in 1844 and General J. Rufino Echenique's in 1841, some works were carried out on the so-called route of progress. In 1863 war broke out against Spain during which the Spanish Squadron bombarded the port of Callao. Again there were revolutions, and the President, don José Balta, was assassinated. The economic situation in Peru became more and more serious; revolutions became more frequent. In 1876, President Mariano Ignacio Prado was elected. It was during his term that the nation suffered one of the greatest national disasters: the war with Chile in 1879. The Republic of Bolivia, with Peru as its ally, was involved in a series of disputes with a Chilean nitrate company, as a result of which Chile declared war on Bolivia; a short time thereafter Chile also declared war on Peru, which was soon defeated by the Chileans because of its economic deficit, its divided citizenry, and its lack of trained soldiers, arms, and ships. There were a few valiant stands at sea, such as that of the monitor *Huáscar*, while General Francisco Bolognesi carried on a bloody but futile defense. President Prado left for Europe "in search of ships." Nicolás de Piérola, secretary of the treasury in 1869, seized the power and declared himself dictator on December 21, 1879, continuing the war and preparing to defend the capital. In January of 1880 the Chileans occupied Lima, which suffered an unforgettable sacking and burning of two of its districts. Piérola fled to the mountains, where he organized the resistance. It was a futile effort. Disasters continued. In October of 1833, General Miguel Iglesias signed the treaty of Ancón, by which the Department of Tarapacá and the provinces of Tacna and Arica were ceded to Chile for ten years. At the end of this period a plebiscite was to resolve the final disposition of this territory. Thus Peru lost a part of the territory which could have helped solve its acute economic problems.

Who was to blame for this disaster? Manuel González Prada (1848–1918), in an address delivered at the Politeama Theater in 1883,[26] recalling these fatal events, said: "While the most insignificant soldier of the invading army had only the name of Chile on his lips, our men from the highest-ranking general to the lowest recruit repeated only the name of a *caudillo;* we were servants of the Middle Ages who invoked the feudal lord." The evil, as always, was in the heritage; the Peruvians bore it within them. In this sense, the Chileans were better prepared. The idea of a fatherland and a nation had some meaning for them, and it led them to victory. The Peruvians, on the other hand, continued to be led by their *caudillos.* They did not fight for Peru, but for their leaders, whether they were Piérola or any other one. "Chile's brutal hand tore our flesh to pieces and crushed our bones, but the true conquerors were our ignorance and our spirit of servitude." The past, the fatal heritage had again become evident. "The Spanish nobility left its degenerating and wasteful legacy; the victor in the struggle for independence produced a line of military men and bureaucrats. Rather than sow wheat and mine ore, the youth of the past generation preferred to let its brain atrophy in the halls of the military barracks and to allow its skin to wither like old parchment in governmental offices. Men fitted for the crude labor of the fields and of the mines sought their livelihood in the spoils which fell to them from the government, and they exercised an insatiable drain on the resources of the national treasury, and the *caudillo,* who distributed bread and honors, was esteemed more than the country. . . . For that reason, in the supreme moment of the struggle, we were not a bronze colossus against the enemy but only a cluster of lead filings. . . . we were all ignorant and bondsmen, and we did not conquer nor could we conquer."

How could we remedy this situation? "If the ignorance of the leaders of the government and the servitude of those governed were the things that defeated us," Gonzales Prada said, "let us resort to *science,* that savior which teaches us to soften the tyranny of Nature; let us adore Liberty, that engendering mother of strong men." But

[26] Collected in *Páginas libres.*

they could not resort to just any science, only to the new science, the science that had already produced great nations. "I am not speaking . . . of a mummified science which is gradually being reduced to dust in our backward universities; I am speaking of the science strengthened by the blood of the century, of the science with ideas of a gigantic radius, of a science which transcends youth and savors of Greek honeycomb; I am speaking of the *positivistic science* which in a single century of industrial application has produced more wealth for humanity than milleniums of theology and metaphysics."

The Destruction of the Past

MANUEL GONZÁLEZ PRADA, like other great Hispanic-American leaders, devoted himself to the difficult task of breaking with that fatal past. The disaster of the war with Chile left no other way open. It was necessary to form another type of man, to re-educate the Peruvians, to orient youth along different lines, for the time being along the road toward the destruction of the past, fearlessly, shamelessly, and boldly. Manuel González Prada, speaking and writing, began the destruction. "Let us break the infamous and tacit pact of speaking in whispers. Let us abandon the crossroads for the highway and ambiguity for the exact word. When we attack error and its followers, let us not strike them with our swords sheathed; let us strike deeply, with a naked blade, clean and shining in the sun. Let truth appear unadorned, beautiful, and chaste, without the veil of satire or the vesture of the apologue . . . let us be true, even though truth bring us misfortune, provided that the torch light the way, for it is of little matter that it burns the hand that lights it and waves it."[27] Denounce, bring to the surface, show all the poverty and misery of a people who had not yet attained its intellectual emancipation—this was the great task of the Peruvian teacher. "We must show the people the horror of their degradation and their misery," he said. "There has never been a good autopsy without cutting into the cadaver, nor did ever a society have a profound knowledge of itself without stripping its skeleton of the flesh." There was no reason to be afraid or to be scandalized: "The people will understand that previously they were used but for the benefit of someone else; now the time has come

[27] A speech in *el Teatro Olimpo* in 1888.

when they must act for their own benefit." It was necessary to attack all the old order, to put an end to all the conventional deceptions, to eliminate all those slogans that promulgate resignation, which is never the resignation of the one who preaches it. "Let us strip the powerful of some of their power and the wealthy of some of their wealth, and we will see whether they accept and preach resignation."[28]

By what means was this destruction of the past to be effected? Who were the men who should bury this past? Manuel González Prada thought for a time that a new political party could succeed in the undertaking. With this in mind he founded the *Unión Nacional,* but he soon realized the inadequacy of this instrument. He had already said in 1898, "Who knows if in Peru the hour of true parties has not arrived! Who knows if we still remain in the era of the solitary apostolate!" Concerning the men who were to assist him in the destruction which must precede reconstruction, he had said in the same famous address, delivered at the Politeama Theater: In the "work of reconstruction and vengeance we do not rely on the men of the past: the old and decayed trees have already produced their deadly flowers and their bitter fruits. We must have new trees that will bear new blossoms and new fruits! Old men to the tomb, the young to work!" Youth answered his call. Many followed him, and with their help he founded the above-mentioned party, in which he placed his greatest hopes: a clean, young, uncontaminated party. Social regeneration was its program.

The new party, as Manuel González Prada conceived it, was to make no compromises with anyone or with anything other than its ideals. It was to be intransigent and irreconcilable. "The Union," he said, "does not attempt to win proselytes or hybrid solidarities; it is breaking political traditions and it is attempting to organize a force which will react against evil ideas and evil habits. Only by being intransigent and irreconcilable shall we find an echo in the soul of the masses and attract their sympathy. . . . In the political order as well as in the zoological, the union of different species produces only hybrid or sterile creatures." The task of destruction must be carried out in a practical way. Everything that stood for falsification was to be destroyed. That entire world of false legislation, laws and

[28] *Propaganda y ataque.*

constitutions which were alien to Peruvian reality, must be destroyed. There were to be no more utopias! A positive sense of reality was needed! The men of the past generation, in spite of the fact that they boasted of a great practical sense, had "promulgated constitutions and laws without educating the citizens to understand them and to obey them. They forged a metal without considering whether the mold could receive it; they decreed digestion without having any means of acquiring bread. . . . What good is free education if we have no schools? What good is the freedom of the press if we cannot read? What good is free enterprise if we have neither capital nor credit nor a piece of land to cultivate?" González Prada and his party sought to carry out social reform before political reform, for all political reforms were futile if urgent social reforms were not previously made. People must be given the means of raising their social level before they are given political freedom. "The *Union Nacional* could condense its program into two lines: to move in the direction of the greatest individual liberty by showing preference for social reforms rather than for political changes. . . . Down with politics, long live social reform."[29]

Manuel González Prada and Positivism

LIKE OTHER MEN such as Sarmiento and Lastarria, the Peruvian leader represents a link between Hispanic-American romanticism and positivism. Like these two leaders, he began by destroying in order to build later upon what he had destroyed. As a romantic he protested loudly against all the falseness of an insane past. His writings and his speeches filled with angry denunciations were directed against everything that he considered prejudices. Like a Jacobin, he made the church a target of his attacks. The Indian was an equal, and he argued vigorously in his behalf. He did not limit himself to destroying; he also tried to formulate a new republic free of all the evils he was intent upon destroying. In this respect he was a realist. He did not believe in building anything not based on reality. He opposed all utopias, and in this respect he was different from many romantics. He believed in *science* because it was always supported by reality. But he did not believe in just any science, as we have already seen—

[29] "*Los partidos y la Unión Nacional,*" a speech delivered in 1898.

183

only in positivistic science. This was the same science used by the great nations which had assumed leadership beginning in the nineteenth century.

González Prada cited on several occasions the positivistic philosophers Comte, Spencer, Mill, and Darwin. Like the majority of the Hispanic-American liberals, he was repelled by Comte. "The most prominent sociologists," he said, "consider sociology as a science in formation and clamor for the advent of a Newton, a Lavoisier, or a Lyell; nevertheless, there is no book in which so many dogmatic and arbitrary affirmations resound as in the works elaborated by Comte's followers or successors."[30]

Prada considered positivistic science one of the best instruments for carrying out the regeneration of Peru, but it was an instrument that few dared to make use of to the ultimate because they feared its consequences, because they were not brave enough to break with all the old prejudices and begin a new structure. There are many, he said, who take up the pen to write on religious freedom and lay education; "but when they are given the chance to accept the principles of positivistic science and apply its logical and tremendous conclusions, when the occasion arises to brandish the facts, to strike a serious blow, then they retreat in fright."[31]

González Prada also used science to combat Roman Catholicism, for he considered science the best instrument to attain truth and destroy all the illusions which keep man in ignorance and bondage. While religion made promises, he said, "science promised nothing and only scrutinized nature to extract at least an atom of truth . . . science dispelled more than one illusion by proving that the earth was not the principal planet in the universe, but an insignificant planet of one of the innumerable worlds in space; by proving that man and earth can disappear tomorrow without the universe suffering from the loss."

To those who spoke of the bankruptcy of science, González Prada replied: "We need only ask if two and two are no longer four, if the three angles of a triangle are no longer equal to two right angles, and if water is no longer composed of oxygen and hydrogen." Not science, but religion was bankrupt. "There is bankruptcy in Catholi-

[30] "*Nuestros indios*," 1904, collected in *Horas de lucha*.
[31] "*Instrucción laica*," 1892.

cism, for it was unable to elevate woman nor could it liberate the slave; and for two thousand years of domination it was unable to convert even one-tenth of humanity." In a comparison of religion and science, he sees the former spreading discord among mankind. "Religion, which forms allies to acquire strength and dominate its allies, considers itself deprived of a legitimate right when it does not rule alone . . . and there is no religion more absorbent, more aggressive, more militant than Catholicism." Science, on the other hand, does not proceed in that manner: "It is conciliatory, peaceful, and tolerant."[32] Whom did science anathematize to prove that a straight line is the shortest distance between two points? asked Prada. Whom did it ever incarcerate to convince that a bacillus produces tuberculosis? Whom did it torture to make him admit that the world revolves around the sun? For González Prada science was one of the most powerful instruments for destroying a world filled with prejudices and falsehoods. For González Prada, who was prepared to destroy everything that was decadent, science became an instrument of destruction, as it had been an instrument of reconstruction for others. He therefore also saw in it a good basis for his so-called anarchy. "Science," he said, "contains anarchistic affirmations, and humanity tends to point itself in the direction of anarchy." Referring specifically to positivism, he declared, "Even Spencer, even the great apostle of anti-revolutionary and conservative evolution, has traces of anarchy."[33]

Against Racial Inequality

"Do NOT PREACH humility and resignation to the Indian," said González Prada, "but rather pride and rebellion." Racial inequality was another of the evils of Hispanic America, especially in countries like Peru and Mexico. The Conquest produced this evil, and independent Hispanic America inherited it. The Peruvian leader knew that one of the realities which must be taken into account was the reality of the native population. It was a reality that could be positive or negative, according to the way in which a solution was sought. The idea of making the Indian an inferior race produced a negative solution. The Indian was not inferior. There are no inferior races; there are only good or evil men, superior or inferior men, depending

[32] *"Catolicismo y ciencia,"* in *Nuevas páginas libres.*
[33] *Anarquía.*

only upon what each one is in himself, not upon the race or nation to which he belongs. "Ethnology is a convenient invention in the hands of some men!" exclaimed Prada. Once the division of humanity into superior and inferior races is admitted, once the superiority of the whites and their right to monopolize the government of the earth are recognized, nothing is more natural than the suppression of the Negro in Africa, the red man in the United States, the Tagalog in the Philippines, the Indian in Peru. It is true that there are also inferior men among the whites. On the basis of this false thesis, the Indian is accused, among other things, of being rebellious against civilization. "Morally speaking," said Prada, "the natives of the republic are inferior to the natives discovered by the conquistadors; but moral depression caused by political servitude is not equivalent to the absolute impossibility of becoming civilized because of physical traits." These are the facts which belie the pessimist. "Whenever the Indian is taught in schools or educated by simple contact with civilized people, he acquires the same moral and cultural level as the descendants of the Spaniards."

The educated Indian is never inferior to the white man under the same circumstances. As mere products of race or representative men, the King of England and William II of Germany are not superior to many men of other races. "Are they worthy of comparison with the Indian Benito Júarez or with the Negro Booker T. Washington? . . . Those who before occupying a throne lived in a tavern, a gambling den, or a brothel, those who from the heights of an empire decree a massacre, sparing neither children, old men, or women, have white skin, but their souls are black." The condition of the Indians will change if they acquire sufficient strength to punish their oppressors. "If the Indian spent on rifles and bullets all the money that he wastes on alcohol and fiestas, if in a corner of his hut or in a crack of a rock he were to hide a weapon, he would change his condition, he would make his property and his life respected. He would answer violence with violence by punishing the *patrón* who steals his wool, the soldier who forces him into the army in the name of the government, the rustler who steals his cattle and his beasts of burden."[34] In short, he concluded, the Indian must redeem himself through his own effort and never through the humanization of his oppressors.

[34] *"Nuestros indios."*

V. POSITIVISM AND NATIONALITY

The Shadow of the Past as an Obstacle to Nationality

THE DISASTER with Chile and the failure of the social organization of Peru set the best of her men thinking upon the necessity of changing the direction which they had followed until that time. Henceforth, no more idealism, no more high-sounding and deceitful words; the time of romanticism had past. A new philosophy was invading Hispanic America, the philosophy which the great nations of the contemporary world were following. This new philosophy was based on science. It was scientific and therefore realistic. Its edifices were solid, for they could only be so constructed by the aid of science. Beginning in 1900 positivism became naturalized in Peru. Peruvian politicians and pedagogues made this doctrine the basis of their ideas. They looked upon it as one of the best instruments to mold Peruvian nationality, and among the positivists Spencer was preferred. The three most eminent Peruvian figures in this reform movement were Mariano Cornejo (1866–1942), a brilliant orator who held important positions and diplomatic posts and who in 1919 served as minister of the interior and president of the Council of Ministers; Javier Prado y Ugarteche, who with Cornejo supported a reformist ideology; and Manuel Vicente Villarán, who directed his efforts toward the field of education to instill a sense of nationality in the Peruvian.

As always, the first obstacle was the past. The first attacks must be directed against it. "For, gentlemen," Cornejo said in a speech on the plebiscite of Tacna and Arica, "if it is true that in the nineteenth century everybody recognizes the strength of law, it is also true that this century is positive in essence, and in order to apply these principles to reality and make them a part of it, it is necessary to use precise means, concrete agreements, and firm guarantees."[35] The war with Chile had made clear the necessity to act in this area. The defeat had also shown Peruvians that they must be more realistic and less dependent upon strength which they did not have. "For," he added, "just as in Darwin's theory natural and artificial selection adapts organisms to their function on earth, in history social selection fits the continents to their destinies. . . . America was made for unity, for

[35] *Discursos parlamentarios y políticos*, First Series (1902).

187

peace, and for democracy." But there was a grave obstacle. "We have inherited a timidity of character from the aboriginal race, a race essentially weak in courage as a result of its fanatical government; for superstition and fanaticism always destroy character. . . . I believe in the theories of Lyell and of Darwin. I believe in a constant evolution which formed the earth and I believe in a latent evolution which in the long run modifies organisms. I believe in atomism, in natural and artificial selection, and that custom produces the variety of species. And I do not know why, after seven centuries of bowing so much, we have not earned for ourselves the distinction of being hunchbacked."

Javier Prado found the Peruvian soil filled with wealth, in contrast to the poverty of Peru's inhabitants. Peru was not rich because it had not developed industry, commerce, and capital. What was the reason for this? After reviewing briefly the historical, social, and geographical policy, he concluded: "The evils are still very serious, but there is a way to combat them. Since these evils in the first place stem from racial influences, how can they be remedied? The race must be changed, "to rejuvenate our blood and our heritage by crossing it with other races; we must increase our population, and what is more, we must change its condition in a way that is advantageous to the cause of progress." He advocated the same well-known remedies: immigration, but a good immigration: "Let us oppose immigration of inferior races . . . which sacrifice the general interest and the future of the country." The other remedy was education. The second condition is to educate, "and to educate by means of work—industry." For there is nothing "which elevates the character of present-day man more, that makes him more respectful of laws and the social order, that makes him more intimately interested in the future of the country, that makes him more practical and prudent, than wealth acquired by his own personal endeavor."[36]

The educator Manuel Vicente Villarán believed that all the evils which characterized Peru had their origins in the Spanish past. The Spanish monarchs and their representatives in the colonies, he said, "fought true science, the serious studies which would have awakened progressive ideas." Hence Peru was unable to attain the degree of

[36] *El estado social del Perú durante le dominación española.*

progress which other younger nations such as the United States had reached. The Spanish government "favored the propagation of theology, scholastic philosophy, Roman jurisprudence, fine arts, abstract and inoffensive things that would not stir up unrest." But something more serious did happen; the situation persisted in spite of the fact that Peru had won her political independence from Spain. Schools where positivistic sciences should have been taught, sciences which could have regenerated Peru, continued to be neglected. There was not a single school of agriculture, commerce, navigation, industrial arts, or of any of the practical professions except for the school of engineering. "Secondary technical instruction is absolutely unknown among us." On the other hand, "we have many who teach us history, literature, Latin, theology, law, philosophy, and higher mathematics; but there is no one to teach us to work the land, to raise cattle, to exploit the forest, to navigate, to engage in commerce, to manufacture useful articles."[37]

Political independence was of no avail. "In spite of independence," said Villarán, "we have kept much of the colonial spirit." Still "we keep alive the same system of decorative and literary education which the Spanish governors implanted for political purposes in South America." If it had not been for that, "Peru should be, for a thousand economic and social reasons, as the United States has been, a land of farmers, planters, miners, merchants, and workingmen; but historical fate and the will of men have decided something else, converting the country into a literary center, a country of intellectuals, and a hotbed of bureaucrats." Bureaucracy was another of the evils which still persisted among Peruvians, making it impossible for them to progress or attain a civic and national sense of responsibility. "The universal and intense desire to attain public positions prevents youth from embracing careers in industry and commerce. Bureaucracy competes with and overwhelms all other industries. . . . We only have a vocation for bureaucracy, and we allow foreigners to take charge of productive works. Thus we shall soon be a colony of foreigners administered by Peruvian functionaries." Bureaucracy is but one form of the expression of the aversion to work inherited from class distinctions, which were established with racial distinctions and which gave

[37] *Las profesiones liberales en el Perú.*

189

rise to the Conquest. "Racial differences contribute to accentuating the aversion toward work. Every white man wanted to be a count or a marquis, and he discovered that the way to attain this rank was by not working: work, the white men said, was for Negroes and Indians." The whites "lived in the cities, spending their incomes, which were more the fruit of oppression than the product of industry. . . . The Indian servant produced the idle and squandering rich." But the most serious consequence was "that a strong association of ideas was established between work and servitude, because *de facto* the only worker was a slave . . . and they came to believe that work was bad and dishonorable."

As a result, "we have, then, through race and birth, a disdain for work, a love for the acquisition of money without any personal effort, a fondness for pleasant idleness, a taste for fiestas, and a tendency toward extravagance." In the same manner "we have acquired an ignorance of industrial and commercial professions and a fondness for literature, rhetoric, and poetry." In order to put an end to this situation, it was necessary to change the course the nation was following; it was necessary to change the habits of the Peruvian. He must exchange his visionary temperament for a more practical one.

"We must correct the erroneous direction which we have given to national education," said Villarán, "so that we can produce practical, industrious, and energetic men, because they are the kind the country needs to become wealthy and therefore strong." Only by so doing could a nation be built capable of withstanding the expansion of other nations. The political liberty already won was a relative liberty, which at any given moment could be lost. It was necessary to change the direction of education so that the country could "withstand the expansion of races from outside; it was necessary to change the course of education in order to succeed in the struggle for work against men more apt than we, coming from Europe and North America; it was necessary to change the course of education in order not to succumb, in short, before the wave of virile people who in the not too distant future will come to our shores and spread throughout our territory."[38] Peru must become like these people; Peru must become a nation like the United States of America. "What the country demands," said

[38] *Ibid.*

Javier Prado, "is the fruit of man's efforts: highways, railroads, transportation, docks, ships, machines, factories . . . the intense and persevering labor of production, of manufacturing, and of the industrial and commercial mobilization of a country firmly oriented toward the development and increase of its great wealth, its material and economic development, and giving at the same time vigor and well-being to its inhabitants." It is for this same reason that "we hope our university will not be a place restricted to theoretical studies, but a center of life and research." This is also the reason, Javier Prado continued, why he considered it a duty to present "from the university, to the youth which has the responsibility for the future of the country, a picture of the development and the greatness of the United States."[39] The powerful nation to the north continued to be the model to be followed. "The race, the tradition, the climate, the territory," said Villarán, "all indicate to us that we must mold practical and sensible men, rather than theoretical and imaginative men . . . endowed with active powers and virtues, not men with moral and esthetic refinements." In order to achieve this end, it would be necessary to bring in foreign teachers. "Just as England was the leader in political organization, North America offers the model for educational organization for free people . . . as a republic we must look to this model, not to the traditional European forms, still more or less contaminated with aristocratic, monarchial, and clerical traditions."[40]

Moralistic Education and Practical Education

ALEJANDRO O. DEÚSTUA, philosopher and educator, was opposed to positivism, for he saw in that doctrine a philosophy alien to the most pressing moral problems of the period. He believed that the most urgent need in education was to mold a class that would lead the nation, this class to be developed at the university. The immediate problem, therefore, was to devote Peru's attention to university education, for it was here that youth was to be taught to sacrifice personal interest for the common good. The evil lay in the governing classes, and it was their reform that needed attention. The levels of

[39] *La nueva época y los destinos históricos de los Estados Unidos.*
[40] M. V. Villarán, *Las profesiones liberales en el Perú.*

education, held Deústua, were but forms of expression of the different social strata which made up a society. Thus, there existed "the primary or popular school, devoted to the education of the working classes; the secondary school, adapted to the needs of the middle classes; and the higher institutions of learning, or universities, devoted to the education of the minds of the class charged with directing national activities."[41] For Deústua these different schools were not steps in the development of a pedagogical function. Primary education was not mere preparation for secondary education, nor secondary for the university. Each of these schools was autonomous in relation to the economic and social ends which they pursued. When despotism or aristocracy was the only form of government, there was only higher, or university, education, since it was all that was necessary for the governors to rule society. Later, when the political power needed the collaboration of economic power, represented by the middle class, there arose the secondary school, adapted to practical subjects necessary for this class. Later still, when the collaboration of the worker became indispensable on the economic and political level, then there arose the primary school, charged with giving to the workers the knowledge which was necessary to their function. In primary education empirical knowledge, factual knowledge, was sufficient. The secondary school demanded a knowledge based on scientific principles. And on the university level there was a need for a thorough knowledge of universal principles in order to discover guiding laws and principles. "The practical knowledge of primary education becomes scientific in secondary education and philosophical in the university. Formal education, therefore, varies according to the level."

On the basis of this thesis, Deústua considered university education the most important. Moral men must be molded before practical men. Hence the university was considered the most important level of education and the men of higher classes more worthy of attention and concern than the illiterates. The illiterate was not to be responsible for the direction of society. He was an unfortunate wretch, but one who, in the field of education, should not receive as much attention as the class that would some day lead him to happiness. But the positivist Manuel Vicente Villarán was definitely opposed to these ideas.

[41] *A propósito de un cuestionario sobre la reforma de la ley de instrucción.*

He considered the formation of an intellectual élite an ideal that could not be attained. The university had a great future, but it was not to come through a miraculous moral regeneration, but rather through the economic evolution of the country. "Where there are no opportunities for activity or remunerative work," he said, "there appears, as a fatal substitute, the industry of living at the cost of the state." The lack of industrialism "predisposes a people to obtain, by revolution or by intrigue, business, favors, and positions." It creates and enlivens "hatred among parties and a common indifference for the general welfare.... The antidote for fiscal parasitism is industrialism." Hence the need for educating first the middle and lower classes. The "excess of education among the upper classes and the lack of it in the lower classes would represent a deepening of the abyss which today separates one class from another." The social evil could not be remedied by the mere education of the upper classes. All the morality that could be acquired through education would not put an end to the many social abuses. "Wherever a few well-to-do educated individuals live together with a multitude of poverty-stricken illiterates, the ease with which the latter are abused stimulates the abuse. . . . These extremes have inevitable consequences, for if a millionaire faces a beggar or a wise man an illiterate, the former will inevitably be the master and the latter will be the slave in spite of any equalitarian constitution, moral discourses, and fraternal protection."[42]

The Indian Problem

THESE MEN, characterized by the same practical sense as González Prada, were to realize the existence of a reality which they must take into account—the Indian. While other countries, like Mexico and Argentina, in this same stage of development regarded the native as a negative element, some of the Peruvian positivists insisted on the positive aspect of the Indian in spite of all his faults, since they were but the product of circumstances that had been brought about by the white man.

Villarán defended this positive point of view of the Indian with great enthusiasm. "Many believe," he said, "that the great majority of the inhabitants, the aborigines, constitute a negative factor in our

[42] "*La educación nacional*," 1908, in *Estudios sobre educación nacional*.

nationality, and in this erroneous idea they place their only hope of strengthening our nation without the Indian, and in spite of him, in bringing people from Europe to replace him and perhaps to eliminate him."[43] The path followed by the United States or Argentina was not the most appropriate one for Peru. The Peruvian Indian, in contrast to the Indians of those countries, made up the greater portion of the population. He had supported the economy of the country for centuries. He was not such a negative element; quite the contrary: an entire society had been able to subsist dependent upon his labor. All the evils had originated from exploitation. This was not the fault of the Indian, but the fault of his exploiters. Hence, it was important to regenerate the Indian by directing his capacity for work along a path that would dignify him and, with him, the nation, of which he was a very important part.

The Indian was looked upon as a parasitical class that did not produce. Such a statement could not be properly made about the Indian, since he had been the object of many forms of exploitation. Certainly the Indian did not produce as he would if the fruit of his labor were destined to his own well-being. Moreover, the Indian lacked a field of action in which to develop his own efforts, since he had been despoiled of his lands and isolated from the rest of society. "Establish means of communication between the cities and the valleys and highlands," said Villarán, "establish commercial routes between the most populous places of the *sierra* and the coast, and millions of those miserable Indians will rise from their forced inertia and within a few years will be perhaps wealthier and more powerful than we."

It was wrong to believe that the Indian was incompetent and a degenerate. "He is today, as in the time of his grandeur, healthy and strong, sober and prolific. The intellectual and manual accomplishments which produced the monuments of Inca civilization can be repeated today and extended by the aid of modern science and skills." Instead of exploiting the Indian, give him the resources necessary for exploitation so that he can make his environment produce. With the aid of science the Indian would become vigorous and active. "If we can succeed in giving him the means by which he can acquire wealth and education, the future will hold for us, we can be certain, un-

[43] *El factor económico en la educación nacional, 1908.*

expected changes." The best way to educate the Indian was to break the isolation to which he had been subjected by placing him in contact with the white man who works. "A distinguished engineer with a profound knowledge of the Indian said that the hammer and the wrench had today a greater educating power than the alphabet." This did not mean that we must "refuse the aboriginal race formal education, but should offer him at the same time the objective education of work and example; school then appears not as the beginning of culture but as its auxiliary."

Mariano Cornejo objected to a projected law denying illiterates the right to vote. To deny the vote to those who could not read, he said, was to take away the last right from the Indian. "You are willing to deprive of its political rights a race that is the basis of a nation"; these are the men "who provide you with the resources for your wealth and who, when there is a national war, cross great deserts and die at the frontier for the honor of the flag, and when there is a civil war come into the streets of Lima barefoot and naked to defend constitutional order. . . . You are willing to deny those men all their rights and leave them only obligations." Love for one's country is not something that can be learned only in schools. "Love for one's country is a natural instinct, the same as love for one's family or humanity. It exists in all peoples close to nature" and, therefore, in the Indian. To think otherwise, on the basis of a purely utilitarian feeling, is to ignore reality completely. More concretely, in defense of the Indian, Cornejo supported a proposition to regulate the Indian's work so that he might obtain from the state protection for his rights. It was futile to talk of the right to work as an argument against this thesis, as the liberal school understood this right; such liberty did not exist in reality and lent itself to multiple abuses. Among liberal schools, he said, "freedom in labor contracts is everything; it must not be forgotten that the laborer has the right to sell his labor at any price that pleases him and in whatever form he wishes." But this thesis is false and passé for the very same reason. Men "are convinced that that freedom does not exist . . . that the individual who struggles against hunger and necessity finds that he is obliged to accept whatever is proffered." For this reason, "today the most conservative legislators are interventionists; they establish the protection of the state for labor and set up a constant vigilance in order to avoid a situation in which, under the appearance of a deceptive freedom, economic necessity may become a fearful chain of oppression that will force the worker to submit to harsh conditions, dictated by the arbitrary domination of his employer." Indeed, "who can deny that that is, in most cases, the condition of the Indian?"[44]

Freedom as a Basis for Progress

MARIANO CORNEJO, in contrast to the Mexican positivists,[45] made freedom the pivot of progress. Like them, he accepted the positivistic thesis of liberty within order, but he placed emphasis on liberty. True progress is achieved only through a liberty protected by order. But order does not mean dictatorship. Cornejo had the opportunity to set forth his ideas on this matter when he opposed the dictatorship of General Cáceres in 1893. "I never excuse," he said, "and I shall always condemn and curse every dictatorship. As far as I am concerned, there is no reason to excuse this crime against humanity." No order justifies dictatorship. Every dictatorship is a violation of law. For that reason "violating the law in the name of order is like blaspheming in the name of God and like committing murder in the name of morality." Order can only be "the respect of the rights defined by law; order is not a condition like right; it is the result of respect towards conditions essential for a social life; it is the respect for rights. Whoever violates rights violates order and brings on disorder." The only order is the order that is legally established. "If you believe that order consists of using arbitrary authority out of fears founded more or less on the possibility that social stability can be changed . . . then you should relinquish immediately the reins of power . . . for then all the crimes of history are justified." Socrates, the Gracchi, and Jesus "all knew that only *freedom* is *the foundation of social order*." He was, therefore, of the conviction "that I am defending at the same time the most vital principles of society: freedom without which there is no progress." Freedom is the only means and foundation of progress.

---

[44] *Discursos parlamentarios y políticos.*
[45] See my work *Apogeo y decadencia del positivismo en México.*

Dictatorship or, more specifically, tyranny is but a form of anarchy, since it is a violation of the law, of the only order possible in a society which is on the road to progress. "I do not know a worse, a more terrible, a more infamous anarchist," said Cornejo, "than the treacherous soldier who by a *coup d'état* hurls the dynamite of revolution into the very center of society." Revolution is the fatal consequence of tyranny. "Tyranny dishonors countries; the revolution that punishes it restores its honor." Dictatorship is satisfactory for people like the Orientals, who still live in a backward stage of society, but it is not good for people who are attempting to advance down the road of progress. "Centralization, which means backwardness, was born in those nations of the Orient where the dagger and poison direct administration. . . . Perhaps centralization is beneficial for warlike peoples, but decentralization is best for working peoples. The Anglo-Saxon race has advanced in labor because it has always been enamored of decentralization."

The best way to attain progress is by means of evolution, said Cornejo, following Spencer. Peru must follow this path if it desires to progress to the point of becoming a nation. Respect for legal order is one of the paths of evolution. Violence only engenders violence. A dictatorship engenders revolution and the latter in turn counter-revolution, thus making all achievements futile. Achievement under these circumstances is like Penelope's weaving: what is done in one day is undone in one night. Whenever a reform is made, said Cornejo, one must "follow a principle which ought to be a guide for all reorganization." This principle is very simple: "Always make reforms that can themselves be improved, never make reforms that can lead to retrogression, for each cursed reaction disables the chariot of progress for half a century." Reforms must always be in accord with reality, in accordance with circumstances. Otherwise there will always be a great danger, the danger of becoming revolutionaries, "of attempting to change in one day, and completely, secular institutions, because when liberal parties are revolutionary, the conservative parties are reactionary, and the latter, in turn, undo the next day the work of the liberal parties."[46]

[46] *Discursos parlamentarios y políticos.*

VI. POSITIVISM AND SOCIAL REGENERATION

The Strangulation of Bolivia

BOLIVIA, the godchild of the Liberator, fared no better than the rest of its sister Hispanic-American republics. Once its political independence was attained and it was separated from Peru, of which it had been a part during the Colonial period, its history was the same: revolutions and dictatorships. The dictatorships were sometimes liberal, sometimes conservative, but always dictatorships, with periods of anarchy. In 1879, as a result of an incident concerning a Chilean nitrate company, the Republic of Chile declared war on Bolivia and invaded its territory. Peru, complying with the terms of a pact signed with Bolivia, came to its aid; but everything was to no avail, and both countries were defeated by the Chilean forces. In 1880, Bolivia was forced to cede to Chile the nitrate zones of its coast and with them its only outlet to the sea. Bolivia thus was left isolated in the midst of high and almost inaccessible mountains.

This fact, said Guillermo Francovich, "led the Bolivians to a brutal consideration of reality and prepared them for the adoption of principles less idealistic than those which eclecticism and Catholicism had pointed out to them. It was then that the doctrines of positivism which had spread throughout the Latin-American countries appeared in Bolivia.[47] A realistic attitude was adopted in opposition to an idealistic character and vision, and within this realism there was an antireligious element. The liberals adopted the views of the new philosophy, converting it into an instrument of what they considered the social regeneration of Bolivia. The first ideological campaigns in that direction found their best arguments in the positivistic doctrines.

Auguste Comte was the first of the positivistic philosophers to exert an influence upon this movement, although his ideas on the religion of humanity were excluded. One of the centers for spreading this doctrine was the "Literary Circle" of La Paz, which was active from 1876. This circle, composed of the most eminent writers of the city, published in 1877 a review in which they began to introduce to the public some of the works of positivism. The outstanding figure in this circle was Agustín Azpiazu. With a sharp mind and a

[47] *La filosofía en Bolivia.*

good scientific background, he was instrumental in promoting a series of studies to examine Bolivian reality. In 1889 he founded the "Geographic Society of La Paz," whose purpose was to acquire a systematic knowledge of the geography of Bolivia. There was another positivistic group in Sucre, headed by Benjamín Fernández, a university professor of public constitutional law. At the university he opposed the principles of natural law held by Ahrens' followers.

The Liberal party found in positivistic doctrines, as has been said previously, a rich arsenal for attacking a past which they considered the source of Bolivian evils, including the last disaster. Politics, which up to that time had revolved around groups with personal interests, was transformed to provide an atmosphere in which real social problems were discussed. The Liberal party opposed the group which held the government in its power; these groups organized themselves into a party known as the Conservatives. The government likewise found an ally in the church, but the discussions were already different. Mariano Baptista, founder of the Conservative party, expressed it thus when he said in 1883, "For the first time in Bolivia the electoral question involves the social question."

The Problem of the Regeneration of Bolivia

WHAT was the cause of all of Bolivia's troubles? What was the source of all of her blunders? How could the country be regenerated? These were the questions that were troubling the men who sought to regenerate the Bolivian nation. They were the same questions, as we have seen, that other Hispanic Americans in their several countries had asked. Gabriel René-Moreno, in his *Notas biográficas y bibliográficas,* tells us something of Nicomedes Antelo, a Bolivian born in Santa Cruz de la Sierra, who resided in Buenos Aires from 1860 until 1882. In Argentina, Antelo had acquired a frame of reference to judge the troubles of his country. "The philosophy of evolution," said René-Moreno, "as it has recently been formulated by the English and German positivists of the new Darwinian school, was professed by Nicomedes Antelo with sectarian fervor and apostolic authority. . . . The Master of the Buenos Aires school was able to read rapidly the works of Lamarck, Darwin, Herbert Spencer, and Haeckel." As a man, "he had pride befitting a Darwinian naturalist, for he was a descendant on the maternal and paternal sides of the common-law wives and the Spanish soldiers who founded Santa Cruz de la Sierra. . . . He was content to be a Latin, though by inclination he could have been more fittingly an Anglo-Saxon."

Bolivia's faults were judged from a naturalistic point of view. "Will the poor Indian be exterminated by the thrust of our race?" asked Antelo. "If the extinction of inferiors is one of the conditions of universal progress, as some of our modern sages say it is and as I believe it is, the consequences, gentlemen, are irrevocable regard-less of how sad they may be. It is like an amputation that is painful but gets rid of the gangrene and saves one's life." Like Sarmiento in Argentina, Antelo believed that with the disappearance of the Indian race and the *mestizos* Bolivia would be regenerated. He like-wise believed that the brains of the Indians and the *mestizos* were cellularly incapable of conceiving and understanding republican free-dom, with the rights and responsibilities that it implied. On an aver-age, he said, "their brains weighed between five, seven, and ten ounces less than the brain of a man of the pure white race. In the evolution of the human species such an encephalitic mass corresponds physio-logically to a psychic period of said species that is today decrepit, to a mental organism too weak to withstand the function and shock of the intellectual, economic, and political forces with which modern civilization operates within a democracy. . . .

"The Indian is good for nothing. But, he does indeed, " Antelo added, "represent in Bolivia a living force, a mass of passive resist-ance, a concrete induration in the viscera of the social organism." On the other hand, we have "the *mestizos*, a caste as hybrid and sterile for the present ethnological task as the mule is for the development of the horse from the ass. . . . The *mestizos*, excited by their appetites, their minds yoked by the instinct of proselytism of the *caudillo* sys-tem, represent in the human species an inferior variety characteristic of a race composed of Spanish impetuosity and Indian pusillanimity." This mixture produced a class that was both turbulent and servile, anarchistic and passive. "Its tendency is, as is well known, toward idleness, quarreling, servility, and intrigue, all sources of disorder and of the *caudillo* system, just as the stupidity and the abject fear of the Inca Indian are fused together to perpetuate a despotic society."

The indigenous race and the *mestizo* will lose the struggle for existence just as men, plants, and animals are today becoming extinct in Australia right before our eyes. This is happening simply because the imported species and the new species already acclimated are better suited for the struggle. Nicomedes Antelo continued, "And for the sake of the efficacy proper to evolution, may the Indian and the *mestizo* of Bolivia disappear as quickly as possible; those two archaic agents—one Inca and the other colonial—may they be destroyed under the foot of European immigration." Antelo found the justification for this thesis in Argentine social life. All of America was aware of the long-drawn-out war that had been waged between the *mestizo* castes of the interior, led by Rosas, and the Creoles of the capital. In this struggle the civilization of the latter had overcome the barbarism of the former. The Bolivian professor living at that time in Buenos Aires witnessed the great material advance of Argentina and the daily advance of its progress. The great spectacle dazzled him. "He looked with amazement," said René-Moreno, "at the almost mechanical precision of the sociological phenomenon by which, as the Indian and *mestizo* disappeared, succumbing in the struggle for existence to the irresistible superiority of the Indo-European races, public order was established among the people, moral and intellectual progress increased by rapid strides, wealth and well-being spread to all areas of the republic."

By comparing this progress with the evils of his country, he realized the need to resort to drastic remedies. Everything was confusion; Bolivian society produced only sterile, bloody militarism with which to protect and defend itself. "It was either the *caudillo* system or revolution." All of the trouble originated, said Antelo, in the "heterogeneity of races, customs, languages, temperament, and even ideas." The only thing that held all this together was "a regime imposed by the sword of the liberators." Antelo's ideas did not change. "Twenty years of subsequent studies in Buenos Aires," said René-Moreno, "following day by day the development of positivistic sciences only confirmed his first convictions. Following the positivists, Antelo held that liberty and order in Bolivia should not be sought except in the area of *material well-being,* by bringing into play all the economic agents which industrial arts suggest and all the natural resources which the country affords. In 1882 as in 1860, his political principle was *work*." Immigration and industrialization could be, in short, the remedies proposed for the regeneration of Bolivia—immigration and industrialization, the same remedies that all of the intellectual emancipators of Hispanic America had dreamed of for their countries.

Spencer and the New Bolivian Order

IN 1889 the Bolivian Liberal party defeated the Conservatives. The revolution offered the generation molded by positivism the desired opportunity. Positivism's influence was felt in all fields. The state was not long in placing under its control all education, civil as well as ecclesiastical. In 1909, said Guillermo Francovich, the first teachers' college was founded under the direction of Belgian pedagogues. The new teachers were products of the doctrine of secularism. In 1913 courses in religion and Christian doctrine were removed from the curriculum of the primary and secondary schools. Positivism also furnished the bases for pitiless studies on Bolivian reality. *Pueblo Enfermo*, by Alcides Arguedas, was one of the most outstanding of these studies.

But at the same time a fanatic and superficial mentality developed that refused to see beyond the experience of realities that transcend the experimental in the material world. Spencer, in the face of this situation, represents a kind of reaction. "If Spencer," said Francovich, "stayed within the purely positivistic traditions, his doctrines had some characteristics that seemed to lead thought back toward generalizations of a philosophical type and toward the solution of religious anxieties."[48] The ideas of Spencerian evolution and progress provided an explanation for changes in conditions, and thereby the desire for the social and political transformation of the Republic of Bolivia was justified. Francovich's thesis regarding the existence of something beyond our experiences opened the doors to religious sentiment.

The most prominent followers of Spencer were two teachers, Luis Arce Lacaze and Daniel Sánchez Bustamante. Arce Lacaze was a professor at the University of Sucre and the author of a book entitled *Filosofía del derecho*, published in 1892. Later, in 1918, he turned

[48] *La filosofía en Bolivia.*

toward the pragmatism of William James. Sánchez Bustamante, a professor in the University of La Paz, also wrote on jurisprudence.

His book *Principios de derecho* shows the influence of both Guyau and Spencer. Both philosophers placed special emphasis on the escape door that Spencer left in regard to the world of the absolute which is beyond the reach of all experience. "The ultimate destiny of man," said Arce Lacaze, "is the one that faith teaches us and that philosophy only treats in one respect: to demonstrate the incompetence of science in these problems by proving that wherever science does broach them, it loses its value and its essential character." For his part, Sánchez Bustamante said, "To erect the mechanism of forces and of interests into a single law is like affirming that mechanism as such is the only reality, and this is what has never been demonstrated and never can be."[49]

Within this current of thought, also influenced by the Argentine philosopher José Ingenieros, was the thought of Ignacio Prudencia Bustillo, professor of legal philosophy in the University of Sucre law school from 1918 to 1921. In his book *Ensayo de filosofía jurídica*, published in 1923, he set forth his philosophical ideas and his ideas on how to raise Bolivian reality to the level of contemporary progress. Bustillo likewise aspired to change this reality. The methods he proposed to effect the transformation were, as will be seen, similar to those proposed by other Hispanic American teachers.

"We could not say now," he affirmed, "up to what point university teaching has made its influence felt on politics. . . . At any rate the verbalistic and charlatan education that our statesmen have received in the great law faculties has not contributed in any way whatsoever to the effective progress of the country." Hence the need to direct efforts down other paths. "Our efforts today must be directed toward providing a *practical education,* one that will be the opposite of the rhetorical education our fathers and we received." We have much to learn from North America in this matter. We must "establish 'model farms' like those set up in the United States by Booker T. Washington for the education of the Negro." On our model farms the "Indians could learn modern methods of cultivating the land." The country needs fewer literary-trained men and more technicians, agron-

[49] Quoted by Francovich.

omists, and mercantile specialists. "All those who, because of money or talent, direct the public destiny ought to see that youth derive their activities from really productive works drawing them away from the practice of law where souls are corrupted."

But if it was not possible to direct young men down other paths, it was at least necessary to set the course of law down more practical roads. "Within a short time," he said, "one could see the result: students would conduct personal investigations, they would understand the intimate meaning of what is called science in the twentieth century." Realism should take the place of the old judicial doctrines. The doctrine we are popularizing, he said, is known in the scientific world as realism. "It means a reaction against natural law, and at the same time it is an effort to employ in judicial, social, and political investigations the same experimental methods that have caused the physical and biological sciences to advance so much." In accord with the new doctrine, "it is no longer necessary to seek a generating principle in the labyrinth of metaphysical disquisitions. It is sufficient for us to observe the modalities of law in the relations that are within our reach, in order to define it exactly . . . it is scarcely a matter of a change in proceedings, but therein lies the entire secret of scientific progress."

Through realism a great step may be taken toward tolerance. "If one recalls," said Bustillo, "the campaign that coincided with the introduction of Herbert Spencer into teaching, he will note that the positivist generations attacked the millenary fortress—religion—without full knowledge or prior investigation. . . . By a singular incomprehension our small-town positivists did not turn toward scientific investigation but toward the vulgarity of irreligiosity. Positivism produced few learned men here, but many sectarians." They did not learn that what makes positivism a valid doctrine is its method of confronting reality by directing it. Bolivian positivists saw in this doctrine only a new form of empty declarations. The positivists did not learn to know their reality; they simply changed their fanaticism. Bustillo then attempted to set positivism on its true path. "Not only is it easy and possible to complete scientific effort by philosophical speculation," he said, "but it is necessary to create a scientific philosophy that synthesizes the isolated results of investigation." We all feel compelled to affirm our criterion, but we find "science incomplete" and "aprioristic philosophy sterile and inconstant. . . . Let us reconcile both disciplines and create a scientific philosophy that will be adequate and have a firm foundation. The man in our day who successfully realizes this attempt will have the glory of rejuvenating and invigorating positivistic philosophy, but to achieve this, he will have to proceed with less intransigence than Auguste Comte."[50]

The New Positivism of Ignacio Pudencio Bustillo

THE REGENERATION of Bolivian education depended in a large measure on the reconciliation of science and philosophy. It was not a matter of going from an a priori fanaticism to a positivistic fanaticism, but rather of reconciling both attitudes by imbuing the Bolivian with a sense of his reality so that he would not be blind to any one of its two aspects, the material and the spiritual. Bustillo had stumbled upon the popular philosophy of his time, intuitive philosophy. It provided the materials for the desired synthesis.

The scientific method was inadequate to discover the multiple facets of reality. There is "an unknown world," he said, "perhaps greater than the one we have succeeded in discovering with the help of our senses and our scientific instruments. It is the world of the nonexperimental—that is, it is the world that does not lend itself to the means of investigation utilized by the scholar." Spencer was already aware of this reality and had pointed it out in his philosophy. For this reason, faced with the obscure and unfathomable problems that nature poses daily, the "scholar shrugs his shoulders and prefers his humble truth to metaphysical hypotheses, which attempt to explain what cannot be perceived in any way."

Could the philosophy in vogue, intuitionalism, offer the desired solution? "The philosophy in vogue," said Bustillo, "dignified by the talent of Bergson in France and by James in the United States, utilizes intuition to probe the world that escapes scientific experimentalism." But this intuition, he added, "little or poorly comprehended, contradictory in its results, constitutes a dangerous way to philosophize, for it lends itself to fantasy and caprice. . . . We cannot abandon it for the solid positions of scientific positivism which, mitigated

[50] *Ensayo de una filosofía jurídica.*

by the idealism of a philosophy based on experimental data, the data of experience, appears to us as a sure support for humanity dragged along forever by contradictory doctrines.

The only solution is a scientific philosophy which combines the transcendental and experimental methods. This is the doctrine that must be formulated. "Observation, the generous fountain of science, is deficient and incomplete. It embraces only a small part of the real world and is not very sure of its results, especially when it chooses as the object of its investigations that which is endowed with life or that which animates the unfathomable breath of the spirit." Hence scientific philosophy must "complement science: where the latter stops, the former must begin, and its hypotheses are those that, by unifying the fragments of scientific knowledge, form a systematic conjunct which resolves the major part of the problems of nature by including in it organized beings and societies."

We are not, however, to understand scientific philosophy as "mere routine and fondness for base and ignoble materialism; it represents, rather, the idealistic side of the human spirit. In the final analysis, what are hypotheses but associations of our imagination which always tends to perfect the real?" Science is thus placed in the service of idealism or the perfection of the real. "The only difference between this *positivistic metaphysics* and *spiritualistic metaphysics* is that the former proceeds from scientific data and the latter from an a priori principle." In order to orient our criteria, we have the lucid view of science, which is the most accurate and corresponds best to our insatiable intellectual curiosity. Following this "method, we can no longer doubt the existence of social laws over which the strict law of causality rules, in spite of freedom that like any other natural phenomenon is subject, in turn, to laws."

In the field of social sciences, Bustillo said, pure deduction becomes a dangerous method. "At first glance it seems destined to cure all the social evils, but it soon causes more serious infirmities. Basically, "inductive reasoning consists of fleeing systematically from *ready*-made ideas, from preconceived opinions, and from all the vices of thought. The inductive method in sociology teaches us to place our faith only in the observation of reality." But if this goes to the extreme, investigation becomes petty, too dependent on data, as if someone had cut its wings so that it could not lift itself into the lofty regions of philosophical generalization." What is the solution? What is the best method? Bustillo concluded that "the best method was eclectic, half-inductive and half-deductive."[51]

VII. POSITIVISM AS EDUCATION FOR FREEDOM

Comte and Argentine Liberalism

AUGUSTE COMTE's influence, said Alejandro Korn, emanated from the Normal School at Paraná. But it was no longer authentic positivism. "In short, Comte upheld the realm of authority and was in disagreement with all democratic tendencies; he had also committed the error of rejecting the concept of evolution." In Comtian positivism the individual was subject to the sociocracy. "These ideas," continued Korn, "were irreconcilable with our milieu; it was necessary for us to affirm evolution and democracy. The Normal School group took from Comte only his theory on the three stages of knowledge and a certain anticlericalism which fundamentally was liberal, not Comtian."[52]

In fact, the Paraná school founded by Domingo F. Sarmiento in 1870 was to be the focal point of Comtian positivism in Argentina, but adapted to Argentina itself. The ideas of the French philosopher were to be adapted, distorted, and placed at the service of the spirit represented by Sarmiento. Positivism and Sarmiento followed the same paths, but the circumstances were different. Spanish America, Argentina in particular, needed an order, but not an order similar to that represented by the despotism of Rosas. Once Rosas was defeated, another order must be established to safeguard the freedom of the individual, the goal of all heroisms and struggles. The new order should be derived from the very will of the individual himself. It was to be a social order for the realization of the highest aims of the individual, and such an order could be effected only by means of education.

The Normal School of Paraná was founded with this in mind, and from this school came the educators of the new Argentine generations.

[51] *Ibid.*
[52] "*Influencias filosóficas en la evolución nacional,*" in *Obras,* III.

The formation of a new Hispanic America, stripped of all the defects of its past, was to begin in this school. The Hispanic America dreamed of by all the leaders of its intellectual emancipation was to take shape. Still without any organized doctrine but with a great will to carry out such an emancipation, Hispanic Americans were soon to find in various European philosophical doctrines, especially positivism, the formulas that would give expression to the realization of these desires.

Pedro Scalabrini, an Italian professor, came to the Normal School at Paraná. Like Ameghino, he had devoted himself to the study of paleontology, but he was also interested in other subjects. He came to Argentina in 1868, and in 1875 he published a book on *Derecho público Argentino,* in which the humanistic ideals of Krause were evident. In 1889 he published a work entitled *Materialismo, darwinismo, y positivismo* and a series of *Cartas scientíficas.* At the Normal School he taught science and philosophy. Comte was one of the subjects that figured prominently in his teaching. Of the forty annual topics in his course in philosophy, four dealt with the official program and the rest were devoted to elucidating Comte's philosophy. Victor Mercantes tells us about his teaching methods: "Scalabrini's purpose in teaching was to produce thinkers; consequently, he refrained from giving opinions; he gave his students absolute freedom to expound, and he never ranted in any discussion by declaring himself for such and such a belief." For him, it was important to think, not to recite. "He had many students, and many of them spread his ideas, not within the closed formalism that commonly destroys great concepts, but with the interpretative freedom to which their teacher had accustomed them."[53] The school which developed here spread Comte throughout Argentina, but it was a Comte adapted to the educational needs of this country. This school rejected the religion, the priesthood, and the apostleship of the Comtian doctrine.

The Individual and His Education for Freedom

BEFORE proceeding, it will be of interest to point out two diametrically opposed interpretations of positivism in Hispanic America: the Mexican and the Argentine. These two interpretations had their ori-

---

[53] "*El educacionalista Pedro Scalabrini,*" *Revista de filosofía,* Vol. V. (Buenos Aires, 1917).

gin in the different circumstances which they were attempting to confront. In Mexico, positivism was adopted because it was considered a good instrument for unifying the nation in the face of the anarchy that followed independence, an anarchy that had bloodied the soil for almost half a century. Mexico was in need of a doctrine which, by unifying the criteria, would bring about an agreement in the political and social fields. The same agreement that was observed to exist in the field of positivistic science was sought in the social field. This science did not discuss, it simply *demonstrated*, and what it demonstrated was within the grasp of any individual who was interested, so that there was no place for disputes or anarchy. Positivistic science always offered a common basis for truths. The Mexican positivists thought that if this common basis of truths could be successfully carried over to the social field, anarchy and revolutions would come to an end. They were determined to establish this common basis of truths in the social field. Their educational systems were directed to this end. They attempted to base the new order on uniformity of opinion. Gabino Barreda, speaking of education, said, "It must be the same for all regardless of what profession a man chooses, for however much the professions may appear to differ, they all must work together since they have a common objective—social well-being." When the time comes that all the members of a society think in a like manner in this field, we shall have put an end to social anarchy. A "common basis of truth"[54] was, then, what was lacking. It was therefore necessary to plan the education of the individual in full detail so that only a minimum was left to his own interpretation. "A sole avenue that lends itself to error," said Barreda, "a single source of real ideas that abandons itself to arbitrariness and to individual whim is enough to ruin an entire educational program regardless of how well put together the rest of it may seem." A scientific education that demonstrates what it teaches is the best instrument. To demonstrate the truth, said Barreda, is "the surest prelude to peace and social order, for it will place all the citizens in a position to appraise all the facts in a similar manner, and for the same reason it will make all opinions uniform as far as possible."

In Argentina, the positivism of the Normal School at Paraná was

[54] See my work *Positivismo en México.*

but the fruit of Sarmiento's ideals. He had insisted on a civilizing task. The principal means for the greatest attainment of civilization in Argentina was to stimulate the individual. Anglo-Saxon nations— the model—were great because every citizen was responsible for his own individual greatness. The politics of civilized individualism were the opposite of the politics of the "barbarian" masses of Rosas. The "individualistic" positivism of Argentina was the best doctrine for the education of the New America. The doctrine of Rosas, supported by the "barbarian" masses and held together by the supreme will of the dictator, was the opposite of creative individualism. The Normal School at Paraná assumed the responsibility of stimulating this individualism by using the doctrine of Auguste Comte, but only in those theses which agreed with this ideal.

The principal animator and chief of the positivistic school of Paraná was J. Alfredo Ferreira (1863–1935), the best-known student of Pedro Scalabrini. Ferreira was also influenced by some of the ideas of the North American teachers whom Sarmiento had brought to the Paraná school. The public school system in Argentina was the result of these influences. Ferreira attempted to set up model schools throughout Argentina The first school of this kind was established in Esquina, in the province of Corrientes, his birthplace. Education in this department was almost nonexistent and in a state of penury. The Argentine educator attempted to save Esquina from disgrace by making it the first "democratic school for both government officials and private citizens: for government officials by teaching them how they should stimulate the citizens to favor beneficial actions and institutions; for parents by showing them how they should be concerned fundamentally for the education of their children; and, in general, for private citizens by teaching them that not everything should be expected from providential governments."[55] Collaborating with Ferreira were some Argentine teachers and two North American teachers, Edith Howe and Cora Hill, brought to Argentina by Sarmiento.

What were the bases of this school for democracy? What were the bases of a school that attempted to stimulate creative freedom of the individual and with it a love for freedom? In his *Bases para un*

[55] In Bassi, *J. Alfredo Ferreira.*

plan de estudios de educación primaria, Ferreira, among other things, affirmed: "The student in the common school ought only to study *directly* things, beings, and natural and social facts of the region in which he lives. The theoretical acquisition of knowledge in a text or from the explanation of the teacher, not derived from observation and induction itself, does not educate or educates poorly. Such knowledge only serves to *oppress* the mind while youth has the scholarly obligation to remember it, and then disappears, leaving only the memory of the painful, fruitless, and harmful task employed by the mind to receive it." Ferreira took the direct observation of things from positivism. Proceeding according to a rigorously scientific method, youth must, he said, continue "advancing into the unknown by means of the known, progressing from the observation of material objects to subjective principles which control them, copying in their individual investigation the intellectual evolution of the race by fulfilling the psychological law formulated by Auguste Comte." Alberdi's ideal of a philosophy that should concern itself with the problems peculiar to Latin America, and more concretely with the problems peculiar to Argentina, appeared in Ferreira's educational ideas. "The student's investigations," he said, "should not extend beyond the area in which he lives, except incidentally for the purpose of making comparisons that may help him to formulate for himself a clear idea of the absolute and relative value of things, beings, and natural and sociological phenomena which he is studying directly."[56]

Direct observation of things stimulates originality and then personality. Ferreira, in contrast to the Mexican positivists, was concerned with multiplicity and not with unity. He hoped that every Argentine would come to think in an original way, since with this thought he would secure his love for liberty. There was no common basis for truth. True reality is rich in variety, and within reality there lies the originality that is the point of departure for freedom. "The student," said Ferreira, "instead of being required to repeat more or less from memory the ideas of his teacher, will have to express his ideas acquired directly from things and facts *in his own language and according to his own intellectual make-up*," since not every individual looks at the same thing in the same way.

[56] *Ibid.*

From this Ferreira drew the same inferences of a political and social character as his predecessors. "If all the students in a class have studied a few descriptions, if they all repeat them with a hopeless uniformity," then there is neither originality nor liberty. "We must realize," he added, "that all the *silent* and *uniform congresses,* the *unilateral political groups,* the republican *caesarism,* have arisen in great part from the uniformity in the classroom. That kind of school," he said, "kills personality; it produces dictatorship. . . . It has contributed, like ignorance itself, like the decadent race, like the great open spaces without an inhabitants, like the laws of historical inheritance, like the evil political education, to leading the country to the abyss of an economic bankruptcy that has no precedence in the civilized world (in complete peace, in complete health); it has led to the sanctioning, as a republican practice, in a nation open to all the most advanced ideas, of a most modern political formula of dictatorship and power for the sake of power, and hence they say, 'I must be governed by reason or by force,'—more commonly and more easily by force." Following these same ideas, Ferreira was opposed to examinations; they were considered a battle "more sterile than all the victories of caesarism over freedom." Examinations dull the personality of the student. "Many of those same brilliant students who have performed brilliantly but to no effect in the classrooms," said Ferreira, "with a certain infantile presumptuousness, which destroys the bases of a solid character, fade away in life. They no longer feel the exterior compulsion of the first lesson or of the next examination, and they do not work. They are like a freed slave who no longer feels the major-domo's whip. They have been given their freedom with all the sacramental formulas, but not having learned to work spontaneously, they are poor citizens in the republic of science." Discussion does not do any damage. Spontaneity is always creative. "Freedom of discussion entails no danger; only slavery is to be feared. All the great original thinkers have gone astray many times; only the young are not allowed to defend an error; for that reason the professor ignores them to teach them a truth which later, with the passing of the years, becomes an academic truth. Hence the student comes to respect the opinion of the teacher more than he does the truth; the examination system strengthens this tendency and contributes effectively to suffocating a sincere and respectful love for science, replacing it with a shameful desire to know only the answers to the examination questions."[57]

Alfredo Ferreira followed the same line of thought as his illustrious predecessors, Echeverría, Alberdi, and Sarmiento. Like them he attempted to destroy the roots of the fatal heritage that was making Hispanic Americans a people outside the civilizing march of humanity. His educational reforms were directed against the Spanish tradition, against all the roots of permanent despotisms. He tried, said his student Angel Bassi, to modify the subconscious mind of the people; he tried "to transform them from absolutists into a democratic people." Like his predecessors he also sought to establish the bases upon which a vigorous nationality could arise, the product of the most vigorous of personalities. These bases, he said, "rested on the general concept that the objective of teaching is not the assimilation of knowledge but rather production itself." His concern with an observable and immediate reality had come from positivism. Positivism refused to recognize the supra-sensible, the metaphysical, which was beyond experience. Ferreira also renounced the study of any reality that was not his own, that was not immediate and within reach of the Argentine man. The world of reality that was outside the real experience of this man was rejected. Studies should be based on the immediate, on what this man could really know. "Of what importance is the River Danube to the Argentine who cannot know it? What should be important to him is the River Paraná and all those realities that are within his grasp. This reality must be the point of departure." Robinson Crusoe was the ideal type of man. Is not that solitary man on the island who studies directly and by himself the things which influence him and which he uses, adapts himself to, invents, and saves himself, asked Ferreira, preferable to the theoretical man who knows many things because he was told them or read them?

The Argentine educator synthesized his ideas in the plan that he drew up specifically for the province of Corrientes and in general for the entire Argentine nation. Here are the principal ideas of his plan: "Education must be experimental, positivistic, and of the present. . . . The plan must answer both present and future needs. . . . For every

[57] *Ibid.*

213

a priori program is troublesome since it sets limitations and precise details, which in practice become broad or narrow and destroy the initiative of both teachers and students, whose physical, intellectual, and moral perfection depend principally on their individual spontaneous work. . . . We must destroy the uniformity of teaching specific subjects and give only general directions within which the action of both teachers and students can develop freely. . . . Examinations are formulas that prove nothing; therefore they are eliminated and replaced by exhibits of work and class demonstrations on what is being done." The result will be a school system with its own character from which will come individuals dedicated to creative liberty.

The Argentine Interpretation of Positivism

ANYONE who, like Ferreira, spoke of freedom of interpretation in education and originality as the end of education would not accept any doctrine literally. Positivism was to be interpreted according to the very circumstances of its interpreter. In a letter sent to P. Lacalde, thanking him for some positivistic propaganda pamphlets, Ferreira said, "Without disregarding the importance of systematic propaganda which is best formulated on the sources themselves, the teachers' books, we here accept the school particularly for the unlimited guidance it gives to the human mind." But, he added, "we also understand that the most pleasant social and subjective creations lose a great portion of their importance when they are taken *literally*. . . . The letter not only kills the interpretative and industrious spirit, but it also helps to kill the institutions themselves or to impede their success." Hence, he concluded, "Comte's great system should be adapted and not immobilized during its birth and growth. Comte himself said that the only absolute principle is that everything is relative. By creating sociology, he gave us this scientific principle of the social concept ruled by natural laws but still modifiable." Social organisms must be for the sociologist the object of study, "modification, and direction and not the object of antiscientific and immoral vexations and hatreds such as I have seen in the minds and on the lips of many *systematic positivists*. . . . If in truth sociologists and statesmen aspire to direct society or effectively influence it, they must adapt themselves to their respective social media. If not, instead of thinkers, they will be mere repeaters of formulas as widely recognized as they are opportune or inopportune, according to the situation." And since we, he added, "are fortunate to have discovered a few great established relative principles, we must contribute something of ourselves and of the active spirit, thus giving them an opportunity to develop. . . . Anything else would make of us only empty, rhetorical chatterers so anathematized by Comte."[58]

Ferreira deduced from Comte several ideas in defense of his own theses. "We do not know the author of the famous motto 'Order and Liberty,' " he said. "By unfurling this banner, we could proclaim the freedom of instruction and the predominance of central power over local power. . . . Positivism is the systematic organ of freedom of exposition and examination because it can withstand every decisive demonstration."[59] As for the control of education by the state, he believed in the independence of education and based his argument on Comte. "Temporal power must renounce every didactic monopoly. . . . The state must renounce every complete system of general education, save the stimuli of certain branches which are threatened by neglect, especially primary education and some institutions of higher special learning, but the academies, even scientific ones must be suppressed." The vigilance "of the government over private institutions must relate not to doctrine but to customs. Every theological and metaphysical theory must be suppressed, leaving to each one the maintenance of his cult and of the instruction that he prefers."[60]

Comtism was only an instrumental philosophy. It, said Ferreira, is no longer the positivism that has been developing. For "every day the relativity of ideas and sciences becomes stronger. . . . it is impossible to know the cosmic universe through the human structure, our science declares only subjective truths." The epoch of absolute truth written in capital letters has passed. The old unilateral doctrines, by virtue of which our illustrious ancestors fought furiously among themselves to be able to leave us a heritage, are rapidly changing into multilateral doctrines to make us more worthy of admiring "the vast and beloved universe." We are also convinced that the indi-

---

[58] *"Carta a P. Lacalde,"* in *La escuela positiva,* Año II (Corrientes, 1896).

[59] *"Síntesis de la política positiva de Comte,"* in *La escuela positiva,* Año V (1899).

[60] *Ibid.*

vidual temperament is almost everything. "Temperament is a synthesis of heritages and adoptions accumulated down through thousands of zoological and even botanical generations. Each one of us reasons much less by rules of logic than with our own temperament." Because of our temperament," some of us view the world through the eye of a needle, while others view it through the grandiose pantheism of Faust. . . . Savages, equals, and equalitarians are more and more in the background."[61]

VIII. POSITIVISM AND THE ARGENTINE BOURGEOISIE

The Generation of 1880

THE GENERATION dreamed of by the leaders of the intellectual emancipation of Argentina seemed to appear in 1880 in Buenos Aires. Spencer, in whose ideas Sarmiento had found an expression of his own ideas, appears as the philosopher of the generation that was to carry out the civilizing period in Argentina. His influence was greater than Comte's, even though his ideas did not produce a school as Comte's had in Paraná: "The men of 1880," said Alejandro Korn, "warmly embraced Spencer's agnostic and evolutionary doctrine while at the same time keeping abreast of the related currents of the universal movement. . . . They professed the individualistic tendencies of English liberalism; they proclaimed the excellence of the experimental method; sometimes they used it, and they distinguished themselves by adhering to a just and honest criterion." But, Korn added, "absorbed by European culture, they placed no value on the innate strength of the Argentine soul, and for the solution of our troubles, they sought exotic remedies. They had the mentality of officeholders and never identified themselves with the masses; men of thought, they lacked a militant push. Others fought with the ideas that they disseminated."[62]

This generation, it is said, leaned more and more toward political and social conservatism. Endowed with rare intelligence, the men of this generation used it for the benefit of their very personal interests. The oligarchy was their greatest expression. They did not accept Comte, since they did not share his idea of a hierarchal, antidemo-

[61] Bassi, *J. Alfredo Ferreira.*
[62] *"Influencias filósoficas en la evolución nacional."*

cratic sociocracy. They were in closer agreement with Spencer's liberalism, which led to a kind of society in which the individual could attain maximum liberty. In some respects this group resembled the Mexican *Científicos,* who for the same reasons were also in close agreement with Spencer. The oligarchy surrounding the Dictator Profirio Díaz was the type of government supported by the Mexican *Científicos.* The Argentine positivists conceived of civilization as the triumph of personal effort as expressed in wealth obtained by means of industrial exploitation. Juan Agustín García, one of the most distinguished members of this generation, criticized this group and was horrified to think of the Argentine republic "as a colossal ranch bustling with railroads and canals, full of factories, with populous cities abounding in wealth of all kinds, but without a single learned man, artist, or philosopher. . . . I should prefer," he said, "to belong to the most wretched corner of the earth where there still lives a feeling for beauty, truth, and goodness." García attributed all of Argentina's evils to Spencer, the evils of public education as well as those of politics. Comte, he said, made an admirable country out of Brazil when he gave it the motto "Order and Progress." Spencer, on the other hand, made it uncivilized and wretched.[63]

Among others who belonged to this generation were José Nicolás Matienzo, Juan Agustín García, Rodolfo Rivarola, Luis M. Drago, Norberto Piñero, Ernesto Quesada, and José María Ramos Mejía. Men like Carlos Octavio Bunge and José Ingenieros, although they did not properly belong to this generation, were influenced by it and moved in its circle or had certain close relationships with members of this group which identified them with the generation. In a short time the influence of the generation of 1880 was felt strongly, dominating all the educational circles, public administration, and business. This generation seemed destined to be the representative of the Argentine *bourgeoisie,* in whose hands "civilization" was to attain its greatest development. Sarmiento's dream of Argentina as the United States of South America seemed to be a fact. But this generation, like others of its kind in all parts of Hispanic America, did not know how to realize or could not put into effect such a dream. Just as they had done in all Hispanic America, the great European *bourgeoisie* made

[63] *Sobre nuestra incultura.*

217

the Argentine *bourgeoisie* mere bookkeepers for their business. Railroads began to cross the pampas, industries flourished in the cities, banks began to multiply, and wealth seemed to increase; but the firms that owned these railroads, industries, and banks were foreign. People spoke of the Argentine essence, but were unable to find it in that civilized world which had little or nothing to do with Argentina.

Many of the best men of this generation persisted in seeking this essence in the past, as Juan Agustín García (1862–1923) had done in his *Ciudad Indiana*. Others, like José María Ramos Mejía (1826–82), persisted in trying to understand the most vigorous figures of the immediate past, like Rosas. But in this past and these figures they saw only what their minds, formed by the latest European philosophies and without any direct contact with Argentine reality, allowed them to see. Paul Groussac, who was a link between the generation of the leaders of the intellectual emancipation of Argentina and the men of this positivist generation, followers of Spencer, had foreseen this result and pointed out its dangers when he said: "In relatively greater degrees and more quickly than the United States, the Argentine republic has come to be the crossroads of nationalities. This migratory onrush has been so violent that it could absorb our national elements; language, political institutions, taste, and traditional ideas. Under the impulse of Spencerian progress, which is really the triumph of heterogeneity, we should be apprehensive lest material considerations gradually dislodge from the Argentine soul its idealistic ambitions, without which all national prosperity is built on sand. In the face of the possible loss of our ideals it would be a small matter for us to become alarmed at the disappearance of our traditions when our very nationality was in danger. . . . And it is, nevertheless, this supreme hour which some have chosen to extol the utilitarian education which has brought us to where we are, and to condemn classical culture which in itself is a school of patriotism and moral nobility."[64]

The Ideal of an Argentine Race

JOSÉ INGENIEROS (1877–1925), the son of Italian immigrants, interpreted Argentine history in relation to the immigrant groups that made up the bulk of the population. The European race represented

[64] In the work cited by A. Korn.

civilization; the autochthonous, barbarism. The struggle of the members of the generation of May against Rosas was regarded as the struggle of the "Euro-Argentine" race against the gaucho or Hispanic-indigenous race. All the leaders of the political independence of Argentina—Moreno, Rivadavia, and the Unitarians—were also included in the Euro-Argentina race. They had fought the gaucho *caudillos* like Rosas and Quiroga after they had defeated Spain. In this struggle the gaucho race had won. But the men who carried out the ideal of the new race and who triumphed were Sarmiento and Alberdi.

Ingenieros said, "The greater part of the grazing lands were occupied by farmers, the gaucho replaced by new settlers, wagons by railroads, and field commanders by school teachers. A new Euro-Argentine race, cultivated, hard working, and democratic, grew up at the expense of the colonial gaucho race, which was illiterate, anarchistic, and feudal." He continued, "Moreno sought from Europe teachers for the schools, capital for industry, and hands for agriculture, and Rivadavia did the same. And the Argentine political exiles did likewise also. When they were in power from 1852 on, they attracted teachers, capital, and laborers to the country." When Alberdi said that to "govern is to populate," Ingenieros noted that he added decisively, "populate with Europeans." And when Sarmiento urged the Argentines "to be like the United States," he declared that Argentina was a bit of Europe sprouting on American soil. None of them was mistaken. Ameghino later repeated "that the white race was, of all the human races, the superior, and it was destined in the future to dominate the globe."

Ingenieros saw the future of Argentina thus: "There are already unmistakable elements of judgment to appreciate the advent of a *white Argentine race* that will soon allow us *to erase the stigma of inferiority* with which the Europeans have always marked the South Americans." At present, he added, in the army, "instead of mercenary natives and gauchos, it is the white citizen who is the custodian of the dignity of the nation." Within fifteen to one hundred years the consequences would be more important and easier to prognosticate. In the Argentine territory, emancipated a century ago by the thought and the action of from one to ten thousand Euro-Argentines, there would live a race "composed of from fifteen to one hundred million whites who during their leisure hours will read the chronicles of the exterminated indigenous races, the histories of the gaucho *mestizos* who retarded the development of the white race, and perhaps the gaucho poems of Martín Fierro, Santos Vega, or the novels of Juan Moreno."[65]

Europe in America. The independence struggle was now directed against America herself, for men of this generation attempted to make America another Europe. The model was North America. The latter, by almost annihilating the Indians, had founded another Europe, young and full of vigor. This was the meaning of "civilization" for Argentina. It was necessary to smother the past by all possible means, to change minds by education and men by immigration. Argentina followed the same path as the rest of the Spanish American countries, but it had greater success. In Mexico, for example, the past was still too deeply rooted. The Indian and the Creole were of such importance that their vigor could not be stifled. The *mestizo*, a synthesis of both races, became the active element of what was to be called the "Mexican *bourgeoisie.*" This *bourgeoisie* never displayed any pride in the fact that it belonged to a European race, although it did scorn the Indian. The *metizo* was the source of progress for the Mexican nation. Justo Sierra, in his essay entitled *México social y político*, interpreted Mexican history from the point of view that the *mestizo* was an agent of progress and the most competent race. The *mestizo* family, he says, "has been the dynamic factor in our history. Sometimes rebelling, sometimes organizing, it has exploited or begun to exploit the riches stagnating in our soil; it has broken the power of the privileged castes. . . . It has facilitated during periods of peace the advent of foreign capital and the colossal improvements of a material order which have been made the last few years. . . . By increasing schools and compulsory education, it fertilized the seeds of our intellectual progress. . . . It has also established law, and within another generation it will have made political liberty a fact."[66]

[65] *"La formación de una raza argentina,"* in *Revista de filosofía*, Vol. I (Buenos Aires, 1915).

[66] See my work *Apogeo y decadencia del positivismo en México.*

The Class Struggle

ARGENTINA thus entered a new stage of social development which gave it special characteristics. The struggle for intellectual freedom seemed to have come to an end. The struggle between the city and the country, the capital and the province, civilization and barbarism had ended. Buenos Aires was the directing center of Argentine life. Industries were increasing, and especially so in the capital. A new struggle was to take place in the nation—the class struggle. The immigration which had stifled the gaucho and the Indian and which had settled the rural problems as seen in Hispanic America spawned a new class, the proletariat, which worked for the new industries. There was an attempt to form a new *bourgeoisie* similar to the great European *bourgeoisie*. But while it was taking shape there arose a class that was inherent in the *bourgeoisie*, the proletariat, its very antithesis. The rural movement, betrayed by Rosas' and other *caudillos'* ambitions and defeated by the Argentine *bourgeoisie*, of which Sarmiento and Alberdi and their generation were an expression, spilled into the city and became proletarian. Juan B. Justo (1865–1928), founder of the Argentine Socialist party, said, "The Argentine people have no glory; independence was a bourgeois glory; the only part the people played in it was to serve the designs of the privileged classes that led the movement."[67] The rural movement, the movement of the mounted rebellion, was crushed by blood and fire, and from its ashes there arose the immigration which completely covered it. But the struggle, the same old struggle, of the oppressed against the oppressors moved to another field, to the city, where the industrialist fought the worker.

The immigrants who had come from a Europe that no longer satisfied their needs brought to Argentina many of their old problems and, if possible, problems that were more serious. In Argentina they encountered a class that enjoyed the fruits of the wealth, that possessed the means of production, that paid wages fixed according to its own interests; it was a class that held great surplus value. There was an immediate tendency to organize the immigrants into groups

[67] Cited by Dardo Cúneo in *Juan B. Justo*.

for their own protection. The Argentine Socialist party was one of the groups organized in their defense.

Juan Bautista Justo, an Argentine, spoke to these men of the past of the land to which they had immigrated. He told them of the deeds of other men who had lived on this land defending their rights with great tenacity; he spoke to them of the feats of a people sacrificed on the altars of the interests of this new class of Argentine *bourgeoisie*. "But soon," he said, "the people had to struggle against this class which directed the movement to defend their means of livelihood, to defend the land on which they lived from rapine and complete domination by the *lords*." The *bourgeoisie* despoiled them of everything; their lands were exploited by this class. "It meant little to the great merchants and exploiters of the cities to control and exploit the land according to new rules."

The old dispute between civilization and barbarism no longer appears in Justo's interpretation of Argentine history. These same struggles now become class struggles: the *bourgeoisie* against the farmhands from the country. The heroes are no longer the men from the city but men from the country. The *bourgeoisie* triumphed in this struggle, crushing the man from the country. "The gaucho," said Justo, "saw his existence threatened, and being incapable of adapting himself to the conditions of the times, he rebelled. In this way the civil wars of 1820 and the following years broke out, for they were a true class struggle. The mounted rebellion was the country people rising up against the 'lords' of the cities. Men, women, and children, the country population en masse resisted their domination." The struggle of these masses was the same struggle that the workers had been carrying on in Europe against the exploiting *bourgeoisie*. "The gauchos defended the terrain in their own way for freedom," but they were defeated. The Argentine *bourgeoisie* had defeated them in several battles. "Their resistance, however, failed. Why did it fail? Because they had no economic ability whatsoever; their insurrection, purely instinctive, only tended to leave things as they were, in an impossible status quo, which would allow them to continue living as they had up to that time. Their triumph would have meant the economic stagnation of the country, its isolation from the rest of the world already revolutionized by steam and electricity.

. . . If the gauchos," he concluded, "had defeated the Argentine *bourgeoisie*, this country would have been for some time a great Paraguay to be conquered later by some powerful foreign *bourgeoisie* which would have been impossible to resist. The rebellion of the country failed because the masses of gauchos lacked any political talent."[68] Their very names were responsible for betraying it and placing it in the service of their ambitions. Rosas, in the name of this class, became its supreme dictator until he was defeated by the Argentine *bourgeoisie*.

IX. POSITIVISM AND SOCIALISM

Education as an Instrument for Social Advancement

IT is interesting to discover how a capable group of Argentine positivists, especially those who were under the influence of the Paraná school, turned toward socialism. From positivism itself they were to deduce the postulates for establishing social justice in Argentina. To be sure, they did not follow communism, for it struck them as an extreme solution that could be avoided, as an unnecessary evil. Some men, like José Ingenieros and Juan B. Justo, modified communism by combining it with Spencerian positivism. Others found in Comte less violent theories for social justice than those deduced from Marxist philosophy.

One of the solutions to the social problem that the class struggle posed was found in raising the level of the worker's education. Pedro Scalabrini attempted to do just this in the Popular Normal School of Esquina, which was placed under his supervision. Víctor Mercante tells us something of this school: "What a beautiful democratic ideal, an educated worker with all the good things of life, a worker who knows how to keep healthy, a worker who knows how to speak, read, and write correctly, who knows how to understand and utilize the facts and the laws of the human, vital, and material order—a worker, in short, who knows how to fulfill the duties of life." In this school diplomas were awarded to tradesmen just as they were to the professional people: "servants, nursemaids, laundresses, farmers, carpenters, blacksmiths, tailors, cobblers." Indeed, "to transform educa-

[68] *Ibid.*

tion into a profession for the boys and girls who complete their studies at the Popular School by awarding diplomas has, according to my way of thinking, great permanent value. The diploma ennobles the profession—just as the diploma of the doctor, the engineer, the lawyer, the school teacher, and the dentist proves their general and specialized preparation—and points out to the student a fixed route, a practical purpose in harmony with his inclinations, his aptitudes known and recognized by his parents or guardian. The important thing is to dignify even the humblest work, to give it standing in society. The Popular School is very close to this ideal." Of course, recognition is given to productive and character-building work. In the eyes of the school, "the laundress in Esquina and the emperor of Germany are equally respectable if they fulfill the duties of their profession with dignity."[69]

Manuel A. Bermudes, a positivist from the Paraná school, in an article entitled *"Educación y socialismo,"* defended the worker's right to education. "Ignorance," he said, "cannot be a source of happiness." Thus he opposed those who held that the extension of elementary instruction was a cruelty. "It is not education that causes the evils in society but rather false moral direction impressed upon the mind." All the masses follow their leaders, "but an educated people will have the good sense to elect or to lean toward the best candidate, and this in itself is an appreciable advantage." It is untrue that the spread of elementary education is an irritating injustice. Quite the contrary. "The poor man who comes to understand his situation will not be alarmed that there are rich men, neither will be disown his humble hut nor his rustic parents." The recognition of the existence of other realities in addition to his own does not necessarily imply unhappiness. Education, to the contrary, helps the individual to recognize his position in society and to assume the responsibility that goes with it. By knowing his place, "he will tend to improve and elevate himself."

It is said that the humble man tends necessarily to be a delinquent, but such is not the case. "That class mistakenly called superior which perverts its instincts in orgies, which rises unjustly and many times opposes justice, that is the worst, the most dangerous class, but it is

[69] Víctor Mercante, *"El educacionalista Pedro Scalabrini."*

the one the people do not know because it refuses to give them the human benefit of sufficient education to recognize it. Education cannot be denied to anyone, for it is necessary for action, for knowing others, and for rising above the level of animals." The time has passed when ignorance was indispensable to guarantee domination, Bermudes said. "Today the perverse do not rule by taking advantage of the intellectual poverty of the masses. Today we are governed by the lofty soul; good men will have more authority and will be followed more readily than the thief, and education is necessary so that the people will know how to distinguish between them." Education is not the source of class hatreds. "Education does not produce hatreds. The social revolution which we are witnessing is the result not of the hatreds of the poor but rather of the injustices of the rich. ... Although it is true," he added, "that our schools waste time pitifully teaching many sterile, useless, and even prejudicial subjects, we cannot deduce from that the uselessness of education but rather the necessity for reforms according to conditions and the exigencies of the moment."[70]

Comtism and Socialism

J. ALFREDO FERREIRA, upon finishing his *Síntesis de la política positiva de Comte,* also pointed out the relationship of Comtian positivism to socialism. He found in positivism a better solution to the social problem than that offered by communism. "Communism's utopia has been beneficial, however, for it has convinced the proletariat that property is of more importance to them than power." Communism with all of its extremes has succeeded in arousing the attention of the worker by forcing him to concern himself with his own problems. "The noble sentiments of communism must be appreciated, but not its vain utopian theories. . . . positivism will resolve the social question better than communism." The proletariat, upon the acceptance of "the felicitious expression of socialism, has accepted the communist problems, but it has rejected their solution."

Positivism has already taken into account these social problems and presents a conciliatory solution for them. "Property," said Ferreira, "has a social origin and objective: a communistic principle

[70] *"Educación y socialismo," La escuela positiva,* Año III (1897).

which positivism systematizes. . . . Property is not an absolute entity entailing the right to use and abuse it." In this respect, "the principal difference between positivism and communism lies in the normal separation of fundamental powers. . . . Plato included women and children as part of communal property. Our proletarians accept only communal ownership of property. . . . Communism does not recognize natural laws in its attempt to suppress all individuality when the two fundamental characteristics of the collective organism are separation and competition among its functions."[71]

In another place, Leopoldo Herrera, a member of this same group of positivists, pointed out the similarities and differences which existed between Comtism and socialism. "Positivism," he said, "accepts completely and incorporates the principle of the destiny of social wealth as its own; but while socialism seeks its solution in a system in which law establishes an obligatory equality, positivism seeks its solution in the constitution of a type of government in which inequalities contribute freely to the proposed objective, under the direction of a common doctrine, which today can only be scientific."

Pointing out the differences, he said: "Socialism calls upon the power of the state for help; positivism depends upon opinion. Socialism faces the problem squarely, while positivism skirts the obstacle. Socialism brings disorder to our social organization and looks for progress from a revolution; positivism does not disturb anything, but by following the law demonstrated by all history under which progress is the development of order, it looks to order for the means of realizing progress."[72] It is simply a matter of different methods; the ends are the same: social justice. Revolutionary violence is not the only means for attaining this justice; positivism possesses other means. This is, in conclusion, what the Argentine positivists, following Comte, tell us. "Positivism is, above all," said Leopoldo Herrera, "a social philosophy."

José D. Bianchi, in an article on the same problem, said: "Socialist plans are in harmony with positivistic policies, even though the propaganda is directly social. Comte's doctrine stems from the government in its conception and application; in order to answer all social needs,

[71] In *La escuela positiva*, Año V (1899).

[72] "*El positivismo y Augusto Comte*," *El positivismo*, Año II, Vol. II (Buenos Aires, 1916).

the socialist theory, equally scientific and philosophical, stems from the opposite pole, its victims, and rises to the abstraction of a governmental system. . . . They are two doctrines that tend toward the same end, social reorganization. One deals specifically with a political factor; the other considers the economic factor." Indeed, he added, "the social problem encompasses improving that great mass without changing the general economy. The scientific spirit can carry out this work. Positivistic politics and socialism lean to that." Nevertheless, it is undeniable that, "if the material life of the individual is not secured and made independent, his political entity will be what it is today: an instrument which can be utilized by anyone who has the economic factor in his power." Comte's philosophy and socialism complement each other. Both attack the same problem from different angles. "Comte's doctrine cannot be consistent with the facts unless socialism offers it the proper elements for the great work."[73]

In another work, entitled *Cuestión social,* Bianchi referred to Darwinism and its theory of the struggle for existence, in which the strongest survive. For Bianchi, the strongest is the one who can unite with the group. The most powerful individuals can never be stronger than well-organized communities. "There is no independent existence," he declared, "apart from the organic connection which Darwin classifies. There does exist another tie, the mutual help in the struggle for life." From this arises the idea of justice, the basis of all society. In this sense, "the socialist crusade is not the campaign of a party struggling to retain unlawfully the power in the continuing succession of the political life of nations; it goes deeper than that, and it attempts to reconstruct the collective organism by calling for the redemption of the body and the soul which is still not realized."[74]

English Positivism and Argentine Socialism

THE *bourgeoisie* of Argentina and other Hispanic-American countries found in Spencer's and Darwin's doctrines the best theoretical justification of their interests, even to the point of converting them into an official philosophy; the Argentine socialists used the same doctrines for the same purpose. Just as the *bourgeoisie* found in Spen-

[73] *"Política positiva y socialismo," La escuela positiva,* Año IV (1898).
[74] *La escuela positiva,* Año V (1899).

cer the justification of its individualism and in Darwin the justification of superiority over those whom it considered less apt, so Argentine socialism found in the same men its justification of the struggles of the proletariat class. This was José Ingenieros' and Juan B. Justo's interpretation of English positivism.

Some of the works of Carlos Octavio Bunge (1874–1918) followed this same interpretation. In his work entitled *La evolución del derecho y la política,* he said: "I find in biology the explanation of the equalitarian process of law, which is also naturally that of politics, morals, and religion; utopian equalitarianism is contrary to the biological principle of human specificity." There follows an explanation of the dialectic according to which humanity develops: (1) Geography determines the formation of races or the specificity of mankind; (2) human specificity produces war and conquest; (3) conquest produces social classes; and (4) social classes make up the state. In this way, "the old ethnic difference is changed into legal political differentiation." It is to the interest of the ruling classes to maintain this new differentiation, and to do so, they struggle to give it efficacy and fundamental principles. "The fundamental principles are based on religious-moral systems; and the efficacy rests on juridical standards that are then fixed into laws." Law is always inequality. "Specificity becomes greater the higher one goes up the animal scale. Man represents the highest development on the animal scale. Hence specificity is greater in man than in any other genus or species."

Up to this point Bunge follows the conclusions of English positivism. But from the same line of thought, the movement of the oppressed peoples was able to deduce conclusions favorable to them. "If the ruling races," he said, "could keep their superiority stationary, the social organization once formed could not be changed. Castes or classes would stay separated *in aeternum.* Succeeding generations would continue indefinitely their political and social supremacy over the conquered. But just as biology teaches us that specificity becomes greater the more complicated the organism is, it also shows us that all organisms, including the most complicated ones, are susceptible to degeneration." Aristocrats who hold power unlawfully degenerate and become parasites. On the other hand, the laboring classes, tempered by activity and continuous work, generally become stronger.

"Several generations of laborers under more or less favorable circumstances generally produce a result that is inverse to that of simultaneous generations of aristocrats. While the latter degenerate, the former grow more robust."

As long as specificity keeps the ruling castes superior, their domination is just; it is imposed by the inevitability of biological and historical laws. The same does not happen "when the dominated attain a vital energy greater than that of their decadent conquerors; then the domination becomes, although still not unjust, at least irritating. The inferior rule the superior! And the latter, as a result of their utilitarian animal instinct, rebel; they initiate a *class struggle*." The ideal of the class struggle is equality. "A heroic equalitarian tendency" will oppose "an infamous aristocracy." In the same way that "the ruling classes previously invented the right to inequality, those who are ruled now invent the right to equality. As a result of the degeneration of the inequalitarian tendency, the opposite tendency triumphs."[75] Such is the source of history.

It is well to point out here another interesting difference in the way in which English positivism was interpreted by the Mexican positivists. Following Spencer, they said, "Society, like every living organism, is subject to the unavoidable laws of evolution, and these laws . . . in their essence consist of a dual movement of integration and differentiation from the homogeneous to the heterogenous, from the incoherent to the coherent, from the undefined to the defined. That is, as every body, every organism, becomes unified or more integrated, its several parts become more differentiated and more specialized, and in this dual movement lies the perfection of the organism which in society is called progress." From this the Mexican positivists deduced the right of the Mexican *bourgeoisie* to maintain the strictest social order. The first thing to do was to make the nation homogeneous, integrate it, give it unity; heterogeneity and differentiation would follow. Order must precede freedom. Freedom is the natural result of a well-established order. As long as the people do not know what order is, they cannot aspire to freedom. The Mexican *bourgeoisie* would take charge of establishing this order. They appointed

[75] "*La evolución del derecho y de la política*," *Revista de filosofía*, Vol. VII (1918).

themselves the guardian of the Mexican people. For the good of the Mexican people they established an iron-handed dictatorship. Within this interpretation they were duly justifying an old attitude with new theories. The Spanish conquistadors in the past had already discussed several theories that justified their rule over conquered peoples. The Indian, yesterday and today, continued to be a person incapable of enjoying freedom. He was morally and intellectually inferior and for that very reason needed a guardian. The Spanish conquistadors in the past and the Mexican *bourgeoisie* in modern times found the justification for their social domination in this supposed inferiority of the Indian, who made up the bulk of the Mexican population.

In Argentina it was necessary to alter this interpretation, since the Indian did not exist there; nor did the justification of the supremacy of a superior race over an inferior one exist. Both the exploiter and the exploited were of the same racial origin. The immigrants belonged to the same race as that already in Argentina. The Argentine *bourgeoisie* belonged to the same race as the working class. They comprised social groups that had social differences but no ethnical differences. The only difference that could develop was in the realm of individual ability. In the struggle for existence the most able come out on top. The ability of the Argentine worker was not previously reduced, as the Mexican's was, by supposedly ethnical inferiority. In his struggle, the Argentine worker knew that he had the same possibilities of succeeding as the *bourgeoisie*. He likewise realized that as an individual he could also attain the same economic level as the highest of the *bourgeoisie*. His world of possibilities was even more open than that of the European worker. Without this concept immigration could not be explained. Each immigrant expected to find in America possibilities for personal success that he could not find in Europe. His struggle, rather than a class struggle, was to attain the greatest possibilities from personal triumph. He did not aspire to destroy the *bourgeoisie*; he simply sought to attain the same advantages, to reach the same plane of economic and social equality. He was therefore closer to Spencer than he was to Marx; he preferred the socialists' solution to the communists'; he only wanted to belong to the *bourgeoisie*, not to destroy it.

In his essay entitled *"El problema del porvenir del derecho,"*

Carlos Octavio Bunge said that socialism implied not only an economic and political tendency but also a moral and emotional impulse,
a super-revolutionary application of the Christian principle. But absolute socialism lacked true scientific bases and the times were not suitable for its acceptance, nor had there yet been formulated a concept
with the same prestige and popularity that the doctrine of social
contract had in its time. "The most feasible formula for socialism
today is the relative and moderate one which is based on the protection of the poor classes by the state." The triumph of socialism," if
it succeeds in the form of communism, will be as passing and deceptive as that of modern democracy." Man progresses and moves ahead
because he perfects himself in relation to his fellow-men. "Therefore, to perfect oneself is to become superior in intelligence and in
character to other men and other nations. And in this concept we
find the biological formula for progress: *to progress is to become
specialized.* A corresponding formula for progress is: *to progress is
to become an aristocrat*—that is to say, to perfect oneself in respect
to other men and other nations in order establish on a real superiority the principle of rule, of power, and of inequality, which constit-
tutes the invariable substance of every practical and effective right."[76]
Communism is impossible, for its principles are contrary to this biological differentiation. Spencer was correct here in his opinion of
Marx. A dialectic in which the worker as an *individual* is the protagonist is preferable to a dialectic in which the *class* plays that role.

José Ingenieros also deduced from Spencer the dialectic that led
the working class toward a more just society and to a greater state
of well-being for its members. The division of classes into those that
possess the means of production and those that do not possess them,
according to Ingenieros, has given rise to a special economic organization. "This economic organization, the inevitable consequence of
the present system of capitalist production, makes slavery and servitude assume a new form destined to be the last." Capitalism contains
at the same time, already in the process of development, the genius
of a new system of production which will signal the way to another
period in the economic history of mankind: the system of social production. With all the means of production held in common and every

[76] *Revista de filosofía*, Vol. VII (1918).

individual converted into an intellectual or manual producer, "the division of society into classes with conflicting interests will disappear and class institutions, whose existence responds to present economic conditions which will then have disappeared, will be replaced by other institutions more in harmony with the historical-social conditions which will prevail in the future. These institutions will have as a basis a scientific concept of life and of society by means of the dual recognition of the essence and the modalities of cosmic and economic factors to which income, progressive development, and the mutual relations of the individual and the species will be subordinated."

Society arrives at socialism through natural and biological evolution. The maximum social solidarity is the fruit of this evolution, a solidarity that has its origin in the very will of the individual. Within this solidarity the individual reaches his maximum development. "The advent of the socialist organization of society," said Ingenieros, "is inevitable and is the essential condition for guaranteeing in the future the free development of all individual talents with a true, beneficent, collective solidarity." By this way "which leads to a maximum social solidarity by effecting the most admirable combination of the highest forms of individualism and altruism, man will approach the solution to his great present social problems . . . he will draw near the supreme formula for well-being; obtain for each individual the maximum satisfaction of his material, intellectual, and moral needs." This was the deduction that was made from Spencer's doctrine, from his theory of evolution applied to the social field. "Because this truth," said José Ingenieros, "which could not escape Spencer in his evolutionary concept . . . is also a fundamental tendency in life and in the social and economic development of human society." The positivism of this English philosopher led to a type of social solidarity that was very different from that which the *bourgeoisie* derived from the same doctrine. It led to altruism as social justice and not as charity or alms."[77]

Positivism and Marxism

"By DEPARTING from the purely bourgeois character, the Argentine positivist Juan B. Justo," said Alejandro Korn, "succeeded in instill-

[77] "*Los sistemas de producción en la evolución de las sociedades humanas,*" *La escuela positiva,* Año IV (1898).

ing a new doctrine which linked positivism to the ambitions of the proletariat and thus gave it a new content."[78] In order to effect this reform, Justo combined the positivistic philosophy of Spencer and the philosophy of Marx, with emphasis on the former. The ideals, the aspirations of his doctrine and action coincide with those of Marxism but depart from Marx in the bases on which its thought rests.

In his book *Teoría y práctica de la historia* he analyzes societies in order to call special attention to the causes of social inequality and the form in which it triumphs. His interpretation is biological. Biology to Justo is the very basis of man's history. The historical process rises from diverse, vital forces which contend and struggle in determined biological conditions, with man dependent upon a technology that becomes more and more powerful. Justo believed that in this struggle for existence technology and co-operation would give man a great superiority. But up to the present, he said, "this had not been possible, since technology was in the hands of a series of institutions "which artificially limit the development and life of great groups of individuals."

"In modern societies," he went on, "technology and co-operation rest on the private ownership of natural resources and on the means of production created by man, and this exclusive domination by a certain class of people over the physical biological means and the tools and materials of work disrupt the conditions of the struggle for existence." With one segment of society, the proletariat, deprived of the principal elements of work, the struggle for existence is very unfavorable, since they only attain, in general, a short life and an incomplete individual development. The monopolization of the means of production, according to Marx, only produces social inequality. Justo sees in this monopolization an attack on nature herself and on the development and progress of the human species. One part is sacrificed when it is left to itself in unfavorable conditions to face the struggle for existence. Sexual selection is also impeded and defeated. In nature, he said, the male seduces the female, displaying like the birds his most beautiful plumage or his best song. In the struggle for love those who can seduce the female with their masculine beauty win. "Those who win in the struggle for love pass on to their off-

[78] Alejandro Korn, *Hegel y Marx.*

spring the characteristics that have made them conquerors, and in this manner the type of beauty of the species is developed." Selection is carried out naturally, and the best of the species is propagated. In human societies this no longer happens, for here an artificial medium, money, exercises a powerful influence. In this case the physically superior no longer win, but rather those who can rely on money. Whatever the origin of the man with a fat pocketbook, the pocketbook is at present the most highly regarded secondary sexual characteristic, with the peculiarity that the principle holds true for both sexes, for just as the wealthy and dissolute man is likely to ruin the beautiful girls of the species, so the ugly wealthy girl is more sought after than the beautiful girl who has no dowry or no future inheritance." In this manner the human species comes to naught.

Nevertheless, in spite of his biological interpretation of the human element, Justo does not reduce his interpretation to this idea. In fact, the human element, that which is fittingly human, rises with history, and history appears in its turn when man passes from a purely biological entity to an individual who uses technology to acquire advantages in the struggle for existence. The point of departure for history is found in technology, in the capacity of man to transform his milieu. "From the time man is intelligent enough to consider himself as animal, he is forced to see the bases of his history in biology. Unconscious activities are the forerunners of every voluntary and conscious activity. The laws of life are the most general laws of history." But with the emergence of technology history becomes detached. "Human toil subordinates history to biology, and at the same time separates it from the latter."

Justo accepts from Marxism its practical interpretation of class inequality and the class struggle, but he rejects every kind of abstractionism. He does not wish to be considered a philosopher but a man of action. Marx above everything else has been a philosopher and has become lost in abstractions to the detriment of the practical. For Justo the theory of the Marxist *surplus value* is only an allegory. He is opposed to the dialectical method. For Hegel's negation of the negation, Justo substitutes what he calls "the affirmation for the sake of affirmation." Marx and Engels gave too much importance to the Hegelian dialectic by assuming that, because of it, scientific socialism was possible. Justo does not agree. "The fact that Marx and Engels," he said, "were proud of their grandiose concept and attributed it to dialectic would not be the only case of such an illusion."[79] For in the past Pythagoras attributed the formulation of some of his theories to the gods. Hegel can give the same basis for a scientific socialism as he can for any kind of reactionism. Justo did not want the proletarian struggle to depend on any such type of abstractions or philosophies. He wanted it to rest on science, a practical science of experimentation, a positive science. "Experience," he said, "is the source of knowledge, the inexorable criticism of illusion."

As for the sciences, he denied that they have any dogmatic character. "Sciences," he said, "are only relative truths"; and these truths are related to man. "No conclusion is ever reached," he continued, "by manipulating these two abstractions, man and nature. There are no physical laws and no intellectual laws: All laws are physical, intellectual, natural, and human. They are written in the world only to be deciphered by our key and they exist only in the understanding and within the reach of this key; hence their relativity." Justo based his interpretation on this experience. As a doctor he saw man for what he is, a biological entity engaged in a struggle for existence, a struggle in which a lack of solidarity is detrimental to human groups.

On the basis of this thesis he was also opposed to the dictatorship of the proletariat, for he considered it a myth that was losing importance in the minds of the people. "The idea of a social transformation that suddenly establishes a perfect order is losing ground in the minds of the people, for they are occupied more wisely with everyday problems."[80] No state, no law can overnight change relations among men by establishing other relations capable of realizing collective ownership. The principal problem is one of training and education, and what is to be done is "to place in the hands of all the people that function of management which the privileged property-owning class now monopolizes."[81] It is not a matter of establishing a dictatorship, but rather of gaining by various means the control of technology which at present lies in a few hands. By gaining that control, inequality will be gradually eliminated, since all individuals will

[79] *El realismo ingenuo.*
[80] *Teoría y práctica de la historia.*
[81] *El Socialismo.*

have the same opportunities and will develop according to their innate possibilities. Education is preferable to revolution so that habits of social co-operation may be formed and technology will thus be in the service of all of society.

X. POSITIVISM AND THE NEW HISPANIC ETHICS

Uruguay and the Problem of Intellectual Emancipation

URUGUAY AND ARGENTINA shared their intellectual development until the so-called "big war" fought against Rosas. Montevideo was a place of refuge for the exiled Unitarians and the members of the Association of May. Juan Bautista Alberdi, Esteban Echeverría, Domingo F. Sarmiento, and other leaders of the intellectual emancipation of Argentina wrote many of their works in this city or planned the defeat of the tyrant. From 1839 to 1851, Uruguay was at war with the Argentine government of Rosas, as a result of which Montevideo underwent an extended siege. Within its defenses many of the works appeared which the generation of leaders mentioned above produced on behalf of intellectual emancipation.

Andrés Lamas (1820–91) was under their influence, especially Alberdi's. At first he had fought Alberdi because of the latter's interpretation of Rosas. Alberdi had praised Rosas in 1837, at the time of the dictator's rise to power, for he saw in it the triumph of the people and the humble classes. "Is it not great," he asked, "is it not beautiful that the common people, who from the ancient times of Greece, from the first centuries of Rome, have plotted on the eastern continent for their emancipation, have now a new world which they govern and with well-founded hopes that the old world will soon be theirs also? All of this leads us to believe that the nineteenth century will become plebeian and we from today hence salute it for that glorious title." Andrés Lamas refuted the young Argentine immediately. He did not agree with him; above everything he was a partisan of freedom; nothing good could be achieved in an aristocratic regime. "If thought is chained," he said, "if there is a man who by taking advantage of our constant political oscillations, or because of a series of coincidences improves himself even by thought itself, how can intelligence be developed? How can the conquest of the American character be made?" Alberdi could not answer him. The reality that Rosas represented prevented him from doing so. "This situation placed me in a difficult position," said Alberdi. "To defend my arguments against his frivolous attacks would have been to concede more than necessary to the despotism of my country; it would have been impossible to explain my arguments without incurring Rosas' persecution." Through Miguel Cané, who was in Montevideo, he explained to Lamas the meaning of what he had said.

Andrés Lamas was soon captivated by the young men in Buenos Aires, for their differences were insignificant. Lamas and Miguel Cané (1851–1905) together published the periodical *El Iniciador* in 1838.[82] The problem of Spanish America's intellectual emancipation was evident in Lamas' introduction to the periodical. "Two chains," he said, "tied us to Spain: one material, visible, and ominous; another no less ominous and burdensome, but invisible, incorporeal, which, like those incomprehensible gases that subtly penetrate everything, is in our legislation, in our literature, in our customs, and in our habits; it binds everything, places the seal of slavery on everything, and belies our complete emancipation." Lamas, like Sarmiento, Alberdi, Echeverría, Lastarria, Bilbao, Rodríguez, Bello, Mora, and other thinkers, struggled in various fields of education and politics to free Spanish America from a heritage which they considered fatal to its development. "We broke the material chain with the strength of our hands and the steel of our lances." The invisible and incorporeal chain "must also disappear if our national personality is to become a reality. To rid ourselves of the corporeal chain was the glorious mission of our fathers; to rid ourselves of the incorporeal chain is ours. There still overwhelms us burdens that the young Spain cannot bear, burdens that she desires to cast off with zeal, patriotism, and the spirit of progress." He concluded, "The least one can do is win the intellectual independence of the nation! Its civil, literary, artistic and industrial independence."[83]

As soon as Rosas was defeated and the siege of Montevideo lifted in 1851, Uruguay began its own independent existence. But with this independence came a period of anarchy: presidents left their office

---

[82] See Arturo Ardao, *La filosofía pre-universitaria en el Uruguay.*
[83] *Ibid.*

without finishing their terms, the influences of various military leaders clashed, and there were revolutions or rebellions in the military barracks. Bernardo P. Berro, a man concerned about the progress of Uruguay, was elected president in 1860. But uprisings broke out again. General Venancio Flores invaded Uruguay from Argentina. In 1865 the General succeeded in entering Montevideo and seizing the presidency. During General Flores' government the Triple Alliance was formed among Uruguay, Brazil, and Argentina to wage war against Paraguay. Flores, in command of the troops fighting the Paraguayans, was well known for his efforts to improve the country in all possible ways. Progress was evident in the railroads that crossed the country, in the encouragement that was given to primary education, and in the new laws that were drawn up. In 1868 revolution broke out again. Bernardo Berro started an armed rebellion. Flores was assassinated, and shortly thereafter Berro; new presidents and new revolutions followed. There were a few short breathing spells during which the progress of the country advanced at a minimum. There seemed to be no end to anarchy. In 1873, Dr. José Ellauri was elected president and a host of university men called "the Girondists of '73" were sent to Congress. It seemed that at last the generation had arrived that was to lead the nation definitely down the desired paths of progress that the Hispanic-American world had not followed. But in 1875, Colonel Lorenzo Latorre seized power in an armed rebellion and appointed a president. After crushing a counterrevolution, Latorre declared himself dictator. From then on the military barracks would be the only competent authority. Latorre's dictatorship was followed by that of Máximo Santos. From 1875 to 1887 the military was the only source of order. Uruguay, like the rest of the Hispanic-American countries, seemed doomed to continue to bear the burden of her terrible heritage. There was no other alternative; it was either anarchy or dictatorship. The intellectual emancipation of Uruguay continued to be an ideal yet to be realized.

The Military versus the Intelligentsia

WHY had the university men failed? Why had the brilliant "Girondists of '73" been defeated? "The famous Girondist congress of Ellauri's time," said Alberto Zum Felde, "was perhaps the most brilliant that the country has ever had because of the wealth of university learning displayed in their debates and the pompous eloquence of their speeches. Without a doubt that congress was the greatest arena in which the second romantic generation displayed its virtues and its faults. These men were educated in the university, founded during the siege, and pure theory was the standard of its faculty. Debaters of a refined style, the intellectuals of Ellauri's insecure and ephemeral government made the parliamentary debates a magnificent tournament of legal erudition and rhetorical eloquence. It was an academy, not a parliament; a literary society is not an organ of government. Those men thought and discussed, with their backs to the country, mixing in lucid dialectics the concepts and the formulas learned in the classrooms or read in European writers. They did not deign to study their own national reality, nor did they face social and economic problems practically."[84] These men attempted to apply to the country standards and laws for which the people were still not prepared. The outcome was failure, and reality again appeared in its most brutal form: the dictatorship of the military barracks.

In 1880 a new generation attempted to oppose the barracks. This new group which tried to save the Uruguayan nation was concentrated in the *Ateneo del Uruguay*. The men of this group sought the means to carry out the emancipation of which Andrés Lamas had spoken. They hoped to set the country along the paths of an order based on the freedom of the individual. But the first members of this new crusade had the same faults as their predecessors, the "Girondists of '73." "Toward 1880," said Zum Felde, "the *Ateneo* stood in opposition to the military; they represented the two conflicting political and social forces. But the young men of the *Ateneo*, a weak, learned minority facing a crude and savage country, persisted in repeating and perpetuating the errors of the old body of principles of their models, the Girondists of '73, to whom was due, in great part, the failure of the university-trained government and the entrenchment of militarism which was its consequence." This group later formed a constitutional party which also was to be characterized by the brilliance of its speeches, the writing of propaganda pamphlets, and an ardent but futile campaign. This was not the way. It was neces-

[84] *Proceso intelectual del Uruguay.*

239

sary to take routes which would lead to more effective results, to take more positive paths more suitable to Uruguayan reality. Those who followed this new path would attain the best results. "Those men of the *Ateneo* who had positive influence on affairs," said Zum Felde, "were those who departed from their literal principles to work within national reality by reconciling pure rights with empirical factors."

How could they defeat the military? Or, in other words, how could they defeat that fixed attitude of Hispanic Americans which nullified their efforts for progress? The only path was that which their own Hispanic-American reality offered. They must go directly to that reality, rely on it, and adapt all reforms to it. If the only possible order, for the present, was the order imposed by the military, they must convert the military into an instrument for the rehabilitation of the country. Power was the most important thing for the military. As long as the military could not be opposed, such rehabilitation could not be effected; but they could orient this power, upon which they depended, toward the mental emancipation of the country. After they have been thus emancipated, the people themselves would take it upon themselves to shake off the bonds of aggression. The first step was to educate, to prepare, the people for the proper use of their rights. This was the program which José Pedro Varela advocated.

Varela, a fervent admirer of the United States, went there to study its educational methods, especially elementary education. Upon his return to Uruguay, he sought an opportunity to put these methods into practice. He quickly became aware of the mistakes of the generation which had come to power with Ellauri. Latorre's military regime, which followed it, showed him the fallacy of their approach. They must use other means if they wanted to give the people freedom and make the nation democratic. It would be necessary to educate the people by broadening public education and establishing public schools on a basis similar to that in the United States. This method would take longer, but the goals, once attained, would be more firmly established. Who was to be responsible for starting this educational program? The military dictatorship itself would be in charge. José Pedro Varela sent Latorre a copy of his book, *De la legislación escolar,* which the dictator received enthusiastically. In his work Varela opposed the theories of the university men on the ground that they were unrealistic. "Institutions established only on paper," he said, "are not adaptable to actual social conditions; while the rural population knows only the absolutism of the *caudillo*, the urban population, directed by the professional group, proceeds along erroneous paths because university teaching inculcates ideal theories which serve only to separate social classes."[85]

Thus there came about the Law of Common Education, written in 1877 with Latorre's approval. The professional group rose against Varela, accusing him of having betrayed his own group, the Uruguayan intelligentsia, by serving tyranny. He, however, answered: "Tyranny is not Latorre's work; it is a spontaneous product of my country's social status. The surest way of combating dictatorship is by changing the moral and intellectual character of the people, and this character cannot be changed except through education." With these words Varela showed his faith in the lofty ideals of the leaders of mental emancipation in Hispanic America. It was important not to combat just a specific dictatorship, but to exterminate the roots of all dictatorships. "I will not exterminate today's dictatorship," he added, "which the people will not exterminate either; but I will end future dictatorships."[86] Thus the intelligentsia would finally overcome the military.

Positivists versus Spiritualists

A NEW SENSE of reality also appeared with Varela's educational reform. The practical, pragmatic, and empirical thought of the North American schools, was brought to the Uruguayans. "Varelian reform," said Zum Felde, "constitutes one of the most important factors of the rationalist, antireligious movement which characterized the intellectual life of the country in the last quarter of the nineteenth century, and the most powerful antecedent of the philosophical campaign undertaken by the *Ateneo* group." This reform was sternly opposed by the church since its principles embodied lay education. On the one hand, it was characterized by a practical rationalist thought, opposed to the purely unrealistic thought of the founders of the *Ateneo*; on the other, it confronted religious dogmatism, while supporting an educational system free from the influence of

85 *Ibid.*
86 *Ibid.*

the church. Rationalism soon penetrated the *Ateneo* and with it some of the theories of scientific positivism. Soon the *Ateneo* was divided into two main groups: those who followed rationalism in its idealistic form and those who accepted a type of rationalism more in harmony with scientific positivism. The first declared themselves spiritualists, the second positivists, and the polemic was begun in the *Ateneo*. The spiritualists accused positivism of being amoral and therefore damaging to the moral regeneration of the nation. The positivists maintained that their philosophy was the most suitable one for attaining this moral reform. Both spiritualists and positivists claimed the right of directing Uruguayan intellectual emancipation.

The polemic began when the *Ateneo* group confronted the Roman Catholic group, attacking the dogmatic and historical foundations of the church. The moral implications of rationalism were brought to discussion in the *Ateneo* itself. Since it was essential to eliminate the old theological morality imposed by the colony, it was desirable to know what moral principles were to take its place. It was on this point that the two attitudes arose: that of the spiritualists and that of the positivists, arguing the right to provide a philosophical foundation for the new moral code.

Carlos María de Pena made the following statement about the struggle which had developed between the representatives of theological dogmatism and the representatives of scientific rationalism, a struggle which brought about the polemic in the *Ateneo*. "The echoes of this great battle," he said, "have reached every corner of the country, greatly disturbing our spirit, provoking us and forcing us to new investigations, and moving the very foundations of the temple of our former deities." The *Ateneo* could not remain aloof and indifferent to this struggle. "Youth follows, so far as present resources and the uneasiness of the times permit, the interesting episodes of this struggle and reaps its great teachings."

He next illustrated how the new philosophy changed the traditional concept of morals without being amoral. "After investigating the genealogy of each being and the genealogy of mankind," he said, "the naturalists have penetrated the seat of the soul!" . . . It seems that the moral world has changed, and that man, an atom lost in eternity, a mixture of the vegetable and the mineral . . . has been toppled from his throne." Nevertheless, he added, "the naturalists have had to recognize that this animal's brain . . . has vibrations which span time and space and go beyond the immensity of the heavens, beyond the deep darkness of the abyss." This being's struggle for existence "has no other purpose than *moral progress,* intellectual and physical, the welfare of the individual, and the perfection of the species." The naturalists have recognized that although man is subject to the laws of heredity, "he has, as no other being, the power of adaptation, the faculty of avoiding, of foreseeing, of minimizing, of overcoming the influence of this law of fate: he has freedom." He thus denied the thesis of those who saw in positivism an amoral doctrine. Positivism does not deny the faculty which makes morality possible when freedom is accepted. "Here are," said Pena, "the great truths which natural philosophy and the sciences offer to those who explore its domains with a lofty spirit and a heart open to the inspirations of a new faith. Here is, if I am not mistaken, the declaration of faith of the youth of the *Ateneo.* The motto on their escutcheon is the struggle for truth, and love of science is their great stimulus. They profess a religious cult of liberty and hate despotism as much as fanaticism and ignorance, which are repulsive to them. Youth has erected this temple because the old ones were narrow and were threatening to crumble . . . the youth of the *Ateneo* accepts the teaching of nature, pays homage to its most eminent interpreters, and at the same time pays a tribute of love and admiration to those moral principles which are like tutelary spirits of our liberty and our civil dignity."[87]

In an address delivered in 1883, José T. Piaggio recalled the great arguments which arose about the new doctrines. He said that in 1875 Uruguayan culture received one of its great shocks. Men's minds were again perturbed. "When the decision was made to establish professorships for preparatory studies, new professors were very scarce." However, they succeeded in fulfilling their duty. It was the period when spirituality was at its height and controversies over essentials began to appear "in the more or less perfect syllogisms of which the novice philosophers availed themselves as a guide in argumentation. . . . Locke came into the picture too early. . . . Krause did not exer-

[87] *"Ecos de una gran contienda," Anales del Ateneo de Uruguay,* Año. I (1881).

cise as much influence as Kant. His system, somewhat extravagant in the domain of science and politics, could not approach the doctrines of the recluse of Koenigsberg." The new ideas agitated thought through a series of lectures. "We were young, perhaps too young, but in our souls burned the flame of pure patriotism, the lofty concept of scientific ideas, the religion of holy memories and flattering expectations."

The lectures at the *Ateneo* made history in the annals of the university. "Ideas changed with each different speaker. No sooner had the voice of a positivist faded away when suddenly the audience in the Fiesta Hall heard the semi-eloquent voice of a young Cartesian. . . . Some ridiculed the doctrines of Spencer and said a great deal about Darwin . . . others were busy criticizing spiritualistic doctrines: Kant, Fichte, they said, were great and eminent philosophers; but if after reading their nebulous works . . . you can give us the numerous pages of those researchers, sociologists or naturalists, certainly if there is a choice between light and darkness, the real and the imaginary, we will take light and the positive."[88] Idealism versus positivism. The choice lay between these two doctrines and its purpose was, as we already know, the moral regeneration of the country.

Positivism as an Amoral Philosophy

THE IDEALISTS or spiritualists, as they preferred to be called, launched an attack on the new philosophy. Positivism, they said, was an amoral doctrine and for that very reason incapable of turning the education of the nation in the direction of regeneration. Segundo Viña said, "Materialism has always been what it is today, in spite of its transformation: the negation of God and therefore of morality."[89] Dr. Prudencio Vázquez y Vega, however, directed the strongest attacks against positivism.

The Uruguayan idealist said: "Parallel to the positivistic movement that has developed among us, there has also arisen a selfish utilitarian movement which we must fight." The followers of positivism were fleeing the field of honor, according to him. "Their tactics are to fight in the darkness of the hallways; they fight in the classrooms with

[88] *Revista de la Sociedad Universitaria*, Año I, Vol. III (1896).
[89] *Anales del Ateneo del Uruguay*, 1881.

the young students, and they gain control through terror by the examinations given at our university." These could not be called honorable tactics, but rather positivistic tactics. For that reason, "spiritualism is down in the arena of the stadium, for it fights out in the open with all kinds of knowledge; it accepts the challenge on all elevated grounds . . . in the classroom it professes, as the highest scientific virtue, the most complete impartiality in the exposition of its systems; it proposes free discussion, the denial of all exclusivism and the most perfect and noble tolerance during the heat of debate."

Vázquez y Vega's philosophical criticism of positivism is this: The absolute, according to Spencer, he said, "is a positive reality. This circumstance is sufficient enough to make it the object of science." The most eminent thinkers of all ages agree in making a profound distinction between phenomena and moral laws. Physical laws have a material basis and they operate through fate; moral laws have as a fundamental basis human personality, and these laws operate freely. Having established the distinction between physical laws and moral laws, Vázquez y Vega added, "Merit and demerit, responsiblity and moral sanction would be incomprehensible facts; the remorse that kills and the moral satisfaction that dignifies and elevates would be inexplicable, impossible phenomena if an inevitable concatenation were the supreme law of human actions." If this were so, "if positivistic evolution is a true doctrine, the most perfect egotism should be the ideal of human nature. . . . The hypothesis of evolution does not explain, according to our way of looking at things, the moral phenomenon of disinterestedness." Free actions which have as their purpose the good of others "are not easily explained by organic evolution. Many of the followers of evolution should understand it in this light since they are egoists through practice, conviction, and doctrine. . . . Moral valor, point of honor, personal dignity, nobility of character, refinement of the mind, great generosity—these are moral endowments that you will never succeed in acclimatizing in the frozen field of positivism."[90]

In another lecture on *"Dominios de la psicología y la moral,"* Vázquez y Vega pointed out the ideals previously mentioned. "To attempt to place morality in the same category as the physical sciences

---

[90] *"Crítica de la moral evolucionista," Anales,* 1881.

is to attempt to encase human actions in a hopeless fatalism, to deny liberty, responsibility, and conscience. . . . There exists an ideal of virtue and of moral perfection that can be judged and comprehended but cannot be measured by a pair of scales or geometric gradation." Vázquez y Vega made it clear that there was a need for a doctrine that would raise the morality of the time, the only remedy for the evils that dominated Uruguay. "You should know," he said, "that the very air we breathe is saturated with paltriness and selfishness, with baseness without name and incredible servilities, and you should know that this situation has produced in great part the utilitarian opinions which look with scientific pedantry upon the rigid and categorical concepts of the morality of duty." In this age in which "a philosophical doctrine is many times sought to conceal or to justify selfish conduct or personal interest, utilitarianism lends itself admirably to such purposes."[91] The positivistic doctrine rather than aiding moral regeneration lends itself to justifying many immoralities.

Angel Solla, a spiritualist and successor to Prudencio Vázquez y Vega, during his professorships at the university began a polemic with Carlos M. de Pena in a lecture entitled *"El positivismo y la metafísica."* "I consider it a bombastic stroke or thoughtless act to attempt to apply the terms befitting a natural or medical science to the ideas and deeds that fall into the domain of another science that has in turn the terms which should express them." What is positivism? Can its objectives and its nature be determined after all with exactitude? he asked. "However strange it may seem at first glance," he answered, "that determination is impossible to make. In the field of positivism there reigns the most fearful confusion. Every one of its adepts has his own doctrine which differs essentially from that of the others, and all of these opposing and contradictory doctrines endeavor to form a body of uniform and compact doctrine." It is quite probable, he added, that there are many positivists who do not even realize "that within their ranks there exist many sects that are carrying on a death struggle to gain pre-eminence." They, like Comte, were eliminating metaphysics and psychology. In turn the disciples abandoned and repudiated the social concept of a teacher like Littré who only accepted a portion of the doctrine. Stuart Mill differed from the two

[91] *"Dominios de la psicología y la moral," Anales,* 1882.

previously mentioned positivists in that he did not accept the proposition that the role of psychology should be given less importance.
Bain and Spencer formed another sect by parting company with rational psychology to base their beliefs on Darwinian conjectures.
When Pena denied, he added, that positivism is materialism, he was
against positivism, for it affirms the opposite. A contradictory doctrine, it was concluded, would ill serve to regenerate the morality
of a people.[92]

Positivism as a Moral Philosophy

THE URUGUAYAN positivists, well versed in the new doctrines,
answered all their opponents' objections, especially the charge that
positivistic philosophy was amoral or immoral. Arechaveleta in a lecture entitled *"La teoría de la evolución es una hipótesis?"* began by
clearly differentiating positivistic philosophy from other doctrines
with which it was confused. To avoid the error generally made by
those who combat the evolutionist theory when they confuse it with
Darwinism or with transformism, Arechaveleta said, we want to give
the definition of the three doctrines formulated by Haeckel, the eminent zoologist from Jena. These doctrines constitute a complete definition of evolutionistic or positivistic philosophy: first, the theory of
evolution; second, the theory of descent; and third, the theory of
selection—or, if you wish the theories of Monism, Lamarchism, and
Darwinism. Two types of explanations of creation have been given,
and from them there have arisen two theories: the theory of supernatural creation and the theory of evolution. The first is based upon
an irrational hypothesis; the second, upon a scientific one. The theory
of evolution has been defended scientifically by Spencer, Huxley,
Haeckel, and others. We support the scientific and the rational in
opposition to the irrational. Hence, "as long as Mr. Vázquez does
not present us with scientific facts, nor with men of learning who can
be compared to those we have just enumerated, we shall hold that
the theory of evolution is scientific and that the opinion of Mr. Vázquez has no basis and was issued without reflection from the platform of the *Ateneo;* it is, in short, a product of the a priori system
of the metaphysicians."

[92] *"El positivismo y la metafísica,"* Anales, 1884.

Arechaveleta, according to his theory, explained idealistic or spiritualistic philosophy as a residue of mental backwardness which as the result of physiological conditions still remained in some men. "The brain," he said, "is the organ of thought, the spiritual cortex, the true sphere of pycho-intellectual activity. All thought produces a change in the gray matter. No thought can be born without this change, nor can its birth be stopped when this change is produced. This change consists of a movement which the present state of knowledge does not as yet allow us to describe with precision. Its direction is determined by the nerve trunks, the fibers and filaments that hold together the cells in the multiple plexi." Indeed, if to these physiological data we add that man in his physical constitution and knowledge is heir to the acquisitions of the past; "that in addition to the innate and irrational nature of the species, he possesses the nature of his immediate ancestors, and that his development follows the path that his heritage has traced for him, we can understand, to a point, how spiritual ideas, more or less religious, idealistic, or rationalistic, whose elaboration began in an epoch that is lost in the darkness of past ages, have continued to be transmitted from generation to generation and are so deeply rooted in many minds. . . . These brain cells which we like to call animistic or spiritualistic, great and small, inherited from our immediate ancestors . . . are the ones that, in the trappings of a monk, were present as very active agents at all the monstrous acts of the Inquisition and were the ones which lighted the bonfires to burn the free thinkers; the ones who committed the massacres of St. Bartholomew." They are the same ones who "today wear civilian dress and wave the flag of tolerance." But "the naturalist physiologist recognizes their filiation and reveals their genealogical tree." These are the same elements which have created the philosophical systems discredited today as sterile. Indeed, concluded Arechaveleta, "slowly and surely science is advancing toward the conquest of those old elements, inventors of sterile systems which have attempted to arrive at the knowledge of prime causes, although science does not have the inhuman purpose of destroying them, but rather a laudable objective of changing them so that they can earn the bread of their soul with the sweat of their brow."[93]

[93] "*¿La teoría de la evolución es una hipótesis?*" *Anales,* 1881.

Julio Jurkowski took as his point of departure the question of whether positivism, improperly called materialism, was an immoral doctrine, as the spiritualists affirmed it was. "As humanity progresses," he said, "it tends not only to material well-being but also to moral perfection, since without the latter the former would be impossible." Those who attack material well-being, considering it a source of immorality, he added, see things superficially. For those superficial moralists it is more important "to propagate a healthy morality than to have railroads and telephones." But reality proves quite the contrary: "Misery impedes the intellectual and moral development of a society; industrial progress, by assuring well-being, favors it. . . . The changes that humanity is undergoing are the result of a fundamental law of organic nature, and these things will necessarily lead humanity to perfection. This is our firm belief; that is the basis of the materialistic doctrine."[94]

"The metaphysical school," said Jurowski in another address, "has always been more exclusivistic and, by almost always occupying official positions, has provided examples of an intolerance which has often reached the greatest excesses and persecutions and has contributed a great deal to retarding the march of civilization." On the other hand, the motto of positivism is "everything through science and for humanity" and not "everything through matter for matter," as it is narrowly interpreted. Man is a simple servant and interpreter of nature; but "while considering himself as a measure of the universe, he has held such a high opinion of himself that he cannot stoop to such a thing."[95]

It is false that positivism does not encourage humanity. Positivism also has its ideas and attempts to realize them by utilizing the best and the surest means. Martín C. Martínez said: "Positivist theory suppresses nothing of the grandeur of humanity; it simply does justice by revealing the essential importance in creation of those small phenomena which only prick the scholar's imagination and which definitely explain the condensations of the worlds, their gravitation, and the elaboration of the species." Positivism takes note of the minute, said Martínez, because from it great facts are derived. Not only

[94] "*La metafísica y la ciencia,*" *Anales,* 1881.
[95] "*El método en metafísica,*" *Anales,* 1881.

does it take note of first causes or first principles; it also takes note of that essential cause which is anonymous because it is small, but which in its entirety constitutes the force which makes the fact possible. The people are the anonymous force without which humanity could not progress. Positivism attempts to do justice to this force. In society it takes into account "the influence of the power of the people, condemned by history to eternal oblivion. . . .

"I do not know," he added, "that the exaltation of the modest virtue which elevates the superior man by diminishing his immense pride and the individual lost in the multitude by showing him that he is an agent of appreciable value in social progress can restrain any heart well tempered in the task by erasing from its spirit the vision of the ideal. . . . Evolutionism has restricted itself to elevating the small, to uniting modest virtues, to showing the influence of general causes, perhaps by reducing the stature of heroes; but it has raised the stature of nations by making history as democratic as nature."

Positivism was therefore the doctrine essential to nations since it dignified their task, however insignificant it might be. Positivism was the philosophy of democracy. The leaders of society, added Martínez, who seek to be the originators of progress are only an expression of its evolution. "The ascent toward the ideal becomes more difficult since it must be the work of collective action; but if that difficulty can discourage those who place little value on the good when it is ostentatious, it does encourage the disinterested servants of progress, for they knew that every advantage attained, even though it be small, is a lasting achievement and because all good, however small it may be, is worth the trouble to create; without this the very future of humanity would be of no consequence to us."[96]

The decline of the morality of the times, according to Rosalío Rodríguez, had nothing whatever to do with the positivistic doctrine or with any other doctrine. "To be sure that cursed cause has never been found in any of the philosophical schools. . . . That positivism does not erase from the consciousness the ideas of good and of justice and that it does not drive from the human heart the sentiment of duty—that, I believe, I could easily demonstrate by simply expound-

[96] *"Ideales positivistas," Anales,* 1884.

ing the doctrines of the great masters." Hence it is a mistake to declare that positivism mutilates human morality and reason. "It is also mutilated by those who constantly resort to a superior principle to explain the phenomena of life; they also mutilate it who, when they have broken a leg or are suffering from a pulmonary infection or any other illness, implore the favor of a divinity to cure them of it. . . .

"Positivism admits the idea of good, the sentiment of duty, and the practice of virtue." Hence "those statements are slanderous which affirm that as a philosophical doctrine it drives the most dignifying sentiments of our personality from the human heart." Positivism, on the contrary, arrives "at the same conclusions as the spiritualistic doctrines; like them it admits that man must do good and eschew evil, and that good is what leads us to the fulfillment of our end." The The only point on which they differ is that "positivism does not wish to recognize in good and in justice simple and abstract principles which always *must have been* imposed in the same fashion on human life; but rather, by following the procedure of analysis, to break down all these simple, alleged ideas in order to find their true basis and finally to understand that good, duty, and justice have no other *raison d'être* than human nature with its needs and its goals."

The only substantial difference between positivism and spiritualism is in the origin of their moral codes. "The metaphysicists stop at the beginning of the journey. They find the idea of good already completely realized, and by regarding it as a simple and irreducible principle, they do not even wish to attempt to analyze it. . . . Our opponents, the metaphysicists of all schools, have created a lamentable confusion between the positivistic doctrine and that selfish and paltry utilitarianism which, under the disguise of a usurped name, begins to reign with pretensions of erecting itself into a philosophical school." Positivism has nothing to do with that attitude. In fact, there are two types of positivism deplorably confused: "One is a false positivism, which we can likewise call indecorous in contrast to the positivism of the great masters. . . . For the positivists," Rodríguez concluded, "as well as for the spiritualists, the good is our north star."[97]

[97] *"Exposición de los fundamentos de la moral evolucionista y su crítica," Anales,* 1884.

The Triumph of Positivism

THE NEW IDEAS finally triumphed and with them a new morality, a practical morality seemingly based on reality. Man no longer expected anything from the transcendental. Henceforth he would have to depend upon himself. Angel Floro Costa, calling himself a "former Darwinian," clearly pointed out the new situation of the new generation formed in positivism. "I myself believe that the great prophet Darwin," he said, "has done us as ill a turn as Cortés did his crew members. Darwin has burned our ships for us, and I have a strong urge to strangle him." Why, it is easy to understand the anger of the metaphysicists! The old heaven was so beautiful, peopled by romantic-like creatures and by a complete fauna of cherubs and sylphs. This is the ethereal mansion sought in vain by the telescope, that indiscreet profaner of the sacred veil of the nebulae! "It was so beautiful to dream of immortality and the absolute supremacy of the spiritual over the material! Man can no longer dream; he must act and act in earnest in a world in which he is the only one responsible for what he does, for what he has done or what he does not do or has failed to do." Costa added, "I stopped being frivolous when I began to study; I stopped laughing at others when I began to cultivate positive sciences a bit. . . . I understood then the waywardness of our new ideas, I understood then the secret of our ferocious intolerance, and I became aware of the inviting and everlasting triumph of our barbarism." Down with all absolute formulas! Down with all a priori theories! This is the motto science has on its banner. "Its banner is the idea of the *relative,* the *democratic* and liberal banner *par excellence,* humanizing and conciliatory, the very opposite of the absolute, the proud *aristocratic, oppressive* banner which has flown up to now over the strongholds of dogma and on the poop deck of spiritualistic metaphysics." At last there was a new philosophical doctrine to take the place of the old colonial one. The philosophy of democracy and liberalism would replace the aristocratic and oppressive philosophy. The intellectual emancipation now had basis.[98]

Nevertheless, man on his own ran the risk of straying from the

[98] Ángel Floro Costa, *La metafísica y la ciencia.*

straight paths that the leaders of the intellectual emancipation had dreamed of. There was the danger that he would become too closely attached to the materialistic and would become an egoist just as the spiritualists had envisioned. The Uruguayan positivists themselves posed this problem. The fear that their ideal would fail was current among them. "I wondered," said E. Fernández, "if positivism as a philosophical system would pervert the conscience, dry up the heart, and precipitate nations into an abyss by snatching from the altars of religion the principles of good, justice, and the dignity of man." He went as far as "alleging that the evils of the present and the wave of corruption and the degeneracy that threatens to envelop the Republic is due to the impetuosity of the positivistic trends. . . .

"But no," he added, "the truly honorable man is not honorable only out of fear of punishment or fear of society's disapproval or of the law or of the divinity, or out of fear of practicing virtue with the complete abandonment of paltry incentives." On the contrary, "the evolutionistic school proclaims that mankind tends on his collective march forward to practice virtue for the sake of virtue itself. . . . Actions which were at first taken selfishly with calculated motives have today become, through habit and custom, actions that are wholly disinterested and altruistic." Positivism is accused of being an ally of personal and arbitrary governments. No philosophical school admits worshipers of gold. The evils that are singled out are not the evils of a philosophical doctrine, but rather those of men. "Positivists, rationalists, Catholics, mystics—in short, followers of all philosophical schools—fall into the great calamity to which the adversaries of positivism refer." As for "those who cloak themselves in the garments of postivistic maxims only to hide a servile and gentle character, they are not positivists but rather degenerate individuals."[99]

In 1890 positivism definitely triumphed in Uruguay. Spencer became a kind of official philosopher, and the University of Montevideo accepted his philosophy in the place of Cousin's and Janet's. The new generation became dominant in the cultural, political, and administrative life of Uruguay. The political situation had changed since 1886, the year the people again elected a president. He was Gen-

---

[99] "*¿La moral de la escuela evolucionista niega la existencia del bien y del deber?*" *Revista de la Sociedad Universitaria*, 1896.

eral Máximo Tajes, who began to return the country to a civil basis and civilians again directed public life; the military was finally defeated. There was an occasional revolution and an occasional dictatorship such as that of Juan Lindolfo Cuestas; but this dictatorship justified itself by the new principles, among which the principle of progress was prominent. In 1903 one of the greatest political figures of Uruguay became president, José Batlle y Ordóñez, who led the country toward the desired liberalism and democracy.

XI. POSITIVISM AND THE POLITICAL EMANCIPATION OF CUBA

The Colonial Failure of Spain in America

WHILE the rest of Hispanic America was engaged in the struggle for its intellectual emancipation and was attempting to find a doctrine to substitute for the one which had dominated her, Cuba continued to follow just the opposite path. She was preparing to gain her political freedom from Spain as soon as she had educated the new generation that was to implement it. The seed planted by the great Cuban masters, Caballero, Varela, Luz y Caballero, and others, was beginning to produce results. After a few frustrated attempts, they prepared the greatest attack, the one that finally was to bear fruit: Cuba won her political independence from Spain in 1898.

Enrique José Varona (1849–1933) was the direct heir of the great Cuban leaders of the struggle for intellectual emancipation. Like his predecessors, he struggled above everything else to win intellectual independence for Cuba before gaining political freedom for the island. At the same time, however, he was a fervent collaborator in the latter struggle. Varona was aware of the fatal Spanish heritage in America. He also realized that political independence alone would not bring complete freedom to his people. All of Hispanic America was engaged in a constant struggle with herself, attempting to destroy one part of her being in order to be completely free. He was also aware of the existence of certain chains more powerful than the material ones with which Spain had held Hispanic America in subjugation. These chains must be destroyed before anything else could be done to give freedom to Cuba. Spain carried this evil in her very soul, and she had innoculated her children on this side of the Atlantic with it. Spain had failed as a colonizing nation; hence it was imperative to break all the ties that bound her to America. "Was the Spanish expansion normal?" Varona asked in 1896. "For it to be so for any society," he added, "the following conditions must coincide: sufficient population, flourishing industry, abundant capital, and sane political ideas. Spain could boast of none of these." As always, there was the eternal model to which our nations must hold. "While in English America," he said, "the spirit of local autonomy springs forth robust and is ever increasing, in Spanish America it is born weak and dies soon thereafter."

All of Spanish America was an example of this pessimistic thesis. Spanish America's political independence was not enough, and for that reason it failed in its greatest aspirations. "In order to understand the great upheavals that characterize Hispanic-American revolutions," said Varona, "and to evaluate their immediate consequences, we must not lose sight of the fact that it was a revolution that was essentially political, conceived, desired, and planned by a single class of the population, in countries in which the population was radically divided; and we must realize that this class sought to use sovereignty for their own profit." We see how Hispanic America became politically independent, but at the same time we see "Chile ruled by an oligarchy *à la* Venice; Argentina trampled underfoot by the horses of the gauchos, Peru governed by the military, Venezuela involved in terrible wars over senseless constitutional reforms, Mexico with ten changes in its form of government and three hundred military uprisings in fifty years. The dismal seeds sowed by Spain were producing their poisonous fruits!" The Spanish heritage was manifest in this terrible form. The legendary dragon's teeth sowed in a fertile soil were producing the best of crops. "Those teeth," said Varona, "were the caste spirit, the spirit of domination and privileges; the monarchial ideal which hides but shines in the depth of the mind; the habit of exploitation that will not relinquish its old power. Everything remains the same; no freedom whatsoever exists. . . . The servile hand continues in servitude, in misery, and in abjection. The same instruments of oppression continue to crush freedom."[100]

[100] *En voz alta.*

Positivism and the Intellectual Freedom of Cuba

ENRIQUE JOSÉ VARONA found in positivism the doctrine that above all would give Cuba her intellectual independence; but it was not in positivism in general, only in that positivism that was capable of stimulating the spirit of freedom by which the Cubans were to gain also their political independence from Spain. Like his master, José de la Luz y Caballero, Varona was opposed to any doctrine in any form that could be used to justify Spanish rule; he was opposed to any doctrine that might induce Cubans to accept this rule. Therefore, he began by rejecting Comte. Varona chose the evolutionism of Spencer, but not in its entirety: He rejected its cosmology and its universal interpretation of cosmology. He wanted nothing that meant the adoption of a totalitarian system, a system that would in any way subjugate the individual; he wanted nothing of metaphysics; he sought only what could be proved by experience; he wanted nothing of idealism; one must be a realist. Reality itself made it clear that Cuban independence was a necessity over and above other solutions that were merely the result of good intentions rather than of urgent necessities.

The island was suffering from many ailments. In order to cure them, it was necessary to work as good realists and root out the cause of the trouble, however painful the operation might be. In reference to the prevalence of graft and the manner in which it could be remedied, he said: "Of what use has a form of legislation been to us, assuming that it has existed. What we need to do is to put a stop to the sources of corruption by beginning at the top, to respect and teach others to respect all our rights, especially those of the human being; to destroy arbitrary inequalities; to fight extra-legal privileges; to spread true culture, beginning with the senses. In a word, we must regenerate, moderate passions, and dignify an entire people." Who is to blame? "Graft does not retreat in the face of force but in the face of *civilization*, and in Cuba barbarism advances. . . . Full responsibility belongs to the class that rules, makes the laws, and establishes authority."[101]

[101] In Vitier, *Historia de las ideas en Cuba.*

Faithful to the educational doctrine of his predecessors, Varona accepted Spencerian positivism because it more closely resembled the ideal of the emancipation that Cuba needed to win political independence. English positivism, he said, "is free from all dogmatism and in a state of complete evolution that does not attempt to place limits on the desire and need to investigate. . . . This school," he added, "makes its assertions without fear, and it has covered a space no less vast than that which still remains to be covered. In this school I found the problem of historical filiation resolved, a problem that the French school of positivism, to its credit, pointed out dogmatically. The solution of this problem is the greatest guarantee of the necessary vigor and vitality for continuing on the road to progress."[102]

Varona rejected Comte for the same reasons Luz y Caballero had rejected Cousin. Comte enclosed human faculties in "the iron circle of a double tyranny when they need the greatest degree of independence to carry out thir evolution successfully. By so doing, he substituted the most rigid and stifling socialism for an illusory anarchy." In order to follow Comte, "one must push our civilization and our political and social organization backward to that model age; everything must be sacrificed, even the noblest attribute of the man of our century, *freedom of conscience;* everything must be sacrificed to that marvelous conformity of beliefs which made all hearts beat in unison." The common background of truths of which the Comtians spoke was to be obtained through the sacrifice of the individual. Spencer's philosophy was opposed to this and justified freedom. "The divergence of opinions," he said, "was the work of evolution, and in this manner the law of progress is fulfilled." Comte was eliminated! In his doctrine there was no freedom, and without freedom there could be no progress. Progress for Cuba, Varona knew, meant its freedom, its independence. "And they come to tell us of a demonstrated faith," he added, referring again to Comtism, "of a doctrine accepted by all intellects at the same time. What chimera is this? And is it presented to us as a model, as an ideal to which we must direct the unity of all beliefs in the Europe of the middle centuries?"[103]

[102] *"El positivismo," Revista de Cuba*, Vol. VIII (Habana, 1880).
[103] *Ibid.*

Bases for a New Educational Method

VARONA found in Spencer's philosophy the elements with which to orient the education of Cubans toward the attainment of their liberties. In reference to the positivistic method, he said: "There are only three steps in this great task which Bacon called interpretation of nature, and it cannot be otherwise, because the process of the mind when it studies the objective is conditioned by that same fundamental relationship of the 'I' to the 'Non-I'; there are only three great moments: the subject gathers from nature all the unrelated data; he subjects them to an elaboration that is characteristic of this method and again compares his work with nature, which has given him the bases. In this manner experience is both at the beginning and at the end; in the center is the mind with its activities." Experience was one of the most positive means for the re-education of Hispanic Americans. Varona, like others of the same mind, saw that one of the defects of the Hispanic American was his lack of a practical sense. The Hispanic American does not know how to go directly to reality; he idealizes it, and when he idealizes it, he forgets it. Varona therefore insisted on the need for experience. On this ladder, he said, "however high we climb, we are always certain of being able to come down on solid ground. This is the conclusion of a logic that has refused to become a blind auxiliary of any empirical or idealistic or any positivistic or metaphysical system. This logic perhaps makes the modest claim that, by following its method, it can be demonstrated that it is neither the exclusive depository of truth nor in its totality a mere fabric of errors." Indeed, it may be well to ask what reality should be the subject of experimentation by *the Cuban*. The Cuban reality to which Varona had referred was crying for reform. Only consciousness of this reality could provoke the reaction necessary for its reform. This was fundamentally what Varona perceived when he asked the Cuban to utilize the best method, experimentation. Besides, this method, as it dignifies man and makes him conscious of his limitations, likewise makes him tolerant of others and provides a basis for a new type of co-existence, an order based upon the conscience of the individual and not on the violence of the person who holds power. "This is another great lesson and perhaps the best one that the true method teaches us," he added. "It teaches us to distrust our own work; it teaches us to look for what justifies the work of others, the adverse work, the contrary work; in a word, it teaches us to be tolerant."[104]

Again referring to psychology, Varona shows how man, if he cannot escape certain deterministic factors, especially natural ones, can indeed by means of education orient these factors. "Religious and moral precepts, the maxims of our conduct, the examples, all the means of education become so many other motives which provoke a struggle and end by being the victors or the vanquished, according to their present strength. Man cannot therefore escape determinism, but he can in a manner train and direct it, which is tantamount to overcoming it. Man is not an automaton, but in order to avoid being one, he must cultivate intelligence as well as feeling. Education is his true redeemer." And he added with a meaning which Cubans with their longing for freedom could appreciate: "Man is not free; he forges his own freedom; he begins by obeying and ends by choosing, but he does not choose out of whim, he chooses by limiting himself." Determinism, here far from being a limitation of Cuba's desire for freedom, justifies freedom. Cuba was destined to be free. By nature, according to Spencer's idea of evolution, the island would gain its independence in a positive and absolute form, as positive and absolute as all determinism is.

The day when, from the examination of physiological conditions and personal psychic data, we can deduce scientifically an individual's character—that is, how he would react in most situations to the stimuli of the milieu in which he is—on that day, he shall know positively how to do what up to now mankind has been doing gropingly. We shall know how to educate. "Positivism offers these means. Psychology, seemingly so poor, has limited itself to describing mental states and to investigating their laws. It has now suddenly opened up for us such perspectives that it overshadows the sciences which until now were rightfully called man's best friends." By means of education man can also learn to overcome great obstacles without futilely sacrificing himself. "Man is not obliged to tunnel through every mountain that stands in his way; by saving the strength that he would expend on a chimerical enterprise, he advances sometimes by taking

[104] *"Conferencias filosóficas," Revista de Cuba,* Vol. VIII (1880).

a roundabout way, and when he finds himself on the other side of the terrible obstacle, when he finds before him the wide and open path, his body and mind still vigorous, he can greet the immovable colossus and turn his back on it shouting with all his strength, 'Forward!' "[105]

Individual Freedom and Social Responsibility

THE NEW DOCTRINE not only had to supply the elements for the intellectual and political emancipation of Cuba; it also had to supply the means for establishing a new order—that is, the principles upon which this order had to rest. It was to be a social order different from the colonial, an order which, while guaranteeing the freedom of the individual, also guaranteed his social collaboration, the only basis for making an authentic independent nation of the island. Otherwise, political emancipation would be a futile task, for other individuals and other forces equally selfish would again enslave the country, as had happened in other Hispanic-American countries. These forces were in the very heart and soul of Hispanic Americans, and they must be destroyed by re-educating the people. Irresponsibility and selfishness must be destroyed. Spencerian positivism also offered these means, for it guaranteed both individual freedom and social collaboration. The individual needs society, but not to the extent of limiting his freedom.

"Far from isolating man and endowing him with some kind of mysterious characteristic called practical reason," said Varona, "which would allow us to deduce all moral law—that is, far from assuming that moral sentiments are already formed at birth in their entirety and their application (the method used by some contemporary moralists to establish science)—we have gone directly to the facts. We have observed that man is a social unity, subject to the actions and reactions of the aggregate of which he is a part, who repeats in his mind, as a kind of reverberation, all of these encounters. We have analyzed one by one the elements of the milieu in which he was placed, one by one the elements of which he was formed, and we have then determined the effect of those elements upon his mind. We have also seen that all this work of elaboration gave us as a result the makeup and perfection of a class of emotional states which pro-

[105] *Ibid.*

duced different acts and judgments, all marked with a characteristic seal which depended upon their very existence. . . . This seal" he added, "was morality; these conditions, solidarity."[106]

The conclusions which Varona derived from Spencerian positivism were different from those derived by the Mexican positivists. While the Mexicans arrived at a type of liberty and morality which justified their limited interests, the Cubans deduced from the same philosophy a liberty that implied responsibility. The Mexicans held that the most able persons were those with the greatest social rights. The most competent had no reason to sacrifice, or at least to limit themselves, for the less competent. Ability, which could even be determined by wealth, placed one individual above others. Society was merely a good and useful instrument available to him, or else a necessary evil because it was also a guarantee of his individuality.

Varona held the reverse. "The individual," he said, "who refrains from harming his fellow-man will not be an obstacle to the activities of other social groups; but if he takes advantage of the group, he will not contribute to the common progress . . . he will enjoy an incomplete life." An incomplete life is one which does not participate in common progress. "The individual who gives aid for the work of the group and receives aid from the group mindful only of the usefulness which the exchange brings him will be a beneficial element in a great number of acts advantageous to the group and to the individuals, but he will necessarily limit his actions and therefore is incompletely determined . . . ; his life will still not be complete." Only the individual "capable of restricting somewhat his personal ambitions and of imposing certain restrictions upon himself in order to assist some other member of the community who needs help, and mindful only of the feeling and progress of the collectivity . . . he is the perfect moral being." Man is moral because he is social; the more social he is, the more moral. "To do no harm, to co-operate, to do good are the maximum precepts that in one form or another solidarity dictates to us."

The individual has certain obligations, and these obligations are to the community to which he belongs. "And to what group do the duties of man toward himself belong?" Varona asked. "To none,"

[106] *"La moral en la evolución," Revista de Cuba,* Vol. IV (1878).

he answered, "because I do not see man as obligated to himself. . . . The preservation of the individual is a necessity, not a duty, because the latter presupposes a dependency, and it is absurd for an individual to be dependent upon himself. . . . We should not confuse individual hygiene with social hygiene," Varona concluded, "nor physical needs with moral precepts."[107]

XII. SPENCER VERSUS HEGEL

The Doctrine of Autonomy versus Separatism

THE PROBLEM of Cuba's political emancipation led to two attitudes and to two ideological currents: one of a traditional character and another of a revolutionary character. The traditionalists favored autonomy from Spain, but without separation; the revolutionaries favored a radical separatism. The autonomists hoped to create a Cuban nationality, but by peaceful means, utilizing legal methods and arguments to persuade the mother country. They wanted an autonomy such as that granted by England to her colonies. Here they were following the ideas of their predecessors Agustín Caballero and Félix Varela. The separatists, on the other hand, favored using revolutionary methods to win complete political independence for the island.

Rafael Montoro (1852–1933) was the leader of the Cuban autonomist movement, a movement which first took the name of the Liberal party and later became completely autonomist. Montoro had spent his youth in Spain, where he came under the philosophical influence that formulated his doctrine. He returned to Cuba when it was scarcely beginning to recover from the long war, which from 1869 to 1879 the Cuban patriots had fought under the leadership of Carlos Manuel de Céspedes. The revolution was crushed. From 1878 to 1892 the island enjoyed relative autonomy conceded to it by Spain. The revolutionaries, however, continued struggling, although almost hopelessly, and José Martí was the greatest figure in this struggle. This was the Cuba that Montoro found upon his return. He immediately undertook a campaign to win authentic autonomy for the island. He used all possible legal means and lectured widely for more than fifteen years. He was opposed to a violent separation, because he hoped to attain separation through peaceful evolution.

In 1881, while expounding his doctrine, he remarked, "The Lib-

[107] Ibid.

eral party requests special laws for Cuba directed toward a greater decentralization within the national unity." To accomplish this, it would be necessary to operate within the law according to a constitutional principle. Article 89 of the constitution of 1876 said, "Overseas provinces shall be governed by special laws"; hence the requisite that the form of local government for the island be necessarily distinct from the form accepted for the government of the Peninsular provinces. "For the peculiar conditions of Cuba require that it be so, since in the social, political, and economic realms she exhibited needs different from those recognized beyond the sea." Montoro sought an insular delegation through which it would be possible to resolve the administrative and economic problems that might arise in purely local affairs. This was to be done in collaboration with the governor-general of Cuba. "It would be necessary, therefore," said he, "to introduce a radical reform in the general budgets of Cuba, to make a distinction between what is national and what is local, and to assign the first to the general budgets of the nation whose vote is incumbent on the Cortes, while reserving the second, the expenditures and revenues of which are purely local by their very nature, for the budgets of Cuba which will be voted upon by the insular deputation." Following the ideas already expressed by Caballero and Varela, he said, "We advocate a constitution for a local responsible government like that which the great English colonies of Canada and Australia have."[108]

Struggling in behalf of these ideas, Montoro returned to Spain to convince its governmental leaders. In the Peninsula he also opened a campaign with this purpose in mind. In a lecture delivered in the *Ateneo* of Madrid in 1894, he presented and justified his program. "Injustice and abuses," he said, "only injustice and inequality cause the respect and love for Mother Spain in the colonies to weaken, since they become stronger and more deeply rooted when the mother country displays a more propitious attitude toward authorizing all the conditions requisite for the development and prosperity of the new societies. In this manner was that beautiful spectacle of the English colonies produced." Montoro's party shrank from any violent outlook, the cause of so many disasters. "Within democracy," he said,

[108] *Nuestra doctrina,* 1881.

"there is revolutionary radicalism which has caused all the great disasters that the modern world bemoans, and there is liberal and progressive democracy whose doctrine is based upon the recognition and the guarantee of the human personality with all its rights and all its necessary limitations. It is this liberal democracy that our party has always tried to represent."[109]

Spain still had time to mend her ways, but the longer she delayed in mending them, the greater the reforms would have to be. Cuba still continued to be faithful to her ties with the Spanish nation, but not for long. The longer Spain delayed, the more difficult it would be for her to keep that loyalty. In 1892, Montoro had told the Spaniards: "Only yesterday the agitation of the minds of the people could have been calmed by modest and gradual reforms. Today these reforms must be more radical. Indeed, tomorrow, my dispassionate voice warns all, tomorrow, those reforms will have to be more transcendental, and perhaps they will come too late. Whether we are in public life or not, a great and formidable clamor will demand them in the name of the people."[110] Nevertheless, as we know, his voice was not heeded. The Constitutional Union party, made up of the Spanish class that defended their rights to patronage, and the supporters of the mother country opposed the autonomist party. Only in the face of the now imminent danger which would set off the revolution of 1895 did the mother country grant a relative autonomy to the island. The Liberal Autonomist party began with this concession to carry out its program, but it was already too late. The people demanded something else—they demanded complete political emancipation of the island.

Hegel and Cuban Autonomy

RAFAEL MONTORO, as has been pointed out, was educated in Spain. There he was under the philosophical influences that guided his political ideas. While still very young, he met in Spain his countryman José del Perojo, who founded the *Revista Contemporánea* in 1875. Perojo had been in Germany taking Kuno Fischer's courses. He was well versed in Kant and German idealism. German philoso-

---

[109] *El programa autonomista*, 1894.
[110] Speech in *el Teatro Tacón* in 1892.

phy was popular in Spain. Don Francisco Giner de los Ríos, together with Salmerón and Sanz de Río, headed the Spanish *Krausista* movement. Others, like Montoro, were followers of Hegel. From Hegel's doctrine the Cuban leader was to derive the thesis for his own doctrine. From Hegel he would also deduce his principles of authority and order, and with them the principles renouncing revolution.

History, according to Hegel's doctrine, follows a path such that all violent efforts to turn it aside are futile. "Historical laws," said Montoro, "rule with an insuperable power over political events, which, when they are considered superficially, seem shifting and variable. . . . Neither in nature nor in history," he added, "are those phantasmagorical appearances possible, those ridiculous transformations of which some dream." All the great reforms that history displays are not the result of a miraculous transformation, but rather the result of silent, continuous, and painful attempts to achieve them. "Consider any of the great reforms of our century," he said, "and you will see how there preceded each one of them a very painful period of attempts and conquest."[111] "That monument of genius and wisdom," as he calls Hegel's *Phenomenology of Mind,* speaks of these troubles, these attempts, and these conquests. Montoro was aware of the great errors committed by Spain and their sad consequences in the colony, but, faithful to the German philosopher, he believed in overcoming these errors and in their dialectical negation.

Historical change will come; sooner or later it must come, it is the inevitable law of history. One must only know how to wait and prepare for its coming. Impatience can do nothing to hasten it. Dialectic moves on its own, and what is to be will be. If the environment is stifling, energy will become taut and, with energy, the will to overcome it. Rebellion is necessary but always within limits—laws; that is, the state. One should not break with the state, for it is the organ of universal history. Only the state itself can carry out the Hegelian *aufheben.*

"From the free people of the colony," he said, there will arise "the free people of the Republic, as naturally as the sprout comes from the seed or as man reaches the age of maturity from inexperience to the enthusiasms of a vigorous youth." The colony is thought

[111] *La ideología autonomista.*

of, following Hegel in his *Phenomenology*, as the historical stage of the slave, still deprived of the freedom of the state although already conscious of its liberty. The autonomists feared that the colony might attempt to gain the liberty of the state before the appointed time. Montoro feared that Cuba would want to become free before its society "was in a condition of plenitude, energy, population, wealth, organization, and culture which would prevent its falling into the fullness of another stronger life." Thinking no doubt of the United States, he feared that Cuba would become independent from Spain, only to fall as the result of a lack of vigor—vigor which can only be attained historically, in the Hegelian way of thinking, under the domination of another nation. Cuba would continue to be a slave. "Under this domination our history would dissolve into the dense and deep history of a dominating nation, in which we would again experience an alien liberty, in spite of the fact that our independence might point with a dramatic irony toward a political fulfillment which is of no value whatsoever without a vital plenitude."[112]

Following Hegel, Montoro felt that America in general and Cuba in particular was discovering itself, preparing itself to take its place in universal culture; that is, making history. Moreover, it appeared that America was rapidly assuming its role in history, while Europe was gradually losing its role. Herein was the so-called *Americanization* of European culture. The United States was giving a new meaning to universal history when it seriously invaded European culture in a manner that appeared to be inevitable. As for Cuba, Montoro said, "We know that the only works that are lasting are those that are not improvised, those that are wisely planned with reflection and with perseverance." In this sense he felt that Cuba was still not mature enough to take its place in history. Before this could occur, "Cuba must strengthen herself thoroughly, practice harsh discipline, and undergo a long apprenticeship." This apprenticeship should be carried out in Cuban political life. It was necessary to begin with harsh civic training.

This training was to prepare Cuba for rising above its colonial history. Referring to the necessity of including a conservative party, he said: "I frankly declare to you that I would look with satisfaction upon a true conservative party among us. I would combat it because

[112] *Ibid.*

I love liberty, but I would not hesitate to consider its existence a fortunate event for our country. The mission of conservative parties indeed cannot be more necessary nor more elevated. They are the depositories of tradition; they represent that spirit of permanence which engenders the solidarity of all generations in the sentiments of the country. Those parties, in short, have the lofty mission of uniting today to yesterday, the present to the past, so that transitions will never be violent or uncertain."[113]

Spencer and Separatism

ENRIQUE JOSÉ VARONA, basing his theories on Spencer's positivism, opposed the Hegelian theories of Rafael Montoro. Montoro was an idealist and an optimist; Varona was a realist and a pessimist. Varona did not believe in the solutions proposed by the Autonomist party. We must be realists. Cuba can go nowhere by legal means. Spain will concede nothing to the island that is not taken from her by force. The long colonial history of Cuba had been nothing but pure deceptions and blows for the patriots. The voices of the autonomists were not the first to seek understanding for the island from the mother country. It had all been in vain. The people of Cuba could not continue to display an idealistic attitude; they must be completely realistic, and reality demonstrated that the only way to put an end to all their troubles was through the complete independence of Cuba. The utopian autonomists, noted Varona, with their intent to keep peace at all costs, were restraining popular initiative and imposing an arbitrary solution. They were struggling for the moral assimilation of the Cuban people with the Spanish people, which, in addition to being an insane desire, assumed the nullification of the Cuban people's personality as a social aggregate with its own peculiar character.

Varona went beyond the autonomists. Cuban independence, if it was to be, must be a complete independence. He favored revolution, and to defend his thesis, he used Herbert Spencer's theory of evolution. This same theory which in other Hispanic-American countries had been used against revolutions, as the Mexican positivists had used it, to Varona would justify the Cuban revolution of independence. Speaking of evolution, he said, "Just as millions and millions of seeds

[113] *Ibid.*

perish for each plant or animal that is produced," in like manner, for every single idea that succeeds in taking root, joining and contributing to human action, "an infinite number of ideas and images pass through the human mind without leaving any trace." In this manner nature and man evolve. All those small influences gradually effect modification, "but so very slowly that the adaptation of individuals is realized in a way that is imperceptible."

This does not imply, however, that at times these changes do not occur by leaps and bounds and that sometimes an evolution occurs in the form of a revolution. "There are times," he said, "when this regular march forward seems to be broken and there seem to arise accidental causes endowed with a particular energy to change and alter everything. Suddenly upheavals and political and religious revolutions seem to break out and change the face of a society." This also is in accordance with evolution; it is one of its forms of expression. "All these small causes noted," he added, "even though they operate by chance and on a limited number of individuals at the same time, gradually *accumulate energy*" until the equilibrium is finally upset. Then "certain ideas appear false and certain institutions absurd. . . . Since the milieu has been gradually and imperceptibly modified, defective adaptation has resulted at one or two points and *malaise* is the logical outcome. Ideas of reform begin to open a path for themselves, and when they have finally taken hold of the minds of a devoted and active minority—for every revolution is the work of a minority—they are not long in taking concrete form and are put into effect by either peaceful or violent means." Then "one sees the old society stripped of its previous form and taking on another form that is more resplendent: a revolution has taken place."[114] Revolution was thus justified as a solution to Cuban problems.

Like a good realist, however, Varona knew that a revolution alone is not sufficient to change society. After the revolution a second task lies ahead, the adaptation of society to new forms. A revolution does not completely modify society; it only brings to the fore a body of ideas according to which it is to be modified. These ideas, through the revolution, are put in a "position to exert a more direct and firmer influence on the mass of followers, the great majority of whom have not

[114] *La moral en la evolución.*

changed in any way." Then a silent struggle between the old and the new begins. The rest of Hispanic America was again engaged in that struggle. The victory of one or the other forces in this struggle, said Varona, is apparent, "because at times it is thought that the old ideas have triumphed under the guise of reaction, while, in fact, what has triumphed is a compromise of ideas and practices in which the old form is mixed with not a few of the new elements. At other times it is believed that revolutions submerge everything, while what they really do is only cast in new molds many old ideas and sentiments." What, in fact, was achieved was an advance forward of some paces, and something as important, as "facilitating the new adaptations that were necessary." A revolution is therefore not a radical break with the past, but a way of facilitating the adaptation of the past to the future. That, then, is evolution, and in that way real progress is made. "How is it that we do not recall," said Varona, "Latin America's revolutions which seem to destroy everything, and once the first, great commotions are over, the same old regime begins to emerge little by little under new names.?"[115] The natural rhythm of evolution is not broken; revolution is simply one of its forms of expression. Cuba, as could be deduced from these ideas, should hurl herself into the revolutionary struggle as the Cuban patriots had already decided. The equilibrium had been upset, the adaptation was defective, and the *malaise* was unbearable. Once the revolution was over, the country would regain the equilibrium that it would have within evolution. The very nature of things proclaimed this necessity. It was not necessary to continue waiting. Revolution was a natural form of the evolution of Cuban society.

XIII. THE LATIN RACE AND POSITIVISM

The Intellectual Transformation of Mexico

To THE ADMIRATION accorded the United States in Hispanic America, there was added the Mexican attitude of distrust, a natural consequence of the war of 1847 with the United States. Mexico felt weak and inferior compared with the powerful "Colossus of the North." This weakness and inferiority was imputed to the racial origin of its inhabitants: Hispanic or Latin. Mexico was looked upon as a weak

[115] *Ibid.*

nation because it belonged to a chaotic, anarchistic race, incapable of organizing itself to carry out works similar to those that had made the United States of North America a powerful nation.[116]

The Spanish race was considered a utopian, idealistic, and visionary race which sacrificed reality to its dreams, a race which scorned every material effort and preferred to maintain itself in a world of futile idealism. It necessarily followed that nations of this race would have to be inferior to people with a practical mind such as those in England and the United States. History bore out these critics. England had defeated theocratic Spain, and her descendants in America had defeated the sons of Spain. North America had prevailed because it had encountered a weak people. No one was to blame for this weakness; it was a racial defect. The Mexicans, instead of organizing themselves, had done nothing from the time of their independence but kill each other over ideas that were only words and over *caudillos* who claimed to incarnate these ideas. Hence the need to tear out the roots of this evil characteristic inherited by the Mexicans.

Education was the best instrument for carrying out this transformation of the Mexicans. But to accomplish the deed there must be a doctrine, an ideology, an instrument of thought that would effect this change. Positivistic doctrine was the adequate instrument. Positivism was a doctrine for practical men, for men like the Anglo-Saxons who had forged their countries into great nations. The same doctrine, it was thought, would endow the Mexicans with a series of qualities without which neither authentic liberty nor an authentic democracy was possible. One of the supporters of this doctrine, Telesforo García, said, "In the country where positivism has its roots in the national character, where it has its proper seat, where the experimental method is applied to every manifestation of life—in England, in short—that is where liberty is most secure and law is best guaranteed." The very opposite takes place in countries where metaphysical philosophies or absolute idealism reign, as in "Germany, the cradle of all absolute idealisms; as in France, the mother of all absolute laws; and as in Spain and Italy and the other nations that have nursed at the breast of those beauties. All these nations have been victims of every kind of tyranny, in spite of the priests who in some

[116] See my works on positivism summarized in this chapter.

places have guillotined men in the name of the absolute and in others have burned them. Positivistic nations like England and the United States have been able to protect their liberties, while metaphysical nations like Germany, France, and Spain, in the name of a liberty taken in a metaphysical sense, have made that liberty an impossibility."

Positivism was also the best means for teaching the Mexicans to organize themselves intellectually and socially. The social order that Mexicans needed so badly depended on the order established in their minds. Hence philosophical doctrines or systems that sought their basis in a world outside the limits of the positive were considered inadequate for their mentality. "How can we reform ourselves," asked Telesforo García, "if we increase the defects of our race, the defects of the Latin temperament, by making it overflow its boundaries instead of rationally erecting a dike to restrain it. We Latins," he said, are "pre-eminently *idealistic* and pre-eminently *mystical*," hence it is absurd that, "instead of disciplining the mind with very strict scientific methods, instead of guiding activity toward well-defined positive ends, we seek contemplation, woo fantasy, court dreams, and regard work as dull; but work should place the crown of the king of nature on the head of man. . . .

"We might say," he continued, "that in history the Latin appears as a synthetic race, and the Anglo-Saxons as an analytical race. The former in order to perfect itself must seek great syntheses, the latter great analyses." Mexicans as members of the Latin family should imbue themselves with the qualities proper to the Anglo Saxons, a practical sense of life and a capacity for material work. But in order that Mexicans can become "great investigators, great experimenters, and very practical," we must "adopt methods and teachings which pursue those ends" instead of adopting methods and systems that increase our racial defects; "we have received from nature in full abundance"[117] qualities which can be produced by educational systems based on metaphysics!

Justo Sierra (1848–1912), one of the greatest of the Mexican educators, emphasized still more the need for Mexicans to change intellectually and socially if they wished to survive in that struggle for life in which, according to Darwin's theory, only the strongest sur-

[117] In *La Libertad, periódico político* (México, 1878–84).

vive. In order to attain this, Mexicans must pass from the *military era,* the era of revolutions and civil wars, to the *industrial era,* the era of work, the era of maximum personal effort. And they must do so "quickly, since the giant growing at our side, coming closer and closer to us as a result of great achievements in manufacturing and agriculture in its border states and the expansion of its railroads, would tend to absorb us and dissolve us if we were weak."[118] History had already spoken some few years previously. Mexico had been defeated by the country to the North, not as the result of the superiority of arms, but rather as the result of the superiority of the North American's intellectual and social organization. The liberals had struggled in vain to give the Mexican people a progressive education and organization. The old vested interests of the clergy and the army inherited from the colony were stronger and were opposed to progress. It was these same vested interests that defeated Mexico, not the arms of the North. Hence at the conclusion of this struggle the reform party resolutely proposed to carry out a program that would put an end to such a situation. This program, said Justo Sierra, consisted of "educating the people with complete freedom from the church and colonizing the country by breaking the barrier of religious intolerance by confiscating all property held by the clergy." Only in this way could Mexicans attain and create what they had needed so desperately and did not have in the war with the North—a national conscience.

This was the task that the generation in whose hands the destiny of Mexico had fallen from 1880 to 1910 attempted to carry out. This generation attempted to establish order in the Mexican conscience and order in their social organization. They established a new kind of national education and tried likewise to establish a new social order. Science was to be the basis of both orders: positivism was the instrument to establish the intellectual order; *porfirismo,* the expression of the social order.

Freedom and Social Order

IN 1878 a new political group appeared in the Mexican capital. General Porfirio Díaz had only recently come into power through a revo-

[118] *Evolución política del pueblo mexicano* (México, 1900–1902).

lution against President Sebastián Lerdo de Tejada. The new group used as its mouthpiece the newspaper *La Libertad*, to which it gave the Comtian positivistic motto of "Order and Progress." Several of the editors had been students of Gabino Barreda (1818–81), the man who had introduced positivism into Mexico and who was responsible for the success of the educational reform he had put into effect at the request of the Benito Juárez's government in 1867. This reform was based on the philosophical doctrine of positivism.

The new group began to agitate public opinion on the idea of order. But according to the editors of *La Libertad* it was a new kind of order that had nothing whatever to do with the order inherited from the colony and defended by the conservatives. The men of this new group called themselves conservatives but liberal-conservatives. "Our goal," they said, is freedom, "but our methods are conservative." They were called conservatives because they were opposed to revolutionary methods to secure freedom. That, they said, was to be reached by evolution, not revolution.

The urgent, the immediate basis on which it would be possible to win this desired freedom was order. The liberals had been unable to understand this; they had wanted to grant the people liberties for which they were not prepared and the result was anarchy. It was first necessary to educate the people, to establish in the mind the realization of liberty and the obligation that it entailed. As long as Mexicans did not have this realization, any set of laws or new constitutions which attempted to establish liberty by a simple decree would fail. This pretension was merely utopian, the fruit of that spirit so alien to the sense of the practical which the Mexicans did not have.

But finally a group of Mexicans with a practical concept of life had appeared; they were trained in the methods of positivistic science. This group was to be charged with the future establishment of an authentic democratic government based on genuine social freedom. In the meantime, while this idea was being effected, it would be necessary above all else to establish an order at any cost. There would have to be an end to the already permanent anarchy, to revolutions and military uprisings. The liberal constitution of 1857 was one of the obstacles to this order; it had been drawn up by men with a utopian outlook and for a utopian country that still did not exist.

The most irritating thing, said Francisco G. Cosmes, one of the editors of *La Libertad*, was that there were still men with such an out-dated mentality that they still believed in the ideas held by the legislators of 1857, "after fifty years of constant struggle for an ideal that once realized produced only disastrous results for the country. ... It is indeed very sad to see the atrocious wounds inflicted by revolutions and civil war on the Mexican Republic still suffering from the bloody consequences, and at the same time to be able to find anyone yet among us who would defend the revolutionary ideal." Justo Sierra, who had also been director of this same newspaper, said, directing his criticism at the lawmakers of 1857, "Our basic law was drawn up by men of the Latin race who believe that a thing is true and capable of being realized if it is logical, who tend to humanize any ideal abruptly and violently, who go in one day from the rule of the absolute to the rule of the relative without transition or gradual changes and by attempting to force the people to practice what only becomes truth in the realm of pure reason. These men, and perhaps we are like them, who confuse heaven with earth, drew up for us an elevated and noble code of laws, but one in which everything tends toward differentiation, toward individual autonomy carried to the extreme, that is to say, to the point that the performance of civil duties seems to cease and everything is converted into individual rights."

It was necessary to counter utopian and anarchist liberalism with a realistic and orderly liberalism, a conservative liberalism. We seek, said Justo Sierra, "the formation of a great conservative party composed of all the elements of order which in our country have sufficient talent to rise to public life. ... Our banner is not a man but an idea. We intend to rally around this idea all those who believe that our country has already passed through the period when aspirations were to be reached by revolutionary violence; we want all those who believe that the precise moment has arrived for the organization of a party that is more kindly disposed toward a practical liberty than toward a proclaimed liberty, a party that is thoroughly convinced that progress rests on the normal development of a society, that is, on order."

"Our banner is not a man but an idea." Those words were the expression of the ideal of a new order, an order whose strength would not depend on the will of the *caudillo,* an impersonal order derived from the Mexicans' own mind. But the order became, at least for the moment, one more utopia. First of all, the people must be educated for order. In the meantime any other order would be good. There seemed to be no solution to the problem. There was the desire to eliminate any kind of order that depended on the will of any *caudillo,* but there was also the need for someone with enough personal prestige to establish the basis of the new order. This someone, of course, could only be a simple instrument, something that was to be transitory as the Mexicans acquired the mental habits for an autonomous order, an order that was beyond any outside force.

For the time being, liberties that were openly of a utopian nature were to be limited. The country must be given confidence, the only means by which it could initiate its regeneration. "Society has already rejected rights," exclaimed Francisco G. Cosmes. "What it wants is bread! Instead of constitutions full of sublime ideas which we have never seen put into practice for one single moment, society prefers the protection afforded by peace, so that it can work quietly; it prefers a feeling of security in its interests and prefers to know that the authorities, instead of plunging hurriedly into the search for the ideal, will hang plagiarizers, thieves, and revolutionaries.... Fewer rights and fewer liberties in exchange for greater order and peace! ... No more utopias! I want order and peace even if it be at the expense of all the rights that have cost me so dearly.... Moreover," he added, "the day is not far off when the nation will say, I want order and peace at the expense of my independence."[119]

How could this order and peace demanded so urgently be attained? Not by an arbitrary act, they declared, nor by personalist governments which had been so fatal to the nation. "There is nothing more odious," said an editorial in *La Libertad,* "nor anything more adverse to progress for us than the rule of one or more men without any fixed policy. This is what we think of as dictatorship." Nevertheless, Mexican reality had produced dictatorship and tyran-

[119] *La Libertad.*

nies. In order to put an end to them, it was necessary to change this reality; but in the meantime it must be taken into account. In order "to put an end to dictatorship *de facto*, it was necessary to find a feasible constitution"; but such a thing was impractical under present circumstances; "we must be content with asking extraordinary authorizations for these extraordinary times." In another of his articles Francisco G. Cosmes said, "We have already acquired an infinity of rights which have only brought misery and *malaise* to society. Let us now try a little bit of honest tyranny to see what effects it will produce." This honest tyranny was to be the tyranny of General Porfirio Díaz.

Gabino Barreda and Comtian Positivism

LET US now return to the scholar who introduced positivism into Mexico. In 1867 there was a definite triumph of the group which, according to Sierra, "was a minority on the day following the North American invasion and became a majority on the eve of the French invasion." On *El Cerro de las Campanas* the deluded Emperor Maximilian paid with his life for the treason of the Mexican clergy and army and the ambition of Little Napoleon. In that same year, in the city of Guanajuato, the physician and lawyer Gabino Barreda (1818–81) delivered his *Oración cívica* in which he presented an interpretation of Mexican history. Barreda emphasized three great periods in Mexican history: the theological, the metaphysical, and the positivistic. The first was represented by the colonial epoch, the second by the war of independence and the struggle against the representatives of retrogression, and the third and last stage began with the triumph of the reformers. According to Barreda, the positivistic spirit which had won its victory in Europe was now winning its last battle in Mexico. Not only was this a Mexican victory, it was a victory for mankind.

Barreda from 1849 to 1851 had taken several courses with Auguste Comte in Paris, where he had gone to complete his medical studies. Upon his return to Mexico he immediately joined the reform movement. In his address *Oración cívica*, he applied the positivistic interpretation to the history of Mexico. However, the motto of Comtian positivism, "Love, Order, and Progress" was changed to "Liberty, Order, and Progress." In this way Mexican reality was fulfilled: The triumphant party, the party of progress, was known as the Liberal party. Barreda's principal problem, like that of his followers, was to attempt to reconcile such opposite terms as "order" and "liberty." Both liberals and positivists soon became engaged in public polemics on what each understood by the term "liberty."

Soon after Barreda had delivered his address, the President of the Republic and the leader of the winning party, Benito Juárez, sent for him to take charge of establishing the bases for the educational reform of the nation. The dreams of the old liberals, of men like José María Luis Mora, were to be realized in this reform. The generation that was to conduct the destiny of the nation in the future must be prepared for the task. Barreda's mission was to transform the mentality of the Mexicans, and the transformation must be radical. Anything that would be the source of any new disorders must be extirpated from their minds. Juárez, said Justo Sierra, realized that the *bourgeoisie*, from whom the men must necessarily be chosen to take the political and social leadership of the nation, were in need of a preparatory education. The revolution that had triumphed with arms was being transformed, in order to stabilize its victory, into an *intellectual revolution*. One step more was being taken toward the nation's independence, which Gabino Barreda called the "intellectual emancipation." The Mexican educator devoted himself to this new task. From the schools he reformed, as well as from his own classrooms, there came the young men who were to lead the country down new paths. This was the beginning of a new experiment, the results of which were of great importance not only to the history of Mexico, but to history in general.

The period of armed revolution had come to an end; the period of the intellectual revolution was beginning. Order at the disposition of certain limited social bodies had been destroyed; a new order was beginning. This new order was to be, as Mora had conceived it, an order that was at the disposition of all society. The old order was based on *corporal violence* and on *intellectual violence* practiced by the army and the clergy respectively. The new order rested on *intellectual conviction*. Mora had said, "The effects of force are rapid but passing; those of persuasion are slow but sure." Freely and without violence, out of pure conviction, Mexicans would eventually suc-

277

ceed in establishing an authentic order, a constructive and progressive order, and only this order would be in accord with the idea of liberty. With complete freedom, Mexicans, once convinced of their social responsibilities, would set up the kind of order that was proper to them.

The state Barreda regarded as "the guardian of material order." It was a social order in which the rights of the individual were limited by the rights of others. Respect for the rights of others was the best guarantee for the respect of one's own rights. This realization, and no other, was the best guarantee for peace and order. Juárez had already expressed this idea when he said, "Respect for the rights of others is peace." Order would thus originate in the mind and would rest on logical conviction. By respecting this order, whose limitations would be set by the state, the individual would enjoy absolute freedom. No force could break the limit of this freedom. Barreda called it the freedom of conscience.

"I hope," he said, "that in the future a complete freedom of conscience, an absolute freedom of exposition and discussion which will admit all ideas and all inspirations, will shed its light everywhere and will make every disturbance that is not spiritual and every revolution that is not intellectual unnecessary and impossible." This freedom would be guaranteed by a material order, accepted by conviction, and protected by the state. "I hope that the material order, preserved at all costs by those who govern and respected by the governed, will be a sure guarantee and a safe way by which to continue ever on the happy road to progress and civilization."[120]

This idea of "a material order" was an attack on another of the sources of disorder which Mora had also pointed out: government as an instrument in the service of certain privileged classes. The government was only to be the guardian of the social order; privileges belonged solely to the sphere of personal effort. In this sphere the individual was to be completely free, but the state could not be in the service of individual privileges. "Their rights will extend only as far as their capabilities take them." But to secure these rights, they must make an instrument of the state. The role of the state is to see that these rights are respected. Nevertheless, Barreda, as a good Comtian,

[120] Opúsculos, discusiones y discoursos (México, 1877).

held that certain privileges such as wealth should be limited by the interests of society. Like Comte, he thought that wealth was a social holding, but he differed from Comte in that he did not admit the intervention of the state in this area. At most he accepted the fact that the wealthy, "once their needs were met and satisfied, should be convinced that what they have in excess they must cultivate and utilize, under the penalty of *moral responsibility*, as a public force which society has placed in their hands for the common good and common progress." He felt that it was not necessary to regulate wealth; what should be done was "to humanize the wealthy."

Gabino Barreda, like his followers later, was soon engaged in a polemic with the old liberals on the definition of freedom. The liberals had not been long in realizing that behind the ideas which the positivists expounded on freedom and order there lurked a new dogmatism with all its political consequences; it was a dogmatism as dangerous as the clerical, for like the latter it attempted to impose certain definite ideas through the medium of a definite educational system. Such a thing was contrary to the freedom of conscience for which the liberals had struggled in the past.

Barreda opposed the idea of freedom held by the Mexican liberals with the positivistic concept of freedom. "Freedom," he said, "is commonly thought of as the right to do anything or to want anything without any regard for the law or the force which directs it. If such freedom did exist, it would be as immoral as it would be absurd, for it would make any discipline, and consequently all order, impossible." True freedom is not incompatible with order. Freedom, he added, consists of submitting wholeheartedly to the law of order that should control it. Something is free when it follows its normal and natural course, when it encounters no obstacles which divert it by separating it from its own law and its own order. Barreda gave the following example from physics: When one says that a body falls *freely*, one is not speaking of a body that falls where it wishes, for it falls according to the law of gravity. On the other hand, when one says that this body does not fall freely, one means that it encounters obstacles that divert its fall. This is true freedom: Man is limited by the society which gives him his laws, and his freedom consists in obeying them.

Spencer and the Evolution of Mexico

THE GENERATION trained by Gabino Barreda, chosen to lead the destiny of the nation down the path of progress, discovered that the limitations of Comtian positivism were rigid. For Comtian positivism, regardless of Barreda's efforts, did not justify the freedom that was of paramount interest to the future Mexican *bourgeoisie*: the freedom to acquire wealth without any restrictions other than the ability of each individual. Comtism in a strict sense subordinated the individual to society in all material areas. This was the meaning of Comte's "sociocracy," and as such it established his positivistic policy. This policy, as well as the Religion of Humanity, was rejected by the Mexican positivists, for both were held to be contrary to the interests for which positivism had been accepted. The important task was to mold the governing class from the Mexican *bourgeoisie*, which was becoming more and more powerful. Anglo-Saxon countries offered a model for this class.

The Mexican *bourgeoisie* theorists soon found a theory which justified their interests. It was the theory of the English positivists John Stuart Mill and Herbert Spencer, especially the latter, and with them Charles Darwin's evolutionism. This doctrine seemed to coincide best with the interests they sought to justify. It was likewise the best expression of the practical spirit which they admired so much. According to these doctrines the Mexican must be educated. English positivism, far from contradicting the idea of individual freedom in the greater part of its expressions, justified it. The liberal regimes of England and the United States stood as great examples, and there stood Spencer opposing the coercive state and Mill defending individual freedom. With both, the state was exactly what Mora had longed for: an instrument of protection for each and every one of the individuals who compose it. The Spencerian idea of progress likewise made it possible to offer, at least in the future, an ideal of freedom such as the people had struggled for on different occasions. To achieve this, there must be a definite degree of progress.

It is here that we again come in contact with that young group of positivists who in the pages of the newspaper *La Libertad* sought a new order and aspired to establish an honest tyranny. This group was no longer following Comte, but Mill and Spencer. How could they then justify ideas that appeared to be contradictory? They found the justification in Spencer's theory of evolution. "I am convinced beyond a shadow of a doubt," said Sierra, "that society is an organism, and even though it is distinct from other organisms and for this reason called by Spencer a superorganism, it has undeniable analogies with living organisms. Like animal organisms, society is also subject to the laws of evolution. According to these laws, all organisms carry out a movement of integration and differentiation in a line that goes from the homogeneous to the heterogeneous, from the indefinite to the definite. In social organisms it passes from social homogeneity to individual differentiation, and then from complete order to complete freedom.

Thus the idea the old liberals continued to defend was not denied. What was denied, by drawing from Spencer's *Principles of Sociology*, was that Mexican society had already reached the high level of progress that was required to obtain this freedom. They did not believe, like the Comtians, that this freedom belonged to a stage of metaphysical transition. On the contrary, they considered it a goal still to be reached. It was not something of the past but of the future. But before such a thing could come about, there must be a social evolution in that direction. For that reason the new Conservatives were opposed to the constitution of 1857; they felt that it was utopian and therefore ahead of its time. Such constitutions were only applicable to countries like the United States, given the high level of progress that they had reached; but they were not suitable for countries like Mexico, which were still on a lower level. "Is it not nonsense," they asked, "to erect a huge edifice on marshy ground without first digging solid foundations?"

The first thing was to seek the material advancement of the country. Liberties were meaningless in countries materially backward. When this advancement was made, liberty in all of her multiple forms would be added in abundance through a process of natural evolution. "The day that we can say that the fundamental charter has given us a million colonists, we shall have found the constitution that befits us. It will no longer be mere words on our lips, it will be the plough in our hands, the locomotive on the rails, and money everywhere. Ideal liberty will soon appear. We prefer normal, slow progress to precipitating matters by violence." These men were partisans, of progress by the route of *evolution*, never by way of *revolution*.

The urgent, the immediate task at hand was to fortify society, integrate it, and make it homogeneous, for as society became more integrated and more homogeneous, it would continue to become better differentiated and defined. As the social order became permanent, individual freedom would continue to develop. Up to this time, according to the positivists, Mexico had been a chaotic country and hence a country that had not complied with the laws of progress pointed out by Spencer. For that reason, before anything else was accomplished, it was necessary to establish order. It was not possible to go from anarchy to true freedom.

The demand for a strong state to assume the task of establishing the order so necessary for the progress of Mexico was now natural and justified. It was now natural, said Justo Sierra, "to demand for a people who live under the worst conditions of life the vitalization of a center which will strengthen the force of cohesion." For, "if the contrary obtains, incoherence will be more and more pronounced and the organism will not become integrated, and this society will be an abortion." It was disorder, said Sierra, that made the Mexican nation one of the weakest and most defenseless of those within the orbit of civilization. While Mexico continued destroying itself, "near us there lives a marvellous collective animal for whose enormous intestine enough food does not exist, and this animal is armed to devour us. . . . In the face of this colossus we are exposed to being a test of Darwin's theory, and in the struggle for existence all probabilities are against us."[121]

The Generation of "Los Científicos"

THE *political evolution* of freedom in the political field would be sacrificed on the altars of what Sierra called the *social evolution*. That

[121] In *La Libertad;* collected in *Periodismo político,* Vol. IV of his *Obras Completas* (México, 1948).

is, all freedom was to be limited on the altars of the social organization of the Mexicans, and this was unavoidable if they were to attain the desired political freedom. It was a very difficult task to root out the disorderly habits from the minds of Mexicans. "Unfortunately," said Sierra, "those innate habits of the Mexican have become a thousand times more difficult to destroy than domination by the privileged classes. Only a complete change in working conditions and thought patterns in Mexico can bring about a transformation of such magnitude," and only a strong state could effect such a change. The day that a group or a party succeeded in organizing itself, on that day the evolution would be on its way. "And man, more vital in democracies than in aristocracies, would then arrive; the function would create the organ."

All the political power and, with it, Mexican freedom were to be handed over to the strong man, General Porfirio Díaz. "So that the President," said Sierra, "could carry out the great task that was imperative, he needed a maximum amount of authority in his hands, not only legal authority but also *political authority* which would allow him to assume the effective leadership of the political bodies, that is, the legislative bodies and the executive power of the states; he needed *social authority,* thus establishing himself as the supreme justice of the peace of Mexican society with its general assent; and he needed moral authority." But all these delegations and abdications of power to one man had to be compensated for by the action of the state in the area which was so important to the leaders of the intellectual emancipation: education. Honorable tyranny was an educational method by which Mexicans were to learn the meaning of freedom.

On November 26, 1867, General Porfirio Díaz, who had revolted against Sebastián Lerdo de Tejada's government with the cry of "no re-election," became the provisional president after the victory of his troops. On December 5 of the same year he yielded the power to General Méndez, but he again took provisional control on February 16, 1877. On September 25, 1880, with Diaz' permission General Manuel González was elected. But in 1884, Díaz definitely returned to the presidency, which he held until May 25, 1911, the date of the triumph of the Mexican Revolution. All the political forces of the country were grouped about General Díaz. His figure came to symbolize the order and the peace for which the men trained in positivism had clamored. Materialism and dehumanization were converted into models of life for the generation which developed during his regime: industry, money, railroads, and always more money. Progress definitely seemed to triumph. The social evolution seemed to be moving forward with gigantic steps; but in the feeling of satisfaction freedom was forgotten, the very thing for which it was said that order had been established. The men of this generation were content with a very special kind of freedom: the freedom to acquire wealth. It was a freedom in which not all classes could participate. The lack of true freedom, Sierra foresaw, was to destroy what had been attained in the sphere of evolution.

A new type of Mexican arose during the Díaz regime. Comparing himself to the liberal generation that had preceded him, he described himself as follows: "We are censured for our lack of beliefs, for our positivism, for our ill-disguised scorn for the institutions of the past." This charge was true, but it was the result of the different kind of *education* that they had received: "You liberals were nurtured in Voltaire and Rousseau, the encyclopedists and the *choix de Rapports* of the French Revolution. The most advanced of you were trained in the lofty metaphysics of the German school, while we studied the logic of Mill and Bain, the philosophy of Comte and Spencer, the science of Huxley and Tyndall, Virchow and Helmholtz." A different kind of education would produce men equally different. "You liberals left the classrooms intoxicated with enthusiasm for the great ideas of 1889, and quoting Danton and the Girondists you rushed to the mountains to battle the clergy, to consolidate the reforms, to defeat the reactionaries, to copy our laws from the beautiful utopias that were currently being used in philosophical transactions." On the other hand, "we, less enthusiastic, more skeptical, perhaps more self-centered, were seeking a new explanation for Newton's binomial, we were interested in natural selection, we studied sociology with enthusiasm, we were little concerned with the heavenly spaces but much so with our earthly destiny. . . . We were engaged in questions that could not be subjected to the measuring tools of observation and experiment. The segment of the world that interests us is the one we can study with the telescope and other instruments of scientific investigation. . . . We do not recognize truth at first sight, to be sure. To reach it we need to make long journeys into the regions of science, painstaking and constant work, and laborious and patient investigation." Because of its ability, the new generation considered itself destined to guide and orient the country. Its methods were sure, perfect, and precise; they were the scientific methods learned in the schools reformed by Gabino Barreda. These methods, these men said, would be applied to the solution of all of Mexico's problems, including political problems. In 1881 they were already talking of a "Mexican School of Political Science." In 1886 several of the men of this generation became members of the House of Representatives; some of them—like Justo Sierra, Pablo Macedo, Rosendo Pineda, Francisco Bulnes, and others—were to become outstanding figures of the Porfirio Díaz regime. All of them were to leave their mark on the period known as the era of *porfirismo*. The era of *"los científicos"* was beginning.

Political Order and Economic Freedom

In 1892 a political group known as the Liberal Union party issued a manifesto to the nation. In the manifesto they pointed out the principles upon which Don Porfirio's regime rested. The purpose of this pronouncement was to support the fourth re-election of General Porfirio Díaz. To this end the party presented a platform that would satisfy the interests of the Mexican *bourgeoisie*, a class that was becoming more and more powerful. The manifesto spoke of analyzing "scientifically" the social situation of Mexico, its problems and its solutions. Soon the opposition and the mass of people in general whose political rights had been taken from them began to call this party by the disdainful and ironic name of *Partido de los científicos*.

The manifesto mentioned, among other things, the need to concede greater freedom to Mexican society, since it appeared that it had now reached a greater degree of progress. It looked as though at last the promised freedom was to be granted. Until recently it had been necessary to give greater power to the Executive. Now it seemed that the time had come to concede greater freedom to the people.

Our party, said the manifesto, "is now in the very midst of establishing a rational discipline. This will allow it to be completely explicit in the expression of its will within the constitutional formula. It will likewise allow it to participate in a more active manner in the management of public affairs by pointing out the paths that lead to its supreme ideal of freedom in perpetual union with order." The new party came forth as the heir to the ideals of the old Liberal party, but with one difference: it was convinced that freedom is not possible if a definite degree of progress has not been previously reached. This order now seemed to be a reality, thanks to Porfirio Díaz' government. Once order was established, liberty could soon take another step forward.

What was this step to be? The party supporting General Díaz felt that conditions were now such that a great degree of freedom could be enjoyed. "We believe that the time has now come to initiate a new era in the historical life of our party; we believe that the transformation of its directive organs into governing organs has already been consummated. We believe that just as peace and material progress have attained this objective, it now falls to the lot of political activity to consolidate order; it is its turn to demonstrate that from this day hence rebellion and civil war will be an accident, and peace based on the interest and will of a people are normal; to obtain this, it is necessary to place peace on the touchstone of freedom." The concession of greater liberties was to demonstrate whether Mexican society had or had not reached the high degree of order that was requisite to attain greater liberties.

The new party proposed a series of liberties for which it believed the Mexican now ready. However, the freedom to vote was still not considered as the most important or as one which should be granted at that time. The people could have other liberties still more important than the right to vote. "The nation," said the manifesto, "would like for its government to be in a position to demonstrate that it regards the present state of peace as a definite fact by reorganizing economically some branches of the administration. . . . It would like for national *freedom of commerce*, through the abolishment of internal customs duties, to be an accomplished fact and not an aspiration that was periodically renewed. Only in this way will peace have permeated future Mexican generations whose resources have been encumbered in order to create our credit and our progress, the way of maintaining progress and of *permitting credit to accumulate a capital gain* which can be converted into a better state of well-being and vigor. Under these conditions peace will never seem dear."

What did these words mean? First, they began by speaking of the need to establish greater liberties, but then they affirmed that the least important of these liberties was the *freedom to vote* or political freedom. The freedom they proposed to be granted immediately was commercial freedom, more fully, *economic freedom* which permitted the accumulation and the formation of capital. What was sought was the reduction of the number of state interventions in the economic field, not in the political field. Political freedom could indeed continue to be sacrificed, if in exchange for it there was obtained what might be called *the right to acquire wealth*, a right, to be sure, that could benefit only those who possessed enough wealth that it could be increased. As is evident, it was not a question of granting the freedom which interested the old Mexican liberals.

Political order and economic freedom were the ideal of the Mexican *bourgeoisie*. The political order maintained by General Díaz should serve the economic freedom of the *bourgeoisie*. Political rights had a secondary character; they were of no concern as long as economic freedom was not in danger. This right was reserved by the *bourgeoisie* in case there should be an attack made on the freedom to acquire wealth. It was to be used only if the government came to oppose these interests. Hence, political freedom, the right to elect leaders, could be limited to the benefit of an order that would satisfy the interests of the Mexican *bourgeoisie*. General Díaz' government represented this order. From this it can be deduced that the concern of the manifesto was the re-election of the President.

The Mexican *bourgeoisie* felt that they had reached their apogee. Their order was identified with the national order, their party with the people. Once national order was secured, then the second step should be taken: the step toward the freedom that was beneficial to their interests. Díaz was the man called to grant his freedom and to see that it should not be obstructed. The Republic, said the manifesto, "is aware that it is the effective cause of the nation's progress and tranquility, but it knows that a man has helped, in the first place, to give a practical form to the general tendencies, and this citizen is the one the convention has chosen . . . to occupy the presidency again! "[122]

The authors of the manifesto added that if Díaz were elected for the fourth time it was not because his services were thought to be indispensable but rather because he had already given proof of his ability to govern in accordance with the interests of the nation. He was not indispensable; he was useful. In this way, the *bourgeoisie* ceded their political rights and those of the Mexican people, since it thus better suited their interests, to the benefit of their economic rights. They had succeeded in making Porfirio Díaz the "honorable tyrant" who satisfied their interests, and for this reason they supported him and would support him as long as he continued to do so. From the very beginning, the theorists of the Mexican *bourgeoisie* made a distinction between what they called *personal dictatorship* and *social dictatorship*. The former was the type of dictatorship of which Mora had spoken; it was the dictatorship which served the interests of a certain group or social body such as the clergy and the army. The second type was merely the dictatorship established to protect what the *bourgeoisie* called the interests of society, that is, their own interests, which they identified with those of the latter.

But fearful that some day General Díaz' dictatorship might become a personal dictatorship or the dictatorship of a group close to him, the authors of the manifesto proposed later the independence of the judicial power, an independence guaranteed by its not being subject to removal. They also proposed the creation of political parties whose purpose was to control the political activities of the Congress and to exercise a kind of vigilance over the Executive. This was a good means to prevent the formation of a personal dictatorship. They accepted only the instrumental dictatorship put at their service, a dictatorship of the *bourgeoisie* for the benefit of the *bourgeoisie*. General Díaz was only a cog in the wheel.

But Díaz, a man of power, with a mentality similar to that which the educators of the *bourgeoisie* had attempted to destroy, would not agree to be a mere tool. The dictator opposed and vetoed all the proposed reforms which in one way or another meant a limit to his

[122] The manifesto of *"Unión Liberal"* is reproduced by Antonio Manero in his book *El antiguo régimen y la revolución* (México, 1911).

political control. He was not disposed to maintain the order that was agreeable to the Mexican *bourgeoisie* except in exchange for a total surrender of political power to him. The *bourgeoisie* would have all the political advantages that they had requested: economic freedom, the right to acquire wealth, but no part of the political power. Díaz was not prepared to share this power. Hence the economic control of the country remained in the hands of the Mexican *bourgeoisie*. José Ives Limantour, one of the signers of the manifesto, was to take charge of the economic control of the country as minister of finance.

What was to happen once the entire political freedom of a people had been delegated in exchange for the economic control of a class? Justo Sierra, with that brilliant intuition which was to set him apart from the rest of the generation to which he belonged, foresaw the future of that political framework of the *bourgeoisie*: "The nation has compounded the power of this man with a series of extra-legal delegations and abdications which belong to the social order. He had not solicited this power, but neither had he side-stepped that formidable responsibility for a moment. And is that dangerous? Horribly dangerous for the future, because it *stamps habits* upon the government, habits that are contradictory, without which there can be great men but not great nations. But Mexico has confidence in that future just as the President had in his star, and it believes that once that confidence is realized without any fear that it may change or that the supreme condition of peace may disappear, everything will come about then, everything in its time. *Let there be no mistaking it.*"[123]

[123] Justo Sierra, *Evolución política del pueblo mexicano.*

Selected Bibliography[1]

GENERAL BIBLIOGRAPHY

Belaúnde, Víctor Andrés. *Hispanic American Culture.* Houston, Texas, 1923.

Crawford, William Rex. *A Century of Latin-American Thought.* Cambridge, Harvard University Press, 1944.

Frondizi, Risieri. *Panorama de la filosofía latinoamericana contemporánea.* Buenos Aires, Minerva, 1944.

Gaos, José. *Antología del pensamiento de lengua española en la edad contemporánea.* México, Editorial Séneca, 1945.

García-Prada, Carlos. *Estudios hispanoamericanos.* México, El Colegio de México, 1945.

Henríquez Ureña, Pedro. *Las corrientes literarias en la América Hispánica.* México, Fondo de Cultura Económica, 1949.

Historia de la cultura en la América Hispánica. México, Fondo de Cultura Económica, 1947.

Insúa Rodríguez, Ramón. *Historia de la filosofía en Hispanoamérica.* Guayaquil, Universided de Guayquil, 1945.

Quesada, Vicente G. *La vida intelectual en la América española.* Buenos Aires, 1917.

Sánchez Reulet, Aníbal. *"Panorama de las ideas filosóficas en Hispanoamérica,"* Tierra Firme, Vol. II, No. 2 (Madrid, 1936).

Vitier, Medardo. *Del ensayo americano.* México, Fondo de Cultura Económica, 1945.

[1] Not all works consulted or cited in footnotes are given here; for example, no works on Brazil or Mexico are included in this bibliography.

Selected Bibliography

ARGENTINA

I. General Bibliography

Alberini. *Die Deutsche Philosophie in Argentinien*. Berlin, 1930.

Estrada, José Manuel. *La política liberal bajo la tiranía de Rosas*. Buenos Aires, Imprenta Americana, 1873.

Ghioldi, Delfina Varela Domínguez de. *Filosofía Argentina*. Buenos Aires, La Vanguardia, 1938.

Groussac, Paul. *Estudios de historia argentina*. Buenos Aires, Edit. Jesús Menéndez, 1918.

Ingenieros, José. *La evolución de las ideas argentinas*. Buenos Aires, Rosso, 1935.

————. Los iniciadores de la sociología argentina. Buenos Aires, Rosso, 1935.

————. *"Influencias de Lamennais durante la emigración argentina,"* Revista de Filosofía, Vol. VI (Buenos Aires, 1917).

Korn, Alejandro. *Influencias filosóficas en la evolución nacional*. Buenos Aires, Claridad, n. d.

Martínez Estrada, Ezequiel. *Muerte y transfiguración de Martín Fierro*. México, Fondo de Cultura Económica, 1948.

Romero, José Luis. *Las ideas políticas en Argentina*. México, Fondo de Cultura Económica, 1946.

Sánchez Viamonte, Carlos. *Historia institucional de Argentina*. México. Fondo de Cultura Económica, 1948.

II. The Romantics and the Positivists

Alberdi, Juan Bautista. *Autobiografía. Con prólogo de* Jean Jaurés. Buenos Aires, El Ateneo, 1927.

————. *Obras completas*. Buenos Aires, La Tribuna Nacional, 1886.

————. *Escritos póstumos*. Buenos Aires, Imprenta Europea, 1895.

ALBERDI, JUAN BAUTISTA, references for:

Baqué, Santiago. *"Influencia de Alberdi en la organización política del Estado Argentino,"* Anales de la Facultad de Derecho, Vol. IV (Buenos Aires, 1914).

Orgas, Raúl A. *Alberdi y el historicismo*. Córdoba, Rossi, 1937.

Peña, David. *"Alberdi, Sarmiento y Mitre,"* Revista de Filosofía, Vol. VIII, IX (Buenos Aires, 1918–19).

Sáenz Hayes, Ricardo. *La polémica de Alberdi con Sarmiento*. Buenos Aires, Edit. Gleizer, 1928.

Bassi, Ángel C. *Ciencia histórica y filosofía de la historia*. Buenos Aires, Talleres Gráficos Argentinos, 1936.

Bunge, Carlos Octavio. *Nuestra América. Prólogo de* Rafael Altamira. Barcelona, 1903.

Echeverría, Esteban. *Obras completas*. Buenos Aires, Imp. Mayo, 1870.

————. *Dogma socialista. Con noticias biográficas de* José María Gutiérrez. Buenos Aires, La Cultura Argentina, 1915.

————. *Lois ideales de Mayo y la tiranía. Prólogo de* Alberdi, *apéndice de* Bartolomé Mitre. Buenos Aires, El Ateneo, 1928.

ECHEVERRÍA, ESTEBAN, references for:

    Bucich, Antonio J. *Esteban Echeverría y su tiempo*. Buenos Aires, Edit. La Capital, 1938.

    Gutiérrez, Juan María. "*Noticias biográficas sobre Don Esteban Echeverría,*" *Obras Completas de E. Echeverría*. Buenos Aires, 1870.

    Sierra, Vicente. "*Las doctrinas sociológicas de Echeverría,*" *Revista de Filosofía*, Vol. I (1915).

Escuela positiva, La, Revista. J. Alfredo Ferreira, director. Corrientes, 1895–99.

Ferreira, J. Alfredo. *Ensayos de ética*. Buenos Aires, Ferrari Hnos., 1944.

FERREIRA, J. ALFREDO, references for:

    Bassi, Ángel C. *J. Alfredo Ferreira*. Buenos Aires, Claridad, 1943.

    Victoria, Marcos. "*El positivismo en la educación argentina,*" *Revista de filosofía*, Vol. I (1915).

García, Juan Agustín. *La ciudad indiana*. Buenos Aires, Claridad, n. d.

————. *Sobre nuestra incultura*. Buenos Aires, Claridad, 1922.

Iniciación positiva, Filosofía de la ciencia y moral social. Buenos Aires, 1938.

Ingenieros, José. *Obras completas. Revisadas y anotodas por* Aníbal Ponce. Buenos Aires, Rosso, n. d.

INGENIEROS, JOSÉ, references for:

    Agosti, Héctor P. *José Ingenieros ciudadano de la juventud*. Buenos Aires, Futuro, 1945.

    Bagú, Sergio. *Vida ejemplar de José Ingenieros*. Buenos Aires, Claridad, n. d.

Justo, Juan Bautista. *Educación pública, escritos y discursos parlamentarios*. Buenos Aires, La Vanguardia, 1930.

————. *Ideario. Compilado y ordenado por* Celso Tíndaro. Buenos Aires, La Vanguardia, 1938.

————. *El realismo ingenuo.* Buenos Aires, La Vanguardia, 1937.

————. *El socialismo.* Buenos Aires, La Vanguardia, 1933.

————. *Teoría y práctica de la historia.* Buenos Aires, La Vanguardia, 1938.

JUSTO, JUAN BAUTISTA, references for:

Cúneo, Dardo. *Juan B. Justo.* Buenos Aires, Americalee, 1943.

Ghioldi, América. *Juan B. Justo.* Buenos Aires, La Vanguardia, 1933.

Korn, Alejandro. *Hegel y Marx. Con una disertación sobre el positivismo.* Buenos Aires, Escuela de Estudios Sociales Juan B. Justo, 1934.

Positivismo, El, Organo del Comité Positivista Argentino. Buenos Aires, 1925–32.

Revista de filosofía. Buenos Aires, 1915.

Sarmiento, Domingo F. *Argirópolis. Con una introducción biográfica de* Ernesto Quesada. Buenos Aires, La Cultura Argentina, 1916.

————. *Conflicto y armonía de las razas en América.* Buenos Aires, La Cultura Argentine, 1915.

————. *Las ciento y une, polémica con J. B. Alberdi, precedida por la* "Carta de Yungay" *a Justo José de Urquiza.* Buenos Aires, La Cultura Argentina, 1916.

————. *Facundo.* Buenos Aires, La Cultura Argentina, 1915.

————. *Mi vida.* Buenos Aires, Colección Estrada, 1938.

SARMIENTO, DOMINGO F., references for:

Guerrero, Luis Juan. *Tres temas de filosofía en las entrañas del Facundo.* Buenos Aires, Imprenta López, 1945.

Martínez Estrada, Ezequiel. *Sarmiento.* Buenos Aires, Argos, 1946.

Rojas, Ricardo. *El pensamiento vivo de Sarmiento.* Buenos Aires, Losada, 1941.

Victoria, Maximio S. *Los orígenes del catolicismo y la Eucaristía.* Buenos Aires, Biblioteca Racionalista, 1936.

BOLIVIA

Arguedas, Alcides. *Historia general de Bolivia.* La Paz, Edit. Arnó Hnos., 1922.

Baptista, Mariano. *Obras completas.* La Paz, 1932.

Bustillo, Ignacio Prudencio. *Ensayo de una filosofía jurídica.* Sucre, Imp. Bolívar, 1923.

Francovich, Guillermo. *La filosofía en Bolivia.* Buenos Aires, Losada, 1945.

René-Moreno, Gabriel. *Notas biográficas y bibliogràficas.* Santiago de Chile, Imprenta Cervantes, 1901.

Taborga, Miguel de los Santos. *El positivismo, sus errores y falsas doctrinas.* Sucre, Imp. La Capital, 1905.

CHILE

I. *General Bibliography*

Amunátegui, Miguel Luis. *Los precursores de la independencia de Chile.* Santiago de Chile, Imprenta de la República, 1870.

Barros Arana, Diego. *Historia de la independencia de Chile.* Santiago de Chile, 1866.

Conferencias conmemorativas en el primer centenario de la Universidad de Chile (1843–1943). Santiago de Chile, Facultad de Filosofía y Educación, 1944.

Donoso, Ricardo. *Las ideas políticas en Chile.* México, Fondo de Cultura Económica, 1946.

Edwards Vives, Alberto. *La fronda aristocrática.* Santiago de Chile, Imp. Universitaria, 1945.

Eyzaguirre, Jaime. *Fisonomía histórica de Chile.* México, Fondo de Cultura Económica, 1948.

Lago, Tomás. *Sobre el romanticismo en 1842.* Santiago de Chile, Universidad de Chile, 1942.

Medina, José Toribio. *"El positivismo en Chile,"* Revista el Pensamiento Latino (Santiago de Chile), 1900–1901.

Muñoz Rayo, Jorge. *"Ensayo sobre la filosofía en Chile."* Unpublished MS.

Pinilla, Norberto. *Panorama y significación del movimiento literario de 1842.* Santiago de Chile, Universidad de Chile, 1942.

Vicuña Mackenna, Benjamín. *Los girondinos chilenos.* Santiago de Chile, Biblioteca de Autores chilenos, 1902.

———. *Historia general de la República de Chile desde su independencia a nuestros días. Colaboran varios autores.* 5 vols. Santiago de Chile, Imprenta Nacional, 1866–82.

II. *Special Bibliography*

Bello, Andrés. *Obras completas.* Santiago de Chile, Imp. Pedro G. Ramírez, 1881.

Bello, Andrés, references for:
Amunátegui, Miguel Luis. *Vida de don Andrés Bello.* Santiago de Chile, Imp. Pedro Ramírez, 1882.
Gaos, José. *"Introducción," Filosofía del entendimiento de Andrés Bello.* México, Fondo de Cultura Económica, 1948.
Méndez Plancarte, Gabriel. *"Prólogo," Antología de Bello, en la serie "El Pensamiento de América,"* México, Ediciones de la Secretaría de Educación Pública, 1943.
Lira Urquieta, Pedro. *Andrés Bello.* México, Fondo de Cultura Económica, 1948.
Bilbao, Francisco. *Obras completas.* Buenos Aires, Imp. Buenos Aires, 1866.
Bilbao, Francisco, references for:
Barra, Eduardo de la. *Francisco Bilbao ante la sacristía, refutación a un folleto.* Santiago de Chile, Imp. Ferrocarril, 1872.
Bilbao, Manuel. *"Vida de Francisco Bilbao," Obras completas de Francisco Bilbao.* Buenos Aires, 1866.
Cúneo, Dardo. *"Bilbao en la Argentina," prólogo a "El evangelio americano."* Buenos Aires, Edit. Americalee, 1943.
Donoso, Armando. *Bilbao y su tiempo.* Santiago de Chile, Edit. Zig-Zag, 1913.
Mandiola, Rómulo. *Francisco Bilbao y sus panegiristas.* Santiago de Chile, Imp. El Estandarte Católico, 1876.
Lagarrigue, Jorge. *La dictature républicaine d'après Auguste Comte.* Rio de Janeiro, Tip. Auguste Comte, 1937.
———. *Le Faux et le vrai positivisme.* Paris, Apostolat Positiviste, 1892.
———. *Trozos del diario íntimo.* Santiago de Chile, Fundación Juan Enrique Lagarrigue, 1944.
Lagarrigue, Juan Enrique. *Dictamen positivista sobre el conflicto entre el Gobierno y el Congreso.* Santiago de Chile, Imp. Cervantes, 1890.
———. *Propuesta de solución para la actual crisis política.* Santiago de Chile, Cervantes, 1890.
———. *Intervenciones religiosas en favor de la paz.* Santiago de Chile, 1942.
———. *Sobre el proyecto de ley contra las huelgas.* Santiago de Chile, 1892.
———. *Hacia la regeneración definitiva.* Santiago de Chile, Cervantes, 1908.
———. *La religión de la humanidad.* Santiago de Chile, 1884.

————. *En servicio de la doctrina altruísta*. Santiago de Chile, Cervantes, 1908.

Lastarria, José Victorino. *Obras completas*. Santiago de Chile, Imp. Barcelona, 1906–14.

Lastarria, José Victorino, references for:
Fuenzalida Grandón, Alejandro. *Lastarria y su tiempo*. Santiago de Chile, Imp. Cervantes, 1893.
Melfi, Domingo. *Dos hombres, Portales y Lastarria*. Santiago de Chile, Nascimiento, 1937.

Letelier, Valentín. *De la ciencia política en Chile y de la necesidad de su enseñanza*. Santiago de Chile, Imp. Gutenberg, 1886.

————. *La evolución de la historia*. Santiago de Chile, Imp. Cervantes, 1900.

————. *La tiranía y la revolución*. Santiago de Chile, Cervantes, 1891.

Letelier, Valentín, references for:
Galdames, Luis. *Valentín Letelier y su obra*. Santiago de Chile, Universitaria, 1937.

CUBA

I. *General Bibliography*

Bachiller y Morales, Antonio. *Apuntes para la historia de las letras y de la instrucción pública en la isla de Cuba. Con introducción por* Francisco González del Valle *y biografía del autor por* Vidal Morales. Habana, Cultural, S. A., 1936–37.

Calcagno, Francisco. *Diccionario biográfico cubano*. Nueva York, Imp. N. Ponce de León, 1878.

Chacón y Calvo, José María. *Ensayos de literatura cubana*. Madrid, Calleja, 1922.

González del Valle, José Z. "*Filosofía en la Habana*," in *De la filosofía en la Habana* (see under Mestre).

Mestre, José Manuel. *De la filosofía en la Habana*. Habana, Imp. La Antilla, 1862.

Mitjans, Aurelio. *Estudio sobre el movimiento científico y literario de Cuba*. Habana, Álvarez y Cía., 1890.

Piñeyro, Enrique. *Hombres y glorias de América*. Paris, Garnier Hnos., 1903.

Vitier, Medardo. *La filosofía en Cuba*. México, Fondo de Cultura Económica, 1948.

————. *Las ideas en Cuba*. Habana, Edit. Trópico, 1938.

————. *Apuntaciones literarias*. Habana, Minerva, 1935.

II. *Special Bibliography*

Caballero, José Agustín. *Philosophia Electiva. Con estudios preliminares de* Francisco González del Valle *y* Roberto Agramonte. *Biblioteca de Autores Cubanos*. Habana, Universidad de la Habana, 1944.

CABALLERO, JOSÉ AGUSTÍN, references for:

González del Valle, Francisco. *Dos orientadores de la enseñanza, El Padre José Agustín Caballero y José de la Luz y Caballero*. Habana, 1935.

Luz y Caballero, José de la. *"Filósofos cubanos," Revista de Cuba*, Vol. III (Habana, 1878).

Luz y Caballero, José de la. *Aforismos y apuntaciones. Ordenados y anotados por* Roberto Agramonte, *retrato de* José de la Luz *por* Martí, *prólogo de* Rafael García Bárcena. *Biblioteca de Autores Cubanos*. Habana, Universidad de la Habana, 1945.

————. *De la vida íntima: Epistolario y diarios. Prólogo de* Elías Entralgo. *Biblioteca de Autores Cubanos*. Habana, Universidad de la Habana, 1945.

————. *Escritos literarios. Prólogo de* Raimundo Lazo. *Biblioteca de Autores Cubanos*. Habana, Universidad de la Habana, 1946.

————. *La polémica filosófica: Cuestión de método. Prólogo de* Roberto Agramonte. Habana, Universidad de la Habana, 1946.

————. *La polémica filosófica: Polémica sobre el eclecticismo*. 3 vols. *Biblioteca de Autores Cubanos*. Habana, Universidad de la Habana, 1946, 1947, 1948.

————. *La polémica filosófica: Impugnación a las doctrinas filosóficas de Cousin. Biblioteca de Autores Cubanos*. Habana, Universidad de la Habana, 1948.

————. *La polémica filosófica; Polémica sobre ideología, moral religiosa y moral utilitaria. Biblioteca de Autores Cubanos*. Habana, Universidad de la Habana, 1948.

————. *Filosofía y pedagogía*. Habana, Cuadernos de Cultura, 1935.

————. *José de la Luz y Caballero como educador. Recopilación de sus escritos, e introducción de* Francisco González del Valle. Habana, Cultural, S. A., 1931.

————. *Obras completas*, in *Obras Escogidas de Autores Cubanos, coleccionadas por* Alfredo Zayas. Habana, 1890.

Luz y Caballero, José de la, references for:
Rodríguez, José Ignacio. *Vida de José de la Luz y Caballero*. Nueva York, Mundo Nuevo, 1874.
Sanguily, Manuel. *José de la Luz y Caballero*. Habana, Edit. O'Reilly, 1890.
Montoro, Rafael. *Obras. Notas epilogales de* José M. Chacón y Calvo. Habana, Edición de Homenaje, 1930.
————. *Ideario autonomista*. La Habana, Cuadernos de Cultura, 1938.
————. *"Kant, el neokantismo y los neokantianos españoles," Revista de Cuba*, Vol. IV (Habana, 1878).
Montoro, Rafael, reference for:
Bustamente y Montorro, Antonio S. de. *La ideología autonomista*. Habana, Imp. Molina, 1933.
Revista Cubana, periódico mensual de ciencias, filosofía, literatura y bellas artes. Enrique José Varona, director. Habana, 1885–93.
Revista de Cuba, periódico mensual de ciencas, derecho, literatura y bellas artes. José Antonio Cortino, director. Habana, 1877–84.
Saco, José Antonio. *Historia de la esclavitud de los indios en el Nuevo Mundo*. Habana, 1833.
————. *Ideario reformista*. Habana, Cuadernos de Cultura, 1935.
————. *La vagancia en Cuba*. Habana, Dirección de Cultura, 1946.
Saco, José Antonio, reference for:
Ortiz, Fernando. *José Antonio Saco y sus ideas cubanas*. Habana, Imp. El Universo, 1929.
Sanguily, Manuel. *Obras*. Habana, Imp. Dorabecker, 1925–26.
Varela y Morales, Félix. *Cartas a Elpidio. Prólogo de Humberto Piñera Llera en el tomo I y un epílogo de* Raimundo Lazo *en el II. Biblioteca de Autores Cubanos*. Habana, Universidad de la Habana, 1945.
————. *El Habanero. Con estudios preliminares de* Enrique Gay y Calbó *y* Emilio Roig Leuchsenring. *Biblioteca de Autores Cubanos*. Habana, Universidad de la Habana, 1945.
————. *Lecciones de filosofía*. La Habana, La Verónica, 1940.
————. *Miscelánea filosófica. Prólogo de* Medardo Vitier. *Biblioteca de Autores Cubanos*. Habana, Universidad de la Habana, 1944.
————. *Observaciones sobre la constitución política de la monarquía española. Biblioteca de Autores Cubanos*. Habana, Universidad de la Habana, 1944.
Varela y Morales, Félix, references for:
Calcagno, Francisco. *"Filósofos cubanos, Varela," Revista de Cuba*, Vol. II (Habana, 1877).

Cuevas Zequeira, Sergio. *El Padre Varela, contribución a la historia de la filosofía en Cuba.* Habana, Tip. Moderna, 1923.

Chacón y Calvo, José M. *"El Padre Varela y la autonomía colonial,"* Homenaje a Varona (Habana, 1935).

Guardia, J. M. *"Filósofos españoles de Cuba, Félix Varela, José de la Luz,"* Revista Cubana, Vol. XV (Habana, 1892).

Rodríguez, José Ignacio. *Vida del Presbítero don Félix Varela.* Nueva York, Imp. O Novo Mundo, 1878.

Varona, Enrique José. *"Conferencias filosóficas,"* Revista de Cuba, Vol. VIII–XV (Habana, 1880–84).

———. *Conferencias filosóficas, Moral.* Habana, Establecimiento Tipográfico, 1888.

———. *Conferencias sobre el fundamento de la moral.* Nueva York, D. Appleton y Cía, 1903.

———. *Cuba contra España. Manifesto del Partido Revolucionario Cubano a los pueblos hispanoamericanos.* Nueva York, América, 1895.

———. *De la Colonia a la República.* Habana, Sociedad Editorial Cuba Contemporánea, 1919.

———. *En voz alta.* Habana, Imp. Comedia, 1916.

———. *"Estética,"* Regista de Cuba, Vol. II (Habana, 1877).

———. *Estudios y conferencias.* La Habana, 1936.

———. *"La evolución psicológica,"* Revista de Cuba, Vol. VI (Habana, 1879).

———. *"Littré,"* Revista de Cuba, Vol. X (Habana, 1881).

———. *"La metafísica en la Universidad de la Habana,"* Revista de Cuba, Vol. VII (Habana, 1880).

———. *"La moral en la evolución,"* Revista de Cuba, Vol. IV (Habana, 1878).

———. *"Ojeada sobre el movimiento intelectual en América,"* Revista de Cuba, Vol. IV (Habana, 1878).

———. *"La psicología en sus relaciones con la fisiología,"* Revista de Cuba, Vol. IV (Habana, 1878).

———. *"La psicología de Bain,"* Revista de Cuba, Vol. II (Habana, 1877).

———. *"El positivismo,"* Revista de Cuba, Vol. III (Habana, 1878).

———. *Las reformas en la enseñanza superior.* Habana, Tip. El Fígaro, 1900.

VARONA, ENRIQUE José, references for:

Cruz, Manuel de la. *Tres caracteres. Bocetos biográficos cubanos.* Key West, Fla., Tip. Revista Popular, 1889.

Homenaje a Enrique José Varona, en el cincuentenario de su primer curso de filosofía. Habana, Dirección de Cultura, 1935.

Varela Zequeira, José. *La figura de Enrique José Varona.* Habana, Cuba International, 1937.

Vitier, Medardo. *Enrique José Varona.* Habana, Imp. Molina, 1935.

PERU

I. *General Bibliography*

Ibérico y Rodríguez, Mariano. *"La filosofía en el Perú," Mercurio Peruano,"* año IV, Vol. IV (Lima, 1921).

Leguía, Jorge Guillermo. *Estudios históricos.* Santiago de Chile, Ercilla, 1939.

————. *Hombres e ideas en el Perú.* Santiago de Chile, Ercilla, 1941.

Riva Agüero, José de la. *Carácter de la literatura del Perú independiente.* Lima, 1905.

Sánchez, Luis Alberto. *La literatura peruana.* Lima, 1928–29.

Valcárel, Luis E. *Ruta cultural del Perú.* México, Fondo de Cultura Económica, 1945.

II. *Special Bibliography*

Cornejo, Mariano H. *Discursos parlamentarios y políticos.* Lima, 1902.

————. *Discursos políticos.* Lima, Imprenta del Estado, 1913.

————. *Discursos políticos.* Lima, Imprenta del Estado, 1919–20.

Deústua, Alejandro. *El problema nacional de la educación.* Lima, Edit. El Sallao, n. d.

————. *A propósito de un cuestionario sobre la reforma de la ley de instrucción.* Lima, Imp. Dávila, 1914.

————. *La reforma de la segunda enseñanza.* Lima, Imp. Centro Editorial, 1916.

González Prada, Manuel. *Anarquía.* Santiago de Chile, Ercilla, 1940.

————. *Bajo el oprobio.* Paris, L. Bellenard, 1933.

————. *Figuras y figurones. Con un estudio crítico de* Rufino Blanco Fombona. Paris, 1938.

————. *Horas de lucha.* Lima, El Progreso, 1908.

————. *Páginas libres.* Santiago de Chile, 1930.

————. *Nuevas páginas libres.* Santiago de Chile, Ercilla, 1937.

————. *Propaganda y ataque.* Buenos Aires, Imán, 1939.

————. *Prosa menuda.* Buenos Aires, Imán, 1941.

————. *El tonel de Diógenes.* México, Tezontle, 1945.

GONZÁLEZ PRADA, MANUEL, references for:

Garra, Eugenio J. *Manuel González Prada.* Nueva York, Hispanic Institute, 1942.

González Prada, Adriana de. *Mi Manuel.* Lima, Edit. Cultura Antártica, 1947.

Iberico, Mariano. "*González Prada pensador,*" in his book *El nuevo absoluto.* Lima, Edit. Minerva, 1927.

Manuel González Prada, por los más notables escritores del Perú y América. Cuzco, Imp. Rozas, 1924.

Sánchez, Luis Alberto. *Don Manuel.* Lima, Edit. Rosay, 1930.

Prado y Ugarteche, Javier. *Discursos.* Lima, Imp. El Comercio, 1905.

————. *El estado social del Perú durante la dominación española.* Lima, Imp. Diaria Judicial, 1894.

————. *Las profesiones liberales en el Perú.* Lima, Imp. La Industria, Lima, n. d.

————. *La evolución de la idea filosófica en la historia.* Lima, Imp. Torres, 1891.

————. *El método positivo en el derecho penal.* Lima, Gil Editor, 1889.

Villarán, Manuel Vicente. *Cuestiones generales sobre el estado y el gobierno.* Lima, Gil, 1938.

————. *Estudios sobre educación nacional.* Lima, Gil, 1922.

————. *Memorias.* Lima, Gil, 1915.

————. *El momento actual de la Universidad Mayor de San Marcos.* Lima, Gil, 1922.

————. *Las profesiones liberales en el Perú.* Lima, Imp. La Industria, 1900.

————. *La Universidad de San Marcos de Lima.* Lima, Gil, 1938.

URUGUAY

Anales del Ateneo del Uruguay. Montevideo, Imp. Ruiz y Becchi, 1881–86.

Ardao, Arturo. *La filosofía pre-universitaria en el Uruguay.* Montevideo, Edit. García, 1945.

Arias C., Alejandro. *Vaz Ferreira.* México, Fondo de Cultura Económica, 1949.

Floro Costa, Ángel. *La metafísica y la ciencia.* Montevideo, Tip. Renand, 1879.

Zum Felde, Alberto. *Evolución histórica del Uruguay*. Montevideo, García, 1945.
———. *Proceso intelectual del Uruguay*. Montevideo, Claridad, 1941.

VENEZUELA

Cova, J. A. *Don Simón Rodríguez*. Buenos Aires, Edit. Venezuela, 1947.
Orrego Luco, A. *Don Simón Rodríguez*. Santiago de Chile, n. d.
Picón, Febres, Gonzalo. *Don Simón Rodríguez maestro del libertador*. Caracas, Artes Gráficas, 1939.
Rodríguez, Simón. *Defensa de Bolívar*. Caracas, Imp. Bolívar, 1916.
———. *"Estado actual de la escuela y nuevo establecimiento de ella,"* *Boletín de la Academia Nacional de Historia* (Caracas, 1946).

Index